DARK WORK

DARK WORK

The Business of Slavery in Rhode Island

CHRISTY CLARK-PUJARA

New York University Press

NEW YORK

NEW YORK UNIVERSITY PRESS
New York
www.nyupress.org

First published in paperback in 2018

Library of Congress Cataloging-in-Publication Data

Names: Clark-Pujara, Christy.
Title: Dark work : the business of slavery in Rhode Island / Christy Clark-Pujara.
Description: New York : New York University Press, 2016. | Series: Early
    American places | "Also available as an ebook"—Title page verso. | Includes
    bibliographical references and index.
Identifiers: LCCN 2015049156 | ISBN 9781479870424 (cloth : alk. paper) | ISBN
    978-1-4798-5563-6 (pb : alk. paper)
Subjects: LCSH: Slavery—Rhode Island—History. | Slave trade—Rhode Island—
    History. | Slaves—Emancipation—Rhode Island—History. | Slaves—Rhode
    Island—Social conditions. | Free African Americans—Rhode Island—History.
    | Rhode Island—Race relations—History.
Classification: LCC E445.R4 C55 2016 | DDC 306.3/6209745—dc23
LC record available at http://lccn.loc.gov/2015049156

References to Internet Web sites (URLs) were accurate at the time of writing.
Neither the author nor New York University Press is responsible for URLs that may
have expired or changed since the manuscript was prepared.

New York University Press books are printed on acid-free paper, and their binding
materials are chosen for strength and durability. We strive to use environmentally
responsible suppliers and materials to the greatest extent possible in publishing
our books.

Manufactured in the United States of America
10 9 8 7 6 5 4 3 2 1

Also available as an ebook

in loving memory of my daddy, Henry Clark, 1932-2014

CONTENTS

Maps, Tables, and Figures

Maps

Tables

Figures

ACKNOWLEDGMENTS

First and foremost, I would like to thank my family and friends. To my parents, Henry and Renee Clark, this book simply would not have been possible without your love and support. To my husband Jesil Pujara, who believed in me in the moments when I did not believe in myself, this book is as much yours as it is mine. To my daughters Priya and Diya, you have brought me immense joy and I am so grateful to be your mother. To my brothers, sisters, and nephew, Matthew Clark, Manuel Clark, Mannix Clark, Cynthia Berliew, Candace Gray-Spann, and Brandon Clark, thank you for your steadfast encouragement. To my friends, who have been there throughout this process, Charissa Threat, Karissa Haugeberg, Amanda Madsen, Ann Budig, and Linn Posey-Maddox, thank you for taking time to listen to me and always offering to help in any way you could. I would also like to thank my church family at Robinson Memorial Church of God in Christ (Omaha, Nebraska): your support throughout my life has been a constant source of comfort.

I first began this research while I was at the Department of History at the University of Iowa–Iowa City. I am immensely grateful for the guidance and support I received from the faculty, staff, and school. I would like to thank the faculty members and staff of the Afro-American Studies Department at the University of Wisconsin, Madison, for enthusiastically embracing and backing my work. To my mentors and colleagues, thank you for the many corrections and suggestions and for your guidance throughout this process.

I would like to extend a special thank-you to Leslie Schwalm, Joanne Pope Melish, Stephen Kantrowitz, Craig Werner, Brenda Gayle Plummer, Christina Greene, Cherene Sherrard-Johnson, and Ethelene Whitmire: your direction and advice have been invaluable. To the editors I have worked with at various stages of this project, Mike Shapiro, David Lobenstien, and Clara Platter, thank you for helping me tell this story with purpose and clarity. To my students, I am grateful for your insightful questions that have challenged both my thinking and methods.

I would also like to extend my acknowledgments to the many librarians, archivists, and staff at the following institutions: the Rhode Island Historical Society, the Newport Historical Society, the John Carter Brown Library (Brown University), the Rhode Island Black Heritage Society, the State Archives of Rhode Island, the Baker Library (Harvard Business School), the John Hay Library (Brown University), the Rhode Island Supreme Court Records Center, the Phillips Memorial Library (Providence College), and the South Kingstown Town Clerk Office for answering my many questions, providing a pleasant working environment, and allowing access to collections over the course of the last several years. This work would not have been possible without your knowledge and hospitality.

Introduction

In 2003, Ruth Simmons, the president of Brown and the first African American to lead an Ivy League university, commissioned a report on the institution's early connections to slavery. The report, released in 2006, confirmed long-standing rumors: slavery had played an essential role in establishing Rhode Island's first college. Enslaved people were among the multiracial workforce that constructed the first buildings, which were built with wood donated by a local slave-trading firm. Furthermore, slaveholders and slave traders dominated the Board of Fellows and Trustees. These "recent revelations" contrasted with the story that Brown had told about itself for at least the last half century—that it was a bastion of tolerance, founded by abolitionists.[1]

Brown, not surprisingly, is far from alone. In the past two decades, all of the Ivy League schools, as well as a wide range of other universities and colleges, are figuring out how to reckon with a history that, for many generations, has been either willfully disguised or unconsciously ignored. Indeed, administrators, alumni, and current students, not to mention the rest of the country, often know little about the relationship between their institution of higher education and the institution of slavery.[2] Brown University's reliance on slave labor and use of donations from slaveholders and slave traders were typical for the region, not the exception but the norm. Throughout the North slavery permeated nearly every business of early America—from trading to banking, from insurance to shipbuilding, from rum distilling to agricultural production, from textiles to tool making. After Brown's report, the investigations spread. Magazines and journals published special issues devoted to slavery in New England; conferences and public forums were held to discuss the legacy of slavery in the region. Descendants of Rhode Island's most dominant slave-trading family, the DeWolfs, released a film and wrote a book about their ancestors' involvement in the American trade in African slaves and its legacy to them.[3] The dawn of the twenty-first century brought a surge of public interest in the history of slavery in the United States, especially outside the American South: slavery, it turned out, was everywhere.

We now know that the institution of slavery was central to the social and economic development of the northern colonies and states.[4] Historians have long noted that the "key dynamic force" in New England's economic success was slave-related commerce.[5] Furthermore, we know that slavery and capitalism, far from being separate and incompatible systems, were utterly interdependent. Indeed, the interchangeability and coexistence of slave and free labor allowed capitalism to exploit the most efficient workers: enslaved cultivators undergirded the growth of the American economy. In sum, slave labor was central to the modern capitalist rise of the United States as an industrial and financial power in the Western world.[6]

In this book I use economic history to investigate how the business of slavery shaped the establishment and growth of lifelong inheritable bondage in the North and how it affected the process of emancipation and black freedom. I define the business of slavery as all economic activity that was directly related to the maintenance of slaveholding in the Americas, specifically the buying and selling of people, food, and goods. The business of slavery, as distinct from the institution of slavery, allowed New England to become an economic powerhouse without ever producing a staple or cash crop—sugar, rice, or cotton.[7] Our understanding of slavery has grown tremendously in the last several decades, but it has been dominated by a few particular visions of enslaved people, particularly the horrors of the Atlantic slave trade and people toiling under the threat of the lash in the hot sun. I would like to continue efforts to expand our comprehension of this peculiar institution. To do so, I focus on the business of slavery and its effect on the lived experience of enslaved people and their "free" descendants. I want to use the seemingly clear realm of economics to explore the often ambiguous experiences of the enslaved: how did the business of slavery shaped the experience of slavery in Rhode Island and what it was like to be both black and free in a society that was economically dependent and invested in black bondage.[8]

Rhode Island is the tiniest state in the North, yet had a surprisingly large role in slavery. In the eighteenth century, Rhode Island merchants dominated the American trade in slaves and provided the West Indies with basic necessities; local merchants also held a relatively large number of enslaved people. In the nineteenth century, after they had begun to legally dismantle slavery, Rhode Islanders still managed to make a profit from black bodies through the manufacture of slave clothing. These deep and lasting economic commitments to the business of slavery shaped the state and black life. The history of New England merchants, tradesmen, businessmen, and abolitionists has been well documented, but the lives and experiences of enslaved and free black people in the region have received comparatively little attention.[9]

Enslaved people lived and labored in Rhode Island from the birth of the colony, in 1636, until slavery was abolished in 1842. These bound people did not labor to build plantations, nor did they toil to produce cash crops like their counterparts in the American South, the West Indies, and South America. Nor were their labors critical to building colonial infrastructure and feeding the locals, like those of their northern counterparts throughout New York and New Jersey. Instead, they labored in the business of slavery. They assisted their enslavers in distilleries that manufactured rum and shops that manufactured barrels, and the barrels of rum were then packed onto slave ships and used to purchase slaves along the West African coast. Enslaved Rhode Islanders also cared for the livestock and cultivated the crops that eventually fed enslaved people in the West Indies. Their work, in other words, reflected the business of their enslavers. Ironically, in the post-Revolutionary period, the free descendants of enslaved Rhode Islanders were almost completely excluded from the business of slavery because they were restricted from working in the new manifestation of the northern industrialization: the factory. Consequently most free black Rhode Islanders worked as domestics, day laborers, and sailors.

Before and after the War for American Independence, white northerners, in one way or another, invested in the business of slavery. However, nowhere was this commerce more important or apparent than in Rhode Island. During the colonial period, the West Indian and Atlantic slave trades were the lifeblood of the colony's economy. Merchants in the two biggest cities, Newport and Providence, transported local agricultural products, especially livestock and cheese, to sugar plantations in the West Indies in exchange for molasses; the same merchants then brought that molasses back to Rhode Island and sold it to local distillers, who used it to make rum, the colony's number one export. Rhode Islanders also trafficked more than 60 percent of all the North American trade in African slaves.[10] And by 1750 Rhode Islanders held the highest proportion of slaves in New England: 10 percent of the total population was enslaved, double the northern average. In contrast, enslaved people made up just 2 percent of population in Pennsylvania, New Hampshire, and Massachusetts and 3 percent of the population in Connecticut.[11] In other words, Rhode Islanders proportionately held five times more slaves than other New Englanders.

Local merchants were the last New Englanders to stop slave trading before the outbreak of war in 1776 and the first to begin slave trading after the peace in 1783. Although Rhode Islanders were among the first to pass, in 1784, a gradual emancipation law ending hereditary slavery, they were among the last northerners to abolish the institution altogether, in 1842.[12] In the antebellum era, Rhode Islanders remained heavily invested in the business of slavery through the textile industry, especially the manufacture of "negro cloth," a coarse cotton-wool material made especially to minimize the cost of clothing enslaved people. Seventy-nine percent of all textile mills in Rhode Island manufactured "negro cloth."[13] These economic commitments to the business of slavery dictated the texture and rhythms of slave life, stalled the emancipation process, and circumscribed black freedom.

While the business of slavery is an important frame for this book, my primary concern is how enslaved and free blacks responded to the restrictions imposed by a socioeconomic system that depended on oppressing people of African descent.[14] There have been a few attempts to write the history of black people in Rhode Island. Those written before the major historical critiques of slavery and emancipation are apologist histories of slavery and lack critical analysis of the institution. The next installments of African American history in Rhode Island were intensely local, focusing on the black experience in Providence, Newport, and the Narragansett Country during or after the American Revolution.[15] The experiences of black Rhode Islanders have also been significant parts of the study of slavery and the process of emancipation in the North.[16] While black Rhode Islanders' experiences form parts of these histories, no single monograph explores the history of black people in Rhode Island from slavery to freedom. This study complicates understandings of the origins of northern slavery and explores how slavery continued to have an enormous influence on the economics, culture, and politics of the North even after it was eliminated by northern states in the post-Revolutionary period.

Though the number of enslaved and free black people in the region never approached the sheer volume of slaves in the South, slavery played a central role in the North and particularly in Rhode Island. The development and maintenance of the institution of slavery in North America required a proslavery consensus among northerners and southerners alike, particularly as their economies grew more complex, more profitable, and more interdependent. The racial ideology of white supremacy and black inferiority was not confined to the southern colonies and states; whites, North and South, created a national ideology that hinged upon their own superiority.[17] I draw on manuscript collections, public records, government documents, business correspondence, and organizational records to reveal the histories of black Rhode Islanders. The result is a detailed account of how white Rhode Islanders' ideological commitments to and financial investments in the business of slavery shaped the institution itself as well as the protracted process of emancipation and the limitations placed on black freedom. Furthermore, placing the experience of black people at the center of my analysis highlights how enslaved and free black people pushed back against their bondage and the restrictions placed on their freedoms.

Though we do not often talk about it, especially those of us living in the North, slaveholding was common throughout the northern colonies. African slaves first entered northern colonies in the 1620s, concentrated in the Dutch encampment that would become New York City.[18] By 1700, 40 percent of New York City residents held slaves. In Pennsylvania one in three residents was a slave of African descent.[19] However, most northern enslavers held just one or two slaves. Consequently, most enslaved people in the North lived in isolation from one another and without the built-in institution of the large farm or plantation had to find alternate means of creating community. Enslaved northerners were jacks of all trades; they labored as carpenters, shipwrights, sailmakers, printers, tailors, shoemakers, coopers, blacksmiths, bakers, weavers, goldsmiths, farmhands, cooks, maids, and caretakers.[20]

Throughout much of the colonial North, the status of enslaved people was ambiguous; in fact, during the seventeenth century, many enslaved people were held as indentured servants.[21] However, by the turn of the eighteenth century most northern colonies had followed the lead of Massachusetts and established slave codes.[22] In the North, the laws of slavery assigned the enslaved a status that simultaneously reduced them to chattel and made demands of them as legal persons—whichever suited their enslavers.[23] This arbitrary treatment of slaves, as chattel in some instances and legal persons in other instances, made northern slavery particularly bewildering and appalling. The limited legal acknowledgment of personhood seemed technically mild but was in practice draconian. For example, enslaved northerners had a right to life and a day in court; however, they were bought, sold, willed, and inventoried. By the early eighteenth century, every northern colony had special laws, procedures, and punishments for people of Native American and African descent. Some restrictions included curfews and provisions against travel and purchasing liquor, holding livestock, and gathering in groups of four or more. Slave codes attempted to prevent running away, theft, drunkenness, damage to public property, assaulting or defaming a white person, disturbing the peace, rioting, and insurrection.[24]

The American Revolution transformed the institution of slavery in the North and led to its slow and uneven destruction. During the war enslaved people ran away in unprecedented numbers, volunteered for military service in exchange for their freedom, and lobbied their enslavers for freedom. The shortage of fighting men and the subsequent use of slaves as soldiers also contributed to the breakdown of bondage. Following the war the enslaved petitioned and filed suit for their freedom in the new democracy. Sometimes they were successful and sometimes they were not. In the three decades after the war nearly all the northern states began to legally dismantle slaveholding, for both the actions of enslaved people and the rhetoric of the Revolution had called slavery into question as never before. In Massachusetts in the 1780s, a series of slave-initiated court cases showed how slavery was incompatible with the state constitution and its declaration of freedom for all. Pennsylvania, Connecticut, Rhode Island, New York, and New Jersey passed gradual emancipation laws between 1780 and 1804, stipulating that children born to slave mothers after a certain date were free but were indentured to their mother's master.[25] Some states freed children when they turned twenty-one or as late as twenty-eight. Piecemeal emancipation allowed white northerners to slowly wean themselves off slave labor. Gradual emancipation laws put an expiration date on legally sanctioned white "mastery" and black "slavery." Yet while these shifts in the legal landscape were transformative, as we shall see, sustaining and growing investments in the business of slavery were equally transformative, ensuring that bondage remained a defining, if now geographically distant, aspect of northern life.

Blacks born after the American Revolution came of age in a country that had complex, contradictory, and contested racial ideologies. While northern citizens were dismantling the use of slave labor, their southern counterparts were committing to it more fully. Furthermore, even within the North, new laws did not mean a new consciousness. While most northern states had begun the process of legally ending black slavery, the white citizenry of the North remained explicitly racist.[26] Black people were free, but they were far from equal; indeed, even the most liberal of the early nineteenth-century northerners considered the notion of equality between the races untenable. What is remarkable is that despite this overt racism, the personal wealth, schools, and churches in black communities all grew in the first three decades of the nineteenth century, largely as a result of the establishment of mutual societies.[27]

Historians have long argued that black freedom was circumscribed in the North.[28] Several have asked what it meant to be a "free" black person in a country that protected race-based slavery. I too pose this question and ask what it meant to be a free black person in a society intimately involved in sustaining chattel slavery throughout the Americas. Blacks in Rhode Island lived in a colony, then a state, that depended on the West Indian rum trade, that dominated the North American slave trade, and that made enormous profits from the plantation societies of the South through the manufacture of "negro cloth." How did these economic realities shape black life?

The experience of enslaved and free blacks in Rhode Island followed the general contours of the larger northern story. Rhode Islanders were engaged in the same economic activities—slave trading and providing West Indian slaveholders with basic necessities—that occupied their neighbors; however, the intensity of their involvement set them apart, making Rhode Island the ideal place to study how the business of slavery shaped the emergence of slavery, the experience of slavery, and the birth of black freedom, however circumscribed, in the North.[29] Rhode Island is the best place to study the impact of the business of slavery because it is both representative of and unique in how slavery shaped and enriched the North. Like their northern neighbors, Rhode Islanders bought and sold people and supplies that kept plantations in the Americas thriving; Rhode Islanders, however, were the most deeply invested in the business of slavery. In other words, Rhode Island is both exemplary and exceptional. Moreover, economic investments in the business of slavery continued and actually increased in the state after passage of the gradual emancipation law. Investments in the business of slavery stunted black freedom. Free blacks were shut out of the emerging industrial economy and increasingly found themselves victims of white violence and restrictive laws that denied them full citizenship, most notably those banning black voting and mandating segregation in schooling. In response to economic, political, and social marginalization, black Rhode Islanders banded together and built institutions to challenge the limitations on their freedom. Thus the experience of free black Rhode Islanders must be understood within this economic reality. To put it bluntly, the lives and the worth of many white Rhode Islanders were predicated on the subordination of black people.

I began researching slavery and emancipation in Rhode Island after Ruth Simmons commissioned the report on Brown University and its connections to the institution of slavery. After reading the report and secondary literature that highlighted Rhode Island's overt investments in slavery, I was surprised to find out that no one had written a history of how those economic ties to the business of slavery had shaped the lives of the enslaved and curtailed the freedom of their descendants. It is my hope that by looking at both the experiences of individuals and the vast realm of economics we can understand how the business of slavery shaped the lives of enslaved and free blacks in the colony and later the state of Rhode Island. I have attempted to reconstruct their lived experience through the documents of the state, the business and personal records of their owners, and the few firsthand accounts left by enslaved and free black Rhode Islanders. The history of Rhode Island must include their stories because they too shaped Rhode Island and the United States of America.

1 / The Business of Slavery and the Making of Race

In 1783 the Rhode Island General Assembly voted to free Amy Allen, who sued for freedom on the basis that she was not black; Allen successfully claimed to be "an abandoned white child raised by an enslaved mother."[1] Her whiteness exempted her from any suspicion of slavery. On the other hand, because blackness was akin to slavery, free blacks had to safeguard their status. In 1785, Jane Coggeshall, who had been emancipated in 1777, petitioned the General Assembly to confirm her freedom, as she feared her former master's family sought to re-enslave her.

> Whereas, Jane Coggeshall, of Providence, a negro woman pre-
> ferred a petition and represented unto this Assembly, that she
> was a slave to Captain Daniel Coggeshall, of Newport; that in
> March, A.D. 1777, the enemy being then in possession of Rhode
> Island, she, together with others, at every risk, effected their
> escape to Point Judith; that they were carried before the Gen-
> eral Assembly, then sitting in South Kingstown, who did there-
> upon give them their liberty, together with a pass to go to any
> part of the country to procure a livelihood; that she hath lived
> at Woodstock and at Providence ever since; that during the
> whole time she hath maintained herself decently and with rep-
> utation, and can appeal to the families wherein she hath lived
> with respect to her industry, sobriety of manners, and fidelity;

that of late she hath been greatly alarmed with a claim of some of the heirs of said Daniel Coggeshall upon her still as a slave; that as she has enjoyed the inestimable blessing of liberty for near eight years, she feels the most dreadful apprehension at the idea of again falling into a state of slavery.[2]

The Assembly voted to declare Jane Coggeshall "entirely emancipated and made free." This black woman, however, was worthy of freedom only because of her "industry, sobriety of manners, and fidelity." In the wake of the Revolutionary War, the members of the Rhode Island Assembly and white northern society in general accepted that whiteness in and of itself was enough to warrant freedom but felt that blackness necessitated certain characteristics to earn freedom. For whites, freedom was an inalienable right; for blacks, it was a privilege. These racial assumptions, however, were a result of decades of legal race-making.

Unlike legislators in Massachusetts and New York, Rhode Islanders did not specifically identify who was eligible for enslavement, nor did they establish the condition as hereditary. They did not see a need to. Rhode Islanders' immersions in the Atlantic economy allowed them to take black slavery for granted. However, it took nearly fifty years for Rhode Islanders to write race-based slavery into law. In 1652, colonial officials in Providence and Warwick banned the enslavement of "blacke and white mankind."[3] Twenty-four years later, in 1676, they prohibited the enslavement of Native Americans.[4] Nevertheless, in 1703, the Rhode Island General Assembly legally recognized both black and Native American slavery, and by 1750 Rhode Islanders held the highest percentage of slaves in New England.[5] This about-face reflected Rhode Islanders' increased participation in the Atlantic economy.[6]

In Rhode Island, it was the business of slavery that brought the disparate towns and villages of this small colony together and encouraged the emergence of slavery. Before they committed themselves to the pursuit of commerce in multiple directions across the Atlantic Ocean, Rhode Islanders sought to restrict and even ban slaveholding; however, once they began to participate in the West Indian and Atlantic slave trades, they wrote slavery into law. By the 1730s, merchants, slave traders, farmers, distillers, and manufacturers had created a niche for themselves in the Atlantic economy, and a series of racist laws served the needs of a local economy already deeply entrenched in the West Indian and Atlantic slave trades.[7] Moreover, the more dominant Rhode Islanders became in the slave trade, the more they relied on slave labor.

By 1750, 10 percent of Rhode Island's population was enslaved— double the northern average. Enslaved people were heavily concentrated in the port cities of Newport, Providence, and the Narragansett Country, also known as South County, which was made up of the rural towns of North Kingstown, South Kingstown, Charlestown, Exeter, Wickford, Wakefield, and Peace Dale. Slave law in the colony also buttressed the business of slavery by explicitly protecting the property rights of slaveholders. Furthermore, these laws elevated all whites to the enslaver class, as it required them to supervise all slaves; at the same time, those laws relegated people of color to the status of dependents or potential dependents. The business of slavery in Rhode Island shaped not only the economy but also social standing and race relations.

Rhode Island had English sponsorship rather than a charter, and no single dominant religion. In other words, unlike other northern colonies, Rhode Island was not founded to promote a particular religious vision, nor was it established for economic gain. All four founders had been expelled from Massachusetts as a result of their "radical" religious beliefs.[8] When Providence, Portsmouth, Newport, and Warwick, the colony's four original towns, were finally united under a charter from the crown in 1644, they shared no central government and lacked even a collective vision. During the last half of the seventeenth century, conditions verged on anarchy as the towns battled over land and land boundaries.[9] As Rhode Island scholar Sydney James writes, "Half the colonial period had gone by before Rhode Island was indelibly on the map—that is, before it enjoyed a flourishing local patriotism and achieved internal order, reasonable immunity from the territorial ambitions of its neighbors, and safety from British plans to merge it with a larger colony."[10]

Amid this instability, there was one certainty: the ocean. Water-based commerce in and around the city of Newport quickly became the basis of Rhode Island's trade economy; it was a likely enterprise for Rhode Island colonists, since water was what united them all (see maps 1 and 2). Rhode Island measures a mere forty by thirty miles, but five hundred of its square miles touch water.[11] By the mid-eighteenth century, Rhode Island had become a permanent and prosperous colony, thanks to local investments in the business of slavery. Colonists supplied sugar plantations in the West Indies with slaves, livestock, dairy products, fish, candles, and lumber. In return, they received molasses, which they distilled into rum. This trade began in the late seventeenth century but flourished after 1730, when rum became a major currency in the slave trade.[12] The West Indian trade propelled Newport out of Boston's shadow and into the status of a major city and helped establish Providence as a major port.[13]

Between 1650 and 1860, an estimated ten to fifteen million Africans were transported to the Americas; nearly every major European power participated in the Atlantic slave trade.[14] And while English colonists in North America were late and minor participants in the slave trade as a whole, Rhode Island slave traders dominated the American trade in African slaves. Newport would become the most important slave-trading port of departure in North America.

The West Indian and Atlantic Slave Trades

In Rhode Island, trade and political power went hand in hand. During the colonial period, most governors were from the merchant class; in fact, many of them were slave traders. The primary duty of the governor, who was elected annually through popular vote, was to negotiate between the General Assembly (the governing body that lived in Rhode Island) and an English authority, either the Board of Trade or the colonial agent in London.[15] In other words, Rhode Island governors brokered trade agreements between the colonies and the mother country; consequently, promoting and protecting Atlantic commerce was in their political interest and was also a personal investment. Peleg Sanford, who acted as governor from 1680 to 1683, exported horses, beef, pork, butter, and dried peas to Barbados in exchange for sugar and molasses. Samuel Cranston won the annual vote for nearly three decades, serving as governor from 1696 to 1725; not coincidentally, he was a slave trader and ship captain.[16] It was under the leadership of Samuel Cranston

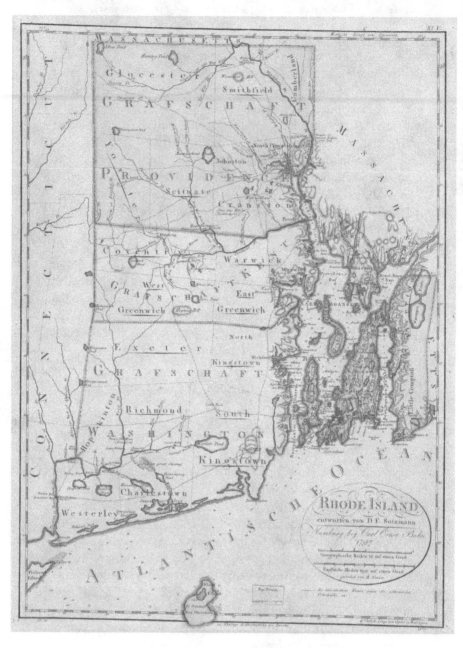

Map 1. Rhode Island. Source: Carl Ernst Bohn, Heinrich Kliewer, and
D. F. Sotzmann, Map of the State of Rhode Island and Providence Plantations (1797), Library of Congress, Map Collections, accessed August 3,
2015, www.loc.gov/item/2011589271/.

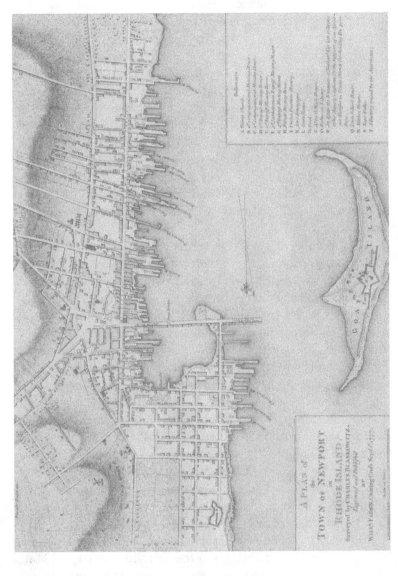

Map 2. Newport. Source: Charles Blaskowitz, Map of Newport, Rhode Island (Charing Cross: William Faden, 1777), Image 81829OD-A53F-4932-87A8-72444179S173, Newport Historical Society.

that Rhode Islanders fully committed to Atlantic commerce. Cranston cracked down on piracy, the major crown complaint against tradesmen.[17] Rhode Islanders relinquished some of their autonomy in exchange for greater access to "legitimate" Atlantic commerce.[18]

Atlantic commerce, the slave trade in particular, brought Rhode Island merchants, tradesmen, and farmers together. Cranston credited the emergence of commerce to the colony's small size and proximity to the Atlantic, saying that "the reason of [commerce's] increase (as I apprehend) is chiefly to be attributed to the inclination the youth on Rhode Island have to the sea. The land on said island, being all taken up and improved in small farms, so that the farmers, as their families increase, are compelled to put or place their children to trades or calling; but their inclinations being mostly to navigation."[19] More and more farmers and merchants recognized Atlantic commerce as their best opportunity for economic security.

Rhode Islanders' eighteenth-century political autonomy and economic success coincided with their entry into Atlantic commerce. Great merchants, including various members of the Malbone, Banister, Gardner, Wanton, Brenton, Collins, Vernon, Channing, Lopez, and Rivera families, collected goods from all who would sell and redirected them to whoever would buy in Africa, the West Indies, and North American port cities. [20] Rhode Islanders exported lumber, beef, pork, butter, cheese, onions, cider, candles, and horses; they imported sugar, molasses, cotton, ginger, indigo, linen, woolen clothes, and Spanish iron. Merchants sent ships primarily from Newport to Antigua, Jamaica, Barbados, Guadalupe, St. Thomas, Marincio, St. Lucia, St. Christopher, Surinam, and the Bay of Honduras. These merchants also transported goods of their neighbors.[21] Rhode Island merchants, like their counterparts throughout the Americas, held a particularly important position in colonial New England because their trade sparked secondary and subsidiary industries that employed most colonists.[22]

Prior to 1696, the English Royal African Company had a monopoly on all English participation in the Atlantic slave trade; Rhode Islanders began sending slave ships as soon as the monopoly was lifted. These voyages grew increasingly common and profitable; in fewer than thirty years they dominated the North American trade in slaves, and the slave trade evolved into one of the pillars of the local economy.[23] The vast majority of the slave ships that embarked from British North America left from ports in Rhode Island, even though it was the smallest and least populated colony (see table 1). In the first quarter of the eighteenth century, Rhode Island slave traders sent 8 slave ships to West Africa and transported 948 Africans back to the Americas. All other New Englanders combined sent just 4 ships transporting 363 Africans. New Yorkers also sent 4 ships transporting 355 Africans, and southern colonists sent just 2 ships transporting 192 Africans to the Americas. Between 1726 and 1750, 123 slave ships embarked from Rhode Island and carried 16,195 African slaves to the Americas; in comparison, only 36 slave ships left from all the other New England colonies, carrying just 4,575 slaves. New Yorkers and Carolinians sent just 3 slave ships carrying 407 and 415 African slaves, respectively, while Virginians sent 2 ships transporting 247 enslaved people. Rhode Islanders' participation in the trade increased even more dramatically over the next twenty-five years. Between 1751 and 1775, Rhode Island slave traders sent 383 slave ships transporting more than 40,000 enslaved Africans to the Americas; all the other colonies combined sent 132 slave ships transporting just less than 18,000 African slaves (figure 2). During the colonial period in total, Rhode Islanders sent 514 slave ships to the coast of West Africa, while the rest of the colonists sent just 189. As historian Jay Coughtry has argued, the North American trade in slaves was essentially the Rhode Island slave trade. Rhode Island slave traders made their money by playing it safe; they sailed small ships that allowed them to avoid long waits for slaves and the subsequent risk of disease on the African coast. In the first half of the eighteenth century, they sold 66 percent of their slaves in the West Indies, 31 percent in North America, and 3 percent in South America.[24]

However, the slave-trading business was not without serious risk and danger. George Scott, a Newport slave trader, nearly lost his life and livelihood when the "human cargo" attempted to take over his ship. During a voyage in 1730, as he transported ninety-six slaves from the coast of Guinea to the West Indies, the male slaves freed themselves from their chains. They killed three white watchmen, a doctor, a barrel repairer, and a sailor—by throwing

Table 1. Number of Slaves Transported to the Americas by British North American Colonists, 1701–50 (with number of voyages)

	1701–25	1726–50
Rhode Island	948 (8)	16,195 (123)
Non-RI New England	363 (4)	4,575 (36)
PA, DE, NJ	137 (1)	148 (2)
New York	355 (4)	407 (3)
Carolinas	48 (1)	415 (3)
Virginia	144 (1)	247 (2)

Source: Compiled through queries from the Trans-Atlantic Slave Trade Database, www.slavevoyages.org/tast/index.faces.

them overboard. Scott's crew then began shooting the slaves and barely suppressed the rebellion.[25] Just two years later, slaves who managed to escape their chains killed Captain Perkins, a Rhode Island slave trader. The rebellion proved costly—several slaves were killed.[26] In the spring of 1765 two Newport merchants, Samuel Vernon and William Vernon, made Thomas Rogers captain of their ship *Othello*. Rogers voyaged to Jamaica to buy slaves, but on the way back the seventy slaves aboard the *Othello* freed themselves and attempted to take over the ship. The slaves armed themselves with "billets of wood," then "seized the master and held him while others beat and wounded him in very dangerous manner." Rogers "suffered a fractured scull" but in the process negotiated with the slaves for nearly two hours. Apparently unsuccessful, he ordered his crew to "fire upon them." One slave was killed immediately; three were wounded and thirteen jumped overboard.[27] In addition to the risk of rebellion at sea, slave traders could lose their "human merchandise" once they transferred it to merchants who oversaw its sale on shore. Newport merchants John Channing and Walter Chaloner sued Henry Livingston, a merchant in Jamaica, for improperly disposing of "80 Negroes belonging to Channing and Chaloner."[28]

Despite the dangers and risks, what had begun as an experiment for wealthy merchants at the turn of the eighteenth century dominated Rhode Island's economy for nearly a century.[29] Slave-trading voyages bolstered the Rhode Island economy as a whole, as the industry employed tradesmen, sailors, scribes, and day laborers, and as slave traders filled their ships with local products to trade on the west coast of Africa. In 1713, Rhode Island slave traders introduced rum to the African coast, where this "new" liquor quickly replaced French brandy as the choice trading good.[30] A half century later there would be "upwards of thirty distil houses" in Rhode Island and eighteen in Newport alone.[31] By 1730, most trades and professions in Rhode Island were tied in one way or another to slaveholding and slave trading. Slave traders employed shipbuilders, sailors, caulkers, sailmakers, carpenters, rope makers, painters, and stevedores (those who loaded and unloaded ships). Coopers made the barrels that stored the rum, which was exchanged for slaves who were sold throughout the Americas.[32] Clerks, scribes, and warehouse overseers conducted the business of the trade.[33] The outfitting of even the smallest sloop required a small army of tradesmen. African slave-trading voyages also required additional crew to control and manage the captives. Merchants, many of whom were slave traders, paid significant taxes to the city of Newport, and the duties collected on the purchase and sale of enslaved people provided funds for public works.[34] The streets of Newport were paved and its bridges and country roads mended through the duties collected on slave imports. In many ways, the business of slavery literally built Rhode Island.[35]

Slave trading buttressed the local economy. For example, the sloop *Adventure*, owned by Christopher and George Champlin, sailed out of Newport in 1773 with eleven men—twice the number needed for a sloop bound for commodities trade with other colonies or the West Indies.[36] Furthermore, the bulk of its departing cargo consisted of local products. The *Adventure* was outfitted with handcuffs and shackles, twenty-six gallons of vinegar, pork, beef, sugar, molasses, wine, beans, tobacco, butter, bread, and flour. Most of these goods were bought from local farmers and merchants to feed the crew on the voyage there and then feed the crew and slaves on the return trip. But the vast majority of the cargo space was reserved for locally distilled rum. The *Adventure* carried 24,380 gallons of rum, which was enough to purchase several dozen slaves; enslaved women cost an average of 190 gallons and men averaged 220 gallons. The *Adventure* reached Africa in five weeks. It took the captain four months of cruising along the coast to acquire sixty-two slaves, along with rice, pepper, palm oil, and gold dust. Fifty-eight slaves survived and were sold in Grenada for between and thirty-five and thirty-nine pounds. The ship's owners received a 5 percent return on their investment.[37] Such voyages were common in Rhode Island. Slave-trading voyages produced profits from 2 to 10 percent; most voyages yielded returns of 5 or 6 percent, and while these profit margins may seem low by contemporary investment standards, investments in the Atlantic slave trade "were less risky and more liquid (that is capital could be extracted) and needed less time to garner returns than all other forms of possible investment in the eighteenth century."[38]

Atlantic commerce enriched the local economy as well as individual merchants. In a 1740 report to the Board of Trade, Governor Samuel Ward declared, "Navigation is one main pillar on which this government is supported at the present." He also reported that Rhode Islanders owned more than 120 vessels, which were "all constantly employed in trade"; all but 10 of them were employed in the slave trade.[39] Most of the vessels sailed back and forth to the West Indies; however, many vessels were employed in trade along the African coast or in neighboring colonies, and a few were even employed in Europe. Ward also noted that five ships, courtesy of Newport merchants, were equipped with crews of almost four hundred men.[40] These merchants thus also provided military support for the colony. Furthermore, Ward bragged that the other New England and West Indian colonies were dependent upon the commerce of Rhode Islanders:

> The neighboring governments have been in a great measure, supplied with rum, sugar, molasses and other West India goods by us brought home and sold to them here. Nay, Boston, itself,

Table 2. Number of Slaves Transported to the Americas by British North American Colonists, 1751–75 (with number of voyages)

	1751–60	1761–70	1771–75
Rhode Island	10,891 (114)	18,062 (165)	12,628 (104)
Non-RI New England	1,175 (10)	5,626 (42)	4,684 (30)
PA, DE, NJ	0 (0)	246 (3)	0
New York	1,457 (14)	1,861 (14)	0
Carolinas	906 (8)	639 (4)	650 (5)
Virginia	137 (1)	0 (0)	530 (1)

Source: Compiled through queries from the Trans-Atlantic Slave Trade Database, www.slavevoyages.org/tast/index.faces.

the Metropolis of Massachusetts, is not a little obliged to us for rum and sugar and molasses which they distil into rum, for the use of the fishermen &c. The West Indies have likewise reaped great advantage from our trade, by being supplied with lumber of all sorts suitable for building houses, sugar works and making casks; beef, pork, flour and other provisions, we are daily carrying to them, with horses to turn their mills and vessels for their own use; and our African trade often furnishes them with slaves for their plantations.[41]

West Indian planters were more dependent on the provisions that Rhode Islanders brought than on the slaves they transported from Africa. Governor Ward's report also noted Providence's entrance into the trade, and in the following decade Providence merchants began to mimic Newport's investments.[42]

The Brown family of Providence exemplifies how local merchants used both the West Indian provisions trade and the Atlantic slave trade to build wealth in colonial Rhode Island. In 1638 Chad

Brown, his wife Elizabeth, and their son John moved to Providence from Salem, Massachusetts. Chad Brown was a surveyor, as was his son John. John Brown had seven children, and his son James Brown, born in 1666, dabbled in mercantile trading. His experimentation led to six generations of Brown merchants. His sons, James and Obadiah Brown, were the first Browns to actively engage in Atlantic trading. In 1721, twenty-three-year-old James set sail for the Leeward Islands in the West Indies as a captain of the sloop *Four Bachelors*, which he owned with four other men from Providence. The profits he made from the voyage allowed him to open a shop in Providence. He sailed for the second and last time in 1727 as the master of the sloop *Truth and Delight*, bound for Marinneco. His store provided Rhode Islanders with an array of everyday goods, such as salt, fish, beef, turnips, sugar, butter, lamb, mutton, iron pots, wood, cotton, linen, leather, looking glasses, hoops for barrels, rum, wine, and brandy. Most of these goods were purchased from surrounding colonies with rum; however, cheese, pork, tobacco, and hoops for barrels were bartered for locally. His younger brother Obadiah worked for him as an agent and a ship captain from 1733 until 1739. Together, these two Brown brothers supplied plantation owners in the West Indies with corn, cheese, tar, horses, shingles, and tobacco.[43]

After John Brown II's death, Obadiah continued to organize voyages and run the store. In 1752, Obadiah Brown moved into the manufacturing business, opening a mill to process cocoa beans, a common trading good in the colonies. He also ran a rum distillery and built a spermaceti candle factory.[44] Obadiah, whose own sons died in childhood, trained his brother's sons in the family businesses—James Brown's sons, James III (b. 1724), Nicholas (b. 1729), Joseph (b. 1733), John (b. 1736), and Moses (b. 1738).

Although James III died in his twenties on a voyage to the Chesapeake, the surviving Brown brothers built a diverse business legacy and were among the most successful and influential merchants in the colony.[45] Nicholas pursued a career in manufacturing—pig iron (crude iron used to make steel or wrought iron) and cotton, as well as international trading with China. Joseph managed the spermaceti candle factory. Moses often served as the supercargo, the officer on a merchant ship in charge of the commercial concerns of the voyage, for family-sponsored voyages. John dabbled in all aspects of the family business and was by far the most ambitious. They sold their goods to West Indian planters. After Obadiah died in 1762, the four brothers continued running the family businesses under the name Nicholas Brown and Company.

The economic foundation that launched the Brown brothers' diverse investments was the business of supplying slave societies with necessities. The Browns also invested directly in the slave trade. James Brown sent the *Mary* on its first slaving voyage from Providence in 1736.[46] He brought back several slaves for the family. While the Browns regularly invested in slave voyages, they did not send another ship until 1759; French privateers captured their ship *Wheel of Fortune*. In 1763, they commissioned another slave-trading voyage on the *Sally*. The voyage was an absolute disaster. One hundred and eight of the 196 slaves died, and the slaves that survived were so sickly that they sold for one-tenth of the price of a healthy slave.[47] The Browns did not send another slaving voyage for over thirty years; however, they remained active in the business of slavery as merchants and investors.

Slaveholding and the Business of Slavery

In Rhode Island, merchants, slave traders, and slaveholders were often one and the same. For example, Aaron Lopez was among Rhode Island's most successful slave traders; this also made him one of the most successful businessmen in eighteenth-century Rhode Island. Between 1761 and 1774, he sent fourteen slave ships to the west coast of Africa. Lopez, a Sephardic Jew, came to Newport in 1752 and joined a candlemaking business with his brother, Moses Lopez, and his uncle and future father-in-law, Jacob Rodriguez Rivera. They also brokered candles, coca, lime, and molasses.[48] In 1760, Lopez held half interest in his father-in-law's brig *Grayhound*. A year later he sent his first voyage; his father-in-law, Jacob Rodriguez Rivera, held half interest, as he would for nearly every slave ship Lopez sent. Lopez's first voyage contained flour from Philadelphia, beef from New York, and, most importantly, 15,281 gallons of rum from local distilleries.[49] Over a fourteen-year period, Lopez was responsible for transporting an estimated 1,116 slaves from West Africa to the West Indies and the American South. Lopez was also a slave owner; he owned five slaves, and his father-in-law owned twelve. Both Lopez and Rivera employed their slaves in candlemaking, specifically the rendering of whale head matter for spermaceti candles.[50] Between 1760 and 1776, Lopez sponsored over two hundred voyages, although only a small fraction (fourteen, or less than 1 percent) were slave-trading voyages.[51] Although the vast majority of Lopez's business was with the other British colonies, the trade with the West Indies was what sustained his entire business because that trade provided him with molasses—the key ingredient for rum, his number one trading good. Lopez used rum to barter with other northern colonies and to purchase slaves. The business of slavery also led to the growth of the slave population. More than any other northerners, Rhode Islanders, as slave traders in West Africa and commodity traders in the West Indies, had direct access to large populations of enslaved people. This relatively easy access to enslaved men, women, and children allowed Rhode Islanders to acquire thousands of slaves in just a few decades.

In 1720, there were an estimated 543 slaves in Rhode Island; by 1750, that number had increased more than sixfold to 3,347 (see table 3).[52] This boom in the slave population directly paralleled the colony's increased participation in the Atlantic slave trade. Between 1726 and 1750, Rhode Island sent more than fifteen times the number of slave ships they had sent in the previous twenty-five years. In 1755, slaves accounted for 19, 18, and 8 percent of the total populations of the Narragansett Country, Newport, and Providence respectively.[53] Slaveholders in the Narragansett Country used relatively large populations of slaves to produce foodstuffs and livestock for trade with West Indian planters, while merchants and tradesmen in Newport and Providence used enslaved people as perpetual apprentices to expand their businesses.

In the two decades preceding the Revolutionary War, Rhode Islanders cemented their place in the Atlantic economy. They were critical suppliers of slaves and food for planters in the American South and the West Indies. Yet as the population of the colony grew the number of enslaved people in Rhode Island remained constant; consequently, slaves who made up of 10 percent of the total population in 1750 (3,347), made up just 6 percent of the population

Table 3. Slave Populations in the Northern British North
American Colonies, 1680–1750 (with percentage of total
population)

	1680	1720	1750
North	1,895 (2)	14,081 (5)	30,172 (5)
Rhode Island	175 (6)	543 (5)	3,347 (10)
Vermont	—	—	—
Massachusetts	170 (<1)	2,150 (2)	4,075 (2)
Connecticut	50 (<1)	1,093 (2)	3,010 (3)
New Hampshire	75 (4)	170 (2)	550 (2)
New York	1,200 (12)	5,740 (16)	11,014 (14)
New Jersey	200 (6)	2,385 (6)	5,354 (7)
Pennsylvania	25 (4)	2,000 (8)	2,822 (2)

Source: Compiled from census data in Ira Berlin's *Many Thousands Gone: The First Two Centuries of Slavery in North America* (Cambridge, MA: Harvard University Press, 1998), 369.

in 1770 (3,761).[54] This was because the slave population in Rhode Island reached a critical mass around 1750, even as the white population more than doubled, primarily as a result of immigration. There was no more room for Narragansett farmers to expand their operations, and the port cities were bursting with new white colonists who did not have resources to purchase slaves. And although the enslaved population plateaued in the mid-eighteenth century, between 1730 and 1770, Rhode Island was home to the largest concentration of blacks in New England. Most of these enslaved men, women, and children lived and labored on large farms in the Narragansett Country.[55]

Historian Ira Berlin famously differentiated a "slave society" from a "society with slaves." In a slave society, slave labor was essential to the economy, and slaveholders constituted the ruling class; in a society with slaves, slave labor was marginal to the overall economy, and slaveholders were part of but did not dominate the elite class.[56] The Narragansett Country was a slave society within a society with slaves. It was a slave society in that slave labor was central to its economy and social hierarchy. Enslaved people cultivated and processed foodstuffs for trade with the West Indies, and that trade was the economic heart of the Narragansett Country. Furthermore, slaveholders dominated local politics and society.[57] Three Narragansett slaveholders served as deputy governor between 1734 and 1752.[58] However, the Narragansett Country, like large farms throughout the North that depended on slave labor, was an anomaly within a region. In other words, the North as a whole was a society with slaves, but a few areas within the North took on some of the characteristics of slave societies.[59]

Located along the southeastern coast of Rhode Island, the Narragansett Country—also known as South County—was first cleared and farmed by Native Americans. The region's rich soil, moderate temperatures, and easy access to Newport made it an ideal place for large-scale commercial agriculture and grazing.[60] There was no staple crop. Instead farmers bred horses, cattle, and sheep, manufactured dairy products (primarily cheese), and cultivated small amounts of Indian corn, rye, hemp, flax, and tobacco.[61] Slave labor was essential to the economy in the Narragansett, as slaves produced nearly all the exported goods.[62] Most Narragansett farmers worked with merchants in Newport and Providence to export their products to markets in the West Indies and the southern colonies, where diary and meat products were sought-after goods because the southern climate was harsh on cattle. Very few Narragansett farmers were large slaveholders or planters, those who held upwards of twenty slaves; in fact, most Narragansett farmers held fewer than five, cultivating a variety of crops, raising livestock, and manufacturing dairy products.[63]

Slaveholders in the Narragansett were both distinct from and similar to their counterparts in Newport and Providence. Like their urban counterparts, they relied on the West Indian market; however, they held twice as many slaves and modeled their lives (if not the scale of their operations) after southern plantation owners. Farmers began moving to the Narragansett Country in the 1690s and would soon amass their wealth from large stock and dairy farms worked by bonded laborers. They initially relied on indentured Native Americans but replaced them with enslaved Africans. By the 1730s, the Narragansett Country was home to between twenty to thirty settler families and their bonds people. African slaves had slowly been brought into the Narragansett from the West Indies starting around 1700, and by 1740 the Narragansett Country had the highest concentration of enslaved people in the colony, many of whom came directly from Africa. By 1755, one out of every three residents was enslaved. In the town of Charlestown blacks were nearly 40 percent of the population (418 blacks and 712 whites). Farmers also employed local Native Americans and hired white day laborers during peak season.[64]

Cheese was the most important dairy product produced by enslaved people in the Narragansett Country, and their enslavers made fortunes in the product. Rhode Islanders produced more cheese than any other colony. Cheese commanded a better price than butter and milk, and Rhode Island planters faced serious competition in butter and milk production from dairy farms in New York and New Jersey. Robert Hazard, a successful Narragansett farmer, owned seventeen acres, had one hundred cows, and produced 13,000 pounds of cheese annually. Enslaved women on his farm were in charge of the care of twelve cows each and were expected to make twelve different cheeses daily. The Champlain farm, also in the Narragansett Country, had forty-two cows that produced 9,200 pounds of cheese annually.[65]

The success of a select few in this region allowed for a rather elaborate and leisurely lifestyle. Narragansett farmers commissioned their own portraits, took long European vacations, and attempted to emulate the English countryside and manor homes (see figure 1). They hired private tutors for their children and dominated local politics. And, like the South's wealthier planters, Narragansett farmers used intermarriage to consolidate their wealth. These farmers rarely performed manual labor—slave labor allowed them the wealth and time to cultivate a life of leisure.[66] While neither their landholdings nor their slaveholdings were equal to those of wealthy southern planters, they were part of the system that sustained and supported the expansion of slavery in the Americas.[67] Narragansett farmers marketed their agricultural goods, produced by slave labor, to distant and international markets.[68] The wealthiest planters hired sloops to ship their goods directly to the West Indies and southern colonies.[69]

Figure 1. John Potter (1716–87), his family, and a young enslaved boy. Potter was a prominent Narragansett farmer. Potter Family Portrait, 1740, Matunuck, RI; Object 53.3, image 002/533, JPG, Newport Historical Society.

Narragansett farmers flourished until the late 1760s, when they could no longer expand. The increase in population on a finite amount of land reduced landholdings and raised land prices—a trend that was occurring throughout New England. By the beginning of the American Revolution, the economic position of Narragansett farmers was deteriorating. Ultimately, their commercial farming operations were disrupted and destroyed by the Revolutionary War. The British occupied Newport, so Narragansett farmers were unable to export their food stuffs and livestock. This led to bouts of famine among the enslaved people in the West Indies—an estimated fifteen thousand slaves in Jamaica died of hunger between 1780 and 1787.[70] The region never recovered its agricultural glory.

All northern colonists, New Englanders in particular, participated in the West Indian and Atlantic slave trades, but Rhode Islanders were the most deeply entrenched.[71] Their domination of the North American trade in African slaves gave them increased access to slaves.[72] Merchants and tradesmen in Newport and Providence put their slaves to work in their homes and shops and on their ships.[73] Farmers in the Narragansett Country put thousands of enslaved men, women, and children to work producing foodstuffs and raising livestock for the West Indian trade. Local slave labor played a key role in the growth of commerce in Rhode Island; moreover, the abundant plantations of the West Indies provided farmers and merchants with a near-perpetual market for their slave-produced goods.

The economic history of Rhode Island reveals how deeply the northern colonies were involved in the development and maintenance of the institution of slavery.[74] Northerners were not peripheral to the development of slavery in the Atlantic world; like their fellow colonists in the South, they relied on an economic system that promoted a white enslaver class and debased people of color. Rhode Island's economic history points to the necessity of a national history of the institution of slavery, one that challenges simplistic regional dichotomies.

Legislating Slavery and Making Race

Rhode Islanders' investments in the business of slavery led to the creation of race-based slave law. In the North, as in the South, slave law reflected the desire and needs of colonists. Throughout most of the northern settlements, especially in the seventeenth century, slave labor was economically marginal. Consequently, the laws referring to the institution were scattered and ambiguous. However, as northerners began to rely more and more on slave labor and the business of slavery, laws were put in place that created and protected enslavement. The legal history of slavery in Rhode Island is unique among British North American colonies because of residents' investments in the business of slavery. Only Rhode Islanders explicitly forbade both African and Native American slavery; they did this in the 1650s and 1670s, when few colonists were invested in the business of slavery. However, as more and more Rhode Islanders made their livelihood from the West Indian and Atlantic slave trades, the General Assembly passed laws that acknowledged and protected both Native American and African slavery. They did this even though colonial lawmakers never explicitly legalized race-based slaveholding; instead, they simply began legislating as if the institution were already in place. While other northern colonists legally identified and justified who was eligible for the institution of slavery, white Rhode Islanders just assumed slavery was legitimate, inherited through the mother, and restricted to people of African and Native American descent.

Slavery was initially ill defined throughout the Northeast colonies. Most northern colonies assigned people of African descent a legal status somewhere between indentured servitude and chattel property. Enslaved blacks were legally recognized as persons before the law; however, they were bought, sold, inventoried, and willed as real estate. Massachusetts was the first colony to formally legalize slaveholding. The Massachusetts Body of Liberties (1641) allowed colonists to hold slaves as long as they were "Captives taken in just warres, and such strangers as willingly selle themselves or are sold to us." In 1670, the word *strangers* was deleted from the statute.[75] In 1704, the General Assembly of Massachusetts officially ruled that children born to slave mothers were indeed slaves. The Assembly also passed several laws restricting the rights of all Africans: emancipation was limited, a curfew was imposed, interracial sex was banned, and severe punishments were issued for striking Christians (who were, by default, white).[76]

A different scenario played out in what would become New York. The Dutch West India Company, which settled New Amsterdam in 1620, imported eleven enslaved Africans in 1626. These slaves could testify in court, bring suit against whites and each other, own property (except real estate or other slaves), and work for wages. In fact, some slaves in New Amsterdam lived under a system referred to as half freedom. Half freedom gave enslaved people control over their person in exchange for labor due to the company.[77] In other words, half-free people lived autonomously except for the days of labor owed to the company. English takeover of New Amsterdam, in 1664, all but obliterated half freedom. The Articles of Capitulation legally acknowledged slaveholding and encouraged chattel bondage, and the English crown allotted land grants to colonists according to the number of slaves owned.[78] The English were also instrumental in attaching race to the institution of slavery. New York laws initially declared that no Christians could be enslaved unless they sold themselves or were captives of war. In 1679, the Provincial Assembly proclaimed that local Native Americans could not be enslaved but that Native Americans from outside the colony could be held in bondage. And in 1706 the New York Assembly declared that "Negroes only shall be slaves" and that a Christian baptism would not alter their condition.[79]

By the first decade of the eighteenth century every northern colony had separate and special laws and punishments to govern people of Native American and African descent. Furthermore, these laws all assumed that all blacks were slaves, even though there was a small population of free black people. This assumption was primarily a reflection of the practice of slavery in the British West Indies. In most northern colonies, both enslaved and free blacks people had curfews, as well as restrictions on what kind of property they could own and on their ability to congregate. The northern colonies restricted the movements and behavior of blacks but allowed blacks to testify against whites in court and did not distinguish between slaves and free people in the prosecution of serious crimes—for example, black and white murderers received similar punishments.[80] Moreover, New Englanders recognized a slave's right to sue and marry, although enslaved married women lost their right to sue under the principle of coverture.[81] New Jersey and Pennsylvania passed sweeping restrictions on enslaved people, but it was New Yorkers, who held the largest number of slaves in the North, who enacted the most stringent and complete system of segregation. Enslaved people in New York could not gamble, hunt, leave home without a pass, or own dogs or livestock. If they violated these or other restrictions, they faced brutal punishments, including having their hands and feet cut off or being burned alive. Although colonies varied in the number and severity of legal restrictions they placed on blacks, "Every colony had laws to guarantee white supremacy."[82] Like their northern neighbors, Rhode Island lawmakers created a legal system in which all people of African and Native American descent, enslaved and free, were subordinate to white colonists.

Native Americans were the first slaves of colonial Rhode Island. Historian Margaret Newell reminds us that "New England armies, courts, and magistrates enslaved more than 1200 Indian men, women and children in the seventeenth century alone." In this, New England was not alone, as Native American slave labor constituted a substantial source of forced labor throughout the British North American colonies.[83] The same year Rhode Island was founded, in 1636, indigenous Pequot were enslaved.[84] The Pequot War (1636–37) established English hegemony in southern New

England and initiated the enslavement of a number of Pequot; it has been described as "one of the most important events in early American history," as it set the stage for English dominance in New England.[85] For Native Americans in New England, slavery resulted either in expulsion from the homeland or in subjugation to enemies; the slave experience for Native Americans was shaped by war, defeat, and capture.

Fewer than thirty years later, Metacom's War (1675–76) cemented English hegemony and led to the enslavement of significant numbers of Native Americans, especially in Rhode Island.[86] Metacom was the first Wampanoag leader to abandon diplomatic talks with English colonists.[87] Persistent English encroachment on the political and physical autonomy of the Wampanoag, combined with the questionable death of a Sassamon (a diplomat), led Metacom to abandon diplomatic avenues in favor of war. He forged an alliance with several Native American communities to drive out the English but could not unite all the Native American communities because of past rivalries, cultural divides, and existing alliances with colonists. The war extended as far north as New Hampshire and as far south as Connecticut. This war, the bloodiest the continent had yet seen, raged until a splinter Wampanoag group, fighting with the English, killed Metacom. One in ten soldiers on both sides was killed or injured, and the war destroyed much of the political and economic strength of the local indigenous people.[88]

During and after Metacom's War, Native American war captives were sold out of Rhode Island. A committee headed by Roger Williams, the founder of Providence, sold Native American prisoners of war into slavery.[89] Many more Native Americans from the now-destitute tribes that had allied with Metacom, including the Narragansett in Rhode Island, entered into indenture contracts with local whites. Some of these contracts bound Native Americans for decades. Native Americans were rarely enslaved for debt prior to 1675, because intact tribes had the resources and political power to pay fines and hire white patrons to represent them in court. After Metacom's War, they could no longer afford to pay goods or cash to avoid bondage as punishment for petty crimes, so they became particularly vulnerable to involuntary servitude. Rhode Islanders quickly became the leading employers of bound Native

American labor in the northern colonies.[90] Several references to Native American slaves appeared in Rhode Island's legislative and colonial records after 1675, and ads for runaway Native American slaves were common throughout the colonial period.[91]

Colonial courts also heard criminal cases involving enslaved Native American perpetrators. In 1712 John Slocum, a Native American who belonged to Giles Slocum, reportedly murdered his master's two small sons. He was hanged publicly in Newport.[92] In 1727, in Newport, a Native American slave named Peter, owned by Jacob Mott, was found guilty of attempted murder. According to the records he "did, sometime past, maliciously endeavor to murder his said master, by discharging at him a gun, loaded with a bullet and sundry shot, shooting him through the hat, so that it was an extraordinary act of Providence, said Mott was not killed." For his crimes, Peter was branded with an R on his forehead and publicly whipped.[93]

Though Native American slavery thrived in the first few decades of the founding of Rhode Island, it dwindled in the late seventeenth and early eighteenth century. In fact, in 1676, officials in Providence and Warwick prohibited the enslavement of Native Americans, declaring, "Noe Indian in this Collony be a slave, but only to pay their debts or for their bringinge up, or custody they have received." And in 1715 the General Assembly prohibited the importation of Native American slaves.[94] Some of this dwindling, albeit slowly, was merely statistical, as most colonial authorities did not recognize the multiple heritages of mixed-race people who were of African and Indian descent; that growing category of people was referred to only as "Negroe," as black, or as African. But more important were the growing conflicts and tensions between colonists and Native Americans. Within the first two decades of the eighteenth century, nearly all the northern colonial governments prohibited Native Americans from moving into, and colonists from bringing Native Americans into, their prospective colonies. Colonists wanted societies where Native Americans did not live at all, even as slaves and servants. The Newport town council made it illegal to sell firearms of any sort to Native Americans, and the town of Portsmouth banished them "to live in the woods." Furthermore, white merchants were not to trade with, sell liquor to, or repair the firearms of Native Americans. Native Americans were viewed as a dangerous population, difficult to control and keep in bondage because they knew the land better than the colonists and were able to escape successfully. Colonists increasingly viewed Native Americans as undesirable neighbors regardless of their status. A 1712 Massachusetts act forbade the importation of additional Native American servants and characterized all Indians as "malicious, vengeful, rude, insolent and ungovernable."[95] Legislators in Rhode Island, Pennsylvania, New Hampshire, and Connecticut all passed similar acts.

The institution of slavery in Rhode Island began as system of bondage for captured and impoverished Native Americans but flourished as a system committed to black bondage. Starting in the first decades of the eighteenth century, white Rhode Islanders replaced a familiar "dangerous" population with black "strangers."[96] By the end of the first decade of the eighteenth century, the few slaves in Rhode Island were primarily not Native Americans but of African descent. First through common practice and then through law, white Rhode Islanders created a race-based system of slavery in which Native Americans and Africans were slaves and whites were the master class. Africans and Native Americans cohabitated both as enslaved people in white households and as free people and fugitive slaves in Native communities. For example, in 1728, Jethro, an enslaved "negro" in Kingstown, Rhode Island, stole a canoe from his enslaver and headed to Martha's Vineyard to "hid among the Indians."[97] The histories of trafficked Africans and the colonization of Native American lands and peoples are intertwined; moreover, "The persistent, symbolic resonance and multifaceted meanings of African-derived peoples and cultures within the spaces of Native America often go unrecognized."[98] In Rhode Island, the Narragansett and the Africans intermarried for generations, and their children did not relinquish their biracial heritage and multiple identities, despite attempts from the state to insist on single-race categories in order to divest Native Americans of their land.[99]

The transition from the practice of slavery to the legalization of slavery took nearly half a century. In 1652, Rhode Island officials from Providence and Warwick, towns not yet involved in Atlantic commerce, prohibited the enslavement of whites and blacks.[100] These officials claimed to speak for the entire colony when they declared: "Whereas, there is a common course practiced amongst English men to buy negers, to that end they may have them for service or slaves forever; for the preventing of such practices among us, let it be ordered, that no blacke mankind or white being forced by covenant bond, or otherwise, to serve any man or his assighnes longer than ten years or until they come to bee twentie four yeares of age, if they bee taken in under fourteen, from the time of their cominge within the liberties of this Collonie."[101] The "common course practiced" probably referred to their slaveholding neighbors in Massachusetts.[102] Perhaps these Rhode Islanders were attempting to set themselves apart: they were not going to be like all the other Englishmen who bought and enslaved "negers." The law protected bound labor but banned lifelong servitude for blacks and whites. Twenty-four years later, in 1676, officials in Providence and Warwick banned lifelong slavery for Native Americans and declared that they were to serve as slaves only to repay debt.[103] Nevertheless, by 1680 there were 175 slaves in Rhode Island of both Native American and African descent. And on May 30, 1696, fourteen enslaved Africans were purchased from the *Seaflower* in Newport, "for betwixt £30 and £35."[104] This was the first record of Rhode Islanders buying slaves directly from Africa. Rhode Island settlers ignored the dictates of a fractured and ineffective colonial government and were not held to any legal account for breaking local law.

In 1703, the transition was complete, as the Rhode Island General Assembly wrote slavery and racism into law. "If any negroes or Indians either freemen, servants, or slaves, do walk in the street of the town of Newport, or any other town in this Collony, after nine of the clock of the night, without a certificate from their masters, or some English person of said family with them, or some lawfull excuse for the same, that it shall be lawfull for any person to take them up and deliver them to a Constable."[105] This act identified blacks and Native Americans as slaves; furthermore, it restricted the movements of all blacks and Native Americans, regardless of their status.[106] Blacks and Native Americans were also identified as likely criminals who should not be allowed out after dark. Blacks and Native Americans, free or enslaved, found after curfew were "to be whipped at the publick whipping post in said town, not exceeding fifteen stripes upon their naked backs." The act also forbade free whites from "entertaining men's servants, either negroes or Indians, without leave of their master or to whom they do belong" after 9:00 p.m., under threat of a five-shilling fine. Finally the act empowered any person, that is, any white person, to detain "any negroes or Indians."[107] In other words, all whites could police all blacks and Native Americans. Whiteness was legally endowed with privilege and power, while people of color were legally identified as suspect and in need of supervision.

Five years later, in 1708, Rhode Island's colonial assembly further endorsed and protected slavery by forbidding whites to socialize with "black slaves" and "Indian servants."[108] Because a collective body, the Rhode Island General Assembly, wrote these two acts, they superseded municipal laws forbidding slavery. Assembly members explicitly attached race to the institution of slavery: "negroes and Indians" were slaves and servants. Whites, on the other hand, had responsibilities in regulating and controlling the behavior of free and enslaved blacks and Native Americans. These laws solidified legal race-making in the colony, serving the needs of the enslaver class while also giving race social and legal meaning. It would take 134 years for Rhode Island lawmakers to completely undo legally sanctioned slavery; in 1784 the General Assembly outlawed hereditary slavery, and in 1842 legislators abolished slaveholding. However, throughout the colonial period Rhode Islanders passed a series of laws to protect the rights of white colonists to hold black and brown people as property.

Rhode Island lawmakers began to refer to and treat enslaved people as property—chattel.[109] In 1714, the General Assembly forbade enslaved people to board ferries alone, even under their masters' direction, without a certificate of ownership carried by their master or mistress or some person in authority. Boatmen and ferrymen who violated the law were fined twenty shillings and were held responsible for any financial damages to the master. By 1728, the practice of race-based slavery extended to an ideology of race with implications beyond bondage. For the first time, people of African descent were explicitly defined as a potentially dependent class. The act for manumitting "negroes" required masters to post a bond of one hundred pounds for each freed person to protect the white public from the burden of supporting freed slaves. Assembly members assumed that blacks would be unable or unwilling to support themselves:

> Forasmuch, as great charge, trouble and inconveniencies have arisen to the inhabitants of divers towns in this colony, by the manumitting and setting free mulatto and negro slaves. Be it enacted by the General Assembly of this colony, and by the authority of the same it is enacted, that no mulatto or negro slave, shall be hereafter manumitted, discharged or set free, or at liberty, until sufficient security be given to the town treasurer of the town or place where such person dwells, in a valuable sum of not less than £100, to secure and indemnify the town or place from all charge for, or about such mulatto or negro, to be manumitted and set at liberty, in case he or she by sickness, lameness or otherwise, be rendered incapable to support him or herself. And no mulatto or negro hereafter manumitted, shall be deemed or accounted free, for whom security shall not be given as aforesaid, but shall be the proper charge of their respective masters or mistresses, in case they should stand in need of relief and support; notwithstanding any manumission or instrument of freedom to them made and given; and shall be liable at all times to be put forth to service by the justices of the peace or wardens of the town.[110]

"Mulattoes and negroes" were now legally defined not only as slaves but as "slave like," even when they were free people. With the hefty penalty for freedom, the government actively discouraged manumission. The only place for blacks in the colony was as slaves. This was also the second time that colonial officials used the term *mulatto*, which suggests that enslaved people were bearing children of white parentage and that some whites were freeing their enslaved children. This was problematic in a society that supported and protected race-based slavery: free people of color were anomalies in this system of racial slavery, which is why Rhode Island lawmakers tried to limit social interactions between whites and blacks. Native Americans were not mentioned. This was most likely the result of mixed-race slaves being simply considered black; however, colonial lawmakers continued to refer to Indian servants.

In 1750, the General Assembly again forbade any person to "sell, give, truck, barter or exchange . . . any strong Beer, Ale, Cyder, Wine, Rum, Brandy, or other strong liquor to any Indian, Mulatto or Negro Servant or Slave." They claimed that liquor was inducing slaves and servants to steal from their masters and was causing public disturbances. Consequently, anyone found supplying Native American and black slaves or servants with liquor would be fined thirty pounds for each offense. Reiterating themes of the 1703 law, this act again restricted any person, including white persons, from entertaining (dancing, gaming, or diversion of any kind) servants and slaves without their owner's permission, "on penalty of forfeiting the sum of Fifty Pounds Old-Tenor . . . for each and every offense." Moreover, "free Indian, Mulatto or Negro" persons found guilty of attending such entertainments would be put to service in a private house for one year, "the Wages accruing by said service, to be for the Benefit of the Town where the Offense shall be committed."[111] Free people of color risked becoming bound servants for socializing with slaves and free whites. In 1757, the General Assembly allowed slaveholders to search private vessels if they suspected that their human property was stowed aboard it. They were also entitled to double damages if a privateer or captain was found guilty of stealing a slave.[112] Rhode Island lawmakers were fully committed to protecting the institution of slavery.

Free People of Color

Slavery also shaped the lives of free people of color. There were so few free people of color in Rhode Island that most census record takers did not bother to designate their actual number; any mention of race was indicated with the assumption that all, or the vast majority, of people of color were enslaved.[113] Not surprisingly, the small population of free people of color faced serious discrimination. In 1703, as we have seen, the General Assembly restricted the rights of all people of color—free, indentured, and enslaved. The law acknowledged that there were indeed free blacks and Native Americans in the colony; however, despite being as "free" as whites, they were to be treated differently than whites. For example, they were subject to curfews and restricted from socializing with enslaved people; violations could result in indentured servitude.[114] These types of laws were particularly devastating for families of color, as it was not uncommon for free families to have an enslaved family member. Such was the case for Anthony Kinnicutt. He was "born free although not wholly of white blood," and he sold small quantities of liquor and other refreshments to passengers going in and out of Providence. Kinnicutt became one of Providence's most successful black entrepreneurs. However, his family was fractured. He married an enslaved woman; consequently, he lived apart from his wife and children until 1774, when he bought his five children. His wife, Margaret, died before he could raise enough funds to free her.[115] Kinnicutt was part of a very small community of property-holding people of color. In 1753 John Read left £100, and in 1745 Jack Howard left his dependents £145.[116] Emanuel Bernoon, manumitted in 1736, ran an oyster bar in Providence; when he died in 1769 he left a house, a lot, and personal property worth £539, 10s to his wife, who supported "herself by taking in washing."[117] At least two free men of color were slaveholders. Tom Walmsey, who was of African and Native American descent, held "Negro Tom Commock," who labored as a sailor. Another black freeman threatened to put his enslaved woman "in his pocket," that is, to sell her if she did not obey him.[118]

Most free people of color did not fare as well as these propertied men. Court records indicate that the free people of color in Rhode Island lived on the margins. Emanuel, a free "negro" man, was indicted for feloniously stealing a "darke bay horse" out of the pasture of Capt. James Clarke of Newport. He pled not guilty but was ultimately convicted and sentenced to a public whipping of twenty-one lashes. Emanuel was also ordered to pay Captain Clarke fifty pounds—two times the value of the horse. He was unable to pay the fine, so he was "sold by the Sheriff for forty-one years for payment of the same."[119] Mercy, a black freewoman, was convicted of stealing two woolen bed blankets, valued at three pounds, from Jeremiah Wilcox of Newport. She was sentenced to "restore twofold" and "be well whipped with Ten stripes on your naked back at the publick whipping post in Newport."[120] These crimes are telling. In the colonial period, holding livestock was a form of financial stability, and firewood and blankets were necessities. Stealing such things was a sign of economic insecurity and desperation.

Race was continually remade in colonial Rhode Island, first by town officials with limited authority and then by a collective body of legislators with central authority. White Rhode Islanders used the law to attach race to both slavery and mastery. First only Native Americans were eligible for enslavement, as the 1652 law explicitly forbade enslaving blacks or whites. In 1676 Native American slavery was also prohibited. These initial bans reflected the opinions or desires of a few town leaders and had little to no meaning to the merchants and tradesmen who were increasingly trading both within the colony and in other colonies across the North. The 1703 law acknowledging black and Native American slavery reflected what was already happening: race-based slavery existed in practice; moreover, white Rhode Islanders took it for granted as participants in the Atlantic economy. As whites increasingly preferred a society in which Native Americans did not participate at all, people of African descent were increasingly the sole candidates for slavery. These laws also required action and obedience from white Rhode Islanders regardless of whether they owned slaves. The 1708 law restricted whites from socializing with or entertaining black slaves and Indian servants. In 1715, the colonial government specifically noted what race of slaves whites could bring into the colony; "imports" of Native American slaves were prohibited, leaving African slaves as the only legal "imports." In 1728, colonial officials restricted slave owners from freeing their slaves by attaching a fee to manumission. Finally, in 1750, free blacks risked bound servitude for socializing in mixed company. *Black* and *slave* became synonyms in this period, and as slavery was understood to be emblematic of dependency, so too was blackness.

2 / Living and Laboring under Slavery

Slaveholding differed from the business of slavery because enslaved people resisted the attempts of their enslavers to turn them into commodities. Unlike the slave traders, who had to deliver relatively healthy, enslaved people, and the merchants who traded foodstuffs in the West Indies, Rhode Island slaveholders had to find ways to coerce and convince enslaved people to work. Such compulsion could not rely solely on threats, verbal abuse, and physical punishments; consequently, slaveholders were compelled to also use inducements in their attempts to control their human property. On July 28, 1725, in Warwick, Rhode Island, Hager, a "negro" slave, was willed ten shillings; her children were bequeathed five shillings each. Their master Captain Peter Green left Hager and her children money to "induce her [Hager] to be kinde to my Wife."[1] In 1749, Joseph Wanton bequeathed all his "Negroes" to his son Edward. There was, however, a catch. He would allow those slaves who were "not willing to live with him" to live with his daughters instead. But if his daughters "decline taking such Negro or Negroes that wants to be sold aforsed, the sd Negro or Negroes shall have the liberty of Chosing a Master or Mistress that will buy them provided they will give as good a price for e'm as another."[2] In 1772, Christopher Gardner testified that his brother's slave Moll had scalded his nephew to death, but she was never prosecuted.[3] These circumstances raise intriguing questions. Why would a master leave his slaves what appears to be a bribe? Did Hager and her children receive their money when Green died, and were they kind to his wife? Why would Wanton allow his slaves to choose their own masters? Did Wanton's slave(s) remain with his sons or elect to live with his daughters or did his daughters sell them? Why did James Gardner not prosecute Moll for murder, especially since his brother had witnessed the alleged crime? Did Gardner punish Moll himself? Did Moll continue to serve the family or was she sold? These questions are impossible to answer, but they serve as a reminder that slavery was a negotiated relationship and that enslaved people were not powerless. The Green, Wanton, and Gardner families had held slaves for over a generation; these experienced enslavers most likely understood that slave management included concessions to enslaved people.

An interesting result of Rhode Island's particular economy is that it dictated geographic patterns of slaveholding in the colony as well as the work done by enslaved people. We know that enslaved people throughout the North did not produce a staple crop; instead, their labor helped to sustain the multitude of slaves that cultivated sugar, tobacco, and rice elsewhere in the Americas. Nowhere was this connection more salient than in Rhode Island. Enslaved Rhode Islanders labored in distilleries where rum was made to purchase slaves, built the slave ships that transported enslaved Africans, served as the crew on those ships as they crisscrossed the Atlantic, and grew the food that sustained the enslaved. Just as the growth of the plantation transformed black life in the South, laboring in the business of slavery transformed black life in North, and Rhode Island in particular. Prior to white Rhode Islanders' commitment to Atlantic commerce, in the first decades of the eighteenth century, the enslaved population was relatively small, scattered, and predominantly Native American. However, as the West Indian and Atlantic slave trades became the cornerstones of the local economy, more and more enslaved people of African descent were brought into the colony. Moreover, those larger webs of trading determined the places where enslaved people lived and dictated the work they performed. Most rural slaves lived on large farms with three or four other enslaved people of African or Native American descent or indentured whites and Native Americans. In the countryside, especially in Narragansett Country, these bound people labored as cow herders, shepherds, and dairy farmers and produced small amounts of grains, vegetables, cheese, and fish. Most urban slaves worked alone or with just one other enslaved or indentured person. In the coastal cities of Newport, Providence, Warwick, and Bristol, these bound people worked as domestics, tradesmen, manufacturers, and shopkeepers. The cumulative labor of all these enslaved people all across the colony undergirded the buying and selling of people and goods on both sides of the Atlantic.

People of color who were enslaved by the progenitors of the business of slavery refused to be treated as objects or products.[4] While few sources reveal the day-to-day experiences of the enslaved, combing public records and private documents allows reasonable conjecture about their lives. Census data, court records, correspondence, private papers, and estate and business records of slaveholders shed light on the activities of the enslaved, while also highlighting the challenges they faced as inheritable and contested property. The agency of many enslaved people countered attempts by enslavers to view and treat them as commodities, even when the enslavers were commodity traders. The white merchants and slave traders who carried out the business of slavery, in colonial Rhode Island, were not just businessmen but active participants in the development and maintenance of American slavery—a system that attempted, unsuccessfully, to dehumanize people of African descent. Many enslaved Rhode Islanders took advantage of the fact that their labors often mirrored those of whites; they assisted their enslavers in their various businesses and were routinely rented out as tradesmen and sailors, positions that afforded increased opportunity to challenge the institution of slavery. Yet most enslaved people in Rhode Island who resisted slavery were not attacking the business of slavery but seeking freedom for themselves, their families, and their communities. Their resistance and lived experiences are critical to understanding how American slavery was contested from every angle. Whether enslaved people found themselves laboring on vast plantations, on small and large farms, in the city, on ships, or in shops, they ran away, lobbied for their freedom, and strove to build full lives within the confines of slavery. Enslaved Rhode Islanders, like counterparts throughout the Americas, refused to be simply property.

Small Slaveholdings and Fractured Families

The absence of plantations in the North made the experience of slavery for enslaved northerners markedly different from that of their counterparts in the middle and southern colonies. Northern slaves often worked alongside and resided in the same homes as their masters. Most enslaved people in the northern colonies lived and labored in the countryside; rural slaveholders held proportionately more enslaved people than their urban counterparts. However, because the colonial populations were often heavily concentrated in urban areas, there were significant numbers of enslaved people living in towns and cities.[5] In Rhode Island enslaved people were just as likely to live in a city as they were to live on a farm.

Because of the patterns of slaveholding, enslaved families, especially urban families, were routinely separated in the colonial North: husbands often lived apart from their wives, parents from children, and sisters from brothers. For sale ads regularly appeared in the *Providence Gazette* stating that a child was being sold "only for Want of Employ."[6] Intimate living conditions among the enslaved and enslavers led most slaves to adapt to and adopt English culture and customs. However, they did not abandon African traditions; in fact, in the North, the heavy population concentration of blacks in New York, New Jersey, and New England allowed for the creation and persistence of a distinct northern black culture. This culture was sustained by a steady increase in the proportion of enslaved people born in the colonies. Between 1700 and 1750, the proportion of black New Englanders who had been born abroad decreased from 70 percent to 50 percent; after 1750, the majority of northern blacks were American born.[7]

Nearly half of enslaved Rhode Islanders labored on large farms raising livestock and cultivating crops for the West Indian trade. Merchants and tradesmen in the port cities, who regularly rented out their slaves to other merchants and tradesmen for shipbuilding and sent them to sea, held the other half of the enslaved population. By the end of the colonial era, in 1774, 10 percent of the slave-owning households in Rhode Island included six or more people of color, and of these households 25 percent had ten or more enslaved people.[8]

During the colonial era, the vast majority of people of African descent in British North America lived under some form of bondage, as did most Native Americans who resided in English settlements.[9] In Rhode Island, the transition from a predominantly Native American slave population to a predominantly African slave population was largely a result of increased access to African slaves via the slave trade and a growing desire to purge Native Americans from white society.[10] Many of the first Africans trickled into the colony from Barbados in the last three decades of the seventeenth century.[11] During that span, white Rhode Islanders purchased just twenty to thirty enslaved Africans a year. Most of these slaves had been in the Caribbean for over a year and could speak and understand some English. The status of these people was ambiguous for most of the seventeenth century. Some were slaves for life, while others were indentured for seven, ten, or even thirty years. Alongside these variant statuses of people of color, the status of white indentured servants remained the same, and their numbers began to dwindle as mortality rates increased and it became more advantageous to own someone for a lifetime rather than for several years. In the eighteenth century, Rhode Islanders began importing slaves directly from Africa as local slave traders began making regular voyages to the continent.[12] Merchants and tradesmen from Newport and the Narragansett Country were the primary buyers. By the end of the first decade of the eighteenth century, most of the enslaved were of African descent and were slaves for life; moreover, their children and their children's children, so deemed the Rhode Island legislature, would inherit their status as lifelong slaves.

For at least the next half century, that geographic pattern, which was dictated by the business of slavery, would persist. More than half of all the enslaved people in the growing colony lived in Newport or the Narragansett Country laboring for tradesmen, merchants, and farmers. According to the 1755 census, 1,234 slaves (648 men and boys and 586 women and girls) lived in Newport, and 1,306 (664 men and boys and 642 women and girls) slaves lived in the Narragansett. The result of these concentrations meant that nearly one-fifth of the total population in Newport and the Narragansett was enslaved.[13]

Laboring in the City, at Sea, and in the Countryside

On June 10, 1745, Captain Robert Morris sold four "Mustees" (someone of African and Native American descent), four "Negroes," and one "Mulatto" (someone of African and European descent) for a total of £956.[14] Such slave auctions were routine in the bustling port city of Newport. These enslaved men and women joined the ranks of thousands of enslaved Rhode Islanders.[15] Samuel Bours, a small shopkeeper who sold everything from Bristol beer to prayer books, owned a slave. John Stevens, a stonecutter, and Richard Johnson, a baker, owned a slave, "and seven of the 11 recipients of tavern licenses granted in Newport owned one to three slaves."[16] In the city enslaved women labored primarily as domestic servants while men labored in local industry (candlemaking and rum distilleries), husbandry, building and metal trades, sailing, whaling, and manual labor (wharf warehousing).[17] One of the many things that made enslaved people so valuable in a commerce-based economy was their versatility—they could be put to work as tradesmen, secretaries, and sailors.

As often the only enslaved person in a household, enslaved people in Newport and Providence lived fairly solitary lives, lodged in an attic, a garret, or a kitchen, working by themselves or beneath a white supervisor.[18] And, like poor people of all races and statuses in the colonies, enslaved northerners often suffered from malnutrition, existing on a diet of "corn meal, stale bread and watery stew." This type of diet was particularly bad for women because it lacked the additional iron, protein, and calcium required for regular menstruation and successful pregnancy. And unlike enslaved people in rural areas, these city dwellers were not allotted vegetable gardens or given leave to hunt to supplement their diets.[19]

Despite the isolation within individual households, the nature of urban slavery allowed enslaved urbanites considerable freedom of movement and association. Because most enslaved men in Newport and Providence worked for merchants and tradesmen, they were often required to traverse the city and had regular encounters with other slaves, servants, and free people. On the other hand, most enslaved women lacked the mobility of their male counterparts, as their labors were primarily confined to the household, where they worked "sweeping, emptying chamber pots, carrying water, washing the dishes, brewing, looking after young children, cooking, baking, spinning, knitting, carding and sewing"; the primary exception to this domestic work was fetching water and running errands, which allowed sporadic and brief contact with a slightly larger world. A few enslaved women acted as "lady maids" to the wives and daughters of the wealthiest slaveholders, and those slaves presumably saw a bit more of the world. This labor, lifelong, menial, and hard, offered few or no opportunities for advancement, autonomy, or adventure. Nevertheless, enslaved northern city dwellers (at least the men) had daily interactions with individuals completely outside the control and domain of their masters.[20] This was especially true in the port cities of Providence and Newport, where enslaved people were rented out for days, weeks, and sometimes years. They traveled between their enslaver's home to their workplaces: shops, ships, or other private homes.

Enslaved northerner urbanities also had greater access to education and religious instruction than their southern counterparts. Sarah Osborn, a white critic of slavery, established an interracial school in the 1750s in Newport, and in the 1760s held Sunday services in her home exclusively for enslaved people; visiting white Baptist ministers conducted the services. By 1765, free and enslaved blacks were attending services; the next year Osborn recorded that thirty-five black women and forty black men regularly attended Sunday evening services. Local clergymen organized schools and classes for blacks, including Reverend Thomas Patten (in the 1750s), Marmaduke Brown (in the 1760s), and Reverend George Bissett (in the 1770s). Mrs. Mary Brett also operated a school for blacks in the 1760s and 1770s.[21]

Such interracial and interclass social interactions were noted and resented by the enslaver class. In 1703, as we have seen, the Rhode Island General Assembly restricted the movements of all blacks and Native Americans, regardless of their status. They were not to be out after nine in the evening. In 1708, the Assembly forbade whites from socializing with "black slaves" and "Indian servants," and finally in 1750 the lawmakers forbade the "entertaining of Indian, negro or mulatto servants or slaves."[22] Authorities were especially concerned about enslaved blacks cavorting with free blacks.

Any free Negro or mulatto who shall keep a disorderly house
or entertain any slave or slaves at unreasonable hours or in
any flagrant manner, such town council be hereby empowered
to examine into said matter—and shall find such free Negro
or mulatto guilty of the same. They may, if they think proper,
break up from the house-keeping such free Negro or mulatto.
And if such free Negroes or mulattoes have been slaves and
manumitted by their masters—town council are hereby
empowered—to put out and bind them as servants for a term of
time, not exceeding four years.[23]

The repeated attempts by lawmakers, across multiple generations,
to control the movement and socializing of enslaved people reveal
that enslaved people made lives for themselves outside the bonds
of slavery.

Because urban slaves often had relative freedom of movement
and association, and because they often possessed sought-after
skills, they had increased opportunities to flee. In 1770, Quam, an
enslaved skilled tradesman, did just that. His enslaver placed the
following ad in the *Providence Gazette*:

Quam, a negro man supposed to be about thirty years of age, by
trade a cooper, went from his master's house in Providence (most
probably in a delirious condition, being often subject to be), on
Sunday the 8th day of July last, and has not been heard of since.

He is of middling stature, slim make, of a serious thought-
ful turn of mind, inclines to talk but little, but speaks pretty
good English, is a good Workman at his Trade, and formerly
lived with Mr. Alexander Frazier, of whom he learnt it. Had
on an old striped flannel jacket, striped shirt, tow trousers
and an old Hat; but took nothing else with him that is known,
although he was uncommonly neat and precise in his dress.

Whoever can give any Account (if living) where he is, so
that his Master may have him again, or will (if he is found living) tenderly and kindly treat him, and return him as soon as
possible to his master, shall have two dollars reward, and all
necessary expenses and charges paid by Job Smith.[24]

Quam's enslaver noted his intelligence and skill and wanted his
runaway treated "tenderly and kindly." Moreover, Quam had some

considerable social freedoms—as he was usually drinking on Sundays, most likely with others. He also had a good command of the language and a marketable skill and had both the means and the opportunity to successfully flee bondage. Skilled enslaved tradesman Caesar, who was "by Trade a Blacksmith, but principally follows Anchor-Making," also absconded from his Newport enslaver. Eber Sweet placed thirteen inquiries in the local paper about Caesar's whereabouts. Despite his efforts Caesar was not recovered.[25] Josiah Lyndon also taught his enslaved bondsman Caesar Lyndon sought-after skills. Lyndon was the Assembly clerk from 1728 until 1767 and served a single term as governor from 1768 to 1769, and Caesar worked as his business agent. In fact, Caesar had his own small lending business; enslaved as well as free blacks and whites borrowed money from him.[26]

As Newport and Providence were port cities, many enslaved Rhode Islanders labored aboard ships. In fact, the demand for sailors was so high that, by 1774, the city of Newport had a female majority because so many men white and black, free and enslaved, went or were sent out to sea.[27] Saint Jago, who was enslaved to Stephen Hopkins—a former Rhode Island governor and a signer of the Declaration of Independence—was part of the crew of the *Blackbird*, a privateer commissioned by Hopkins in 1762. Jago also worked as a rigger, fitting the ropes and chains used to support the masts and control the sails of the ship, on a twenty-ton schooner.[28] Enslaved Rhode Islanders, like their northern port city counterparts, were also routinely involved in shipbuilding and voyage preparation. On June 23, 1747, two enslaved men, "Negro Mingo" and "Negro Toney," were rented out to help prepare the *Swan* for a West Indian voyage. "Negro Anthony" was rented six times in a two-year period to help outfit trading ships.[29] John Banister, a prominent Newport merchant, regularly rented out all three of these men. Slaveholding women also "rented out" their bondsmen: widows James, Thurston, and Wanton sent their "negroes" to work on the *Apollo*, as did Lidia Rodam, who rented out multiple bondsmen.[30] These men were a part of a long history of enslaved people, engaged in nearly every aspect of maritime labor: they and other enslaved men worked as pilots, sailors, canoe men, divers, linguists, porters, stewards, cooks, cabin boys, and riggers.[31]

Like many enslaved men before him, Benjamin Freebody sailed out of Newport, which had become, by the 1730s, the center of North American slave trading. He sailed from Rhode Island to West Africa, to Grenada, to Pensacola, to the West Indies, and finally to New York. It was from New York City on April 8, 1784, nearly a decade after his journey began, that he posted a letter to his enslaver, reminding him of his promise to emancipate him and reporting his beleaguered condition:

> Dear Master I belong to you and without your goodness would grant me any liberty to be a free man as you often Promised me should when I was with you I was not content but wanted my liberty but I have Sincerely wish I'd never had left you the swill that was given to the hogs I have often wishd for young Malboar can inform how I was used I'm at present in a very low state of health and without a friend or a Copper to bless I hope your goodness will comply with my request to let me know if I'm to be free or remain a slave if your goodness will consent to give my discharge I would wish a line from your own hand and then I would know what Id had to depend upon I'm at present at work to discharge a debt my Spirits is very low and I really believe in a declining state of health my Sincere Prayers and well wishes for you and all your family which is all at present from poor Benjamin Freebody.[32]

Two months later, June 16, 1784, Benjamin wrote to Samuel again, this time imploring him not to sell him: "Being well assured of your goodness which I have experienced for many years. . . . I hope and trust you will not sell me to any man without my consent." His flattery was one of the many strategies employed by enslaved people to combat arbitrary power. He also reported that he and Dick, who was most likely owned by Samuel Freebody, received only "one doller" and "2 sea vests osnabrig for 2 frocks and as much bais as made a shirt and trousers" in all their time at sea. Freebody was hinting that they, and therefore Samuel Freebody, had not been properly compensated for their labor; it was not usual for slaves who were rented out to receive clothing or cash in addition to the fee paid to their master.[33] In some respects, Freebody represented a typical enslaved Rhode Islander—his labors were shaped by the business of slavery in that he was rented out as a sailor; however, unlike most enslaved people, he left a firsthand account of his experiences and his desire to be a free man. There is no record of Samuel Freebody's response, so we do not know if Samuel ever manumitted Benjamin; however, Samuel did report having slaves in his household in 1800.[34] Enslaved sailors, like Freebody, often had to contend with multiple masters and to navigate multiple layers of oppression. Freebody had to appeal to his first master to save him from his master abroad, while making a case for his ultimate goal—freedom.

Enslaved Rhode Islanders were just as likely to labor on farms as they were to labor in cities, and in the Narragansett Country they raised livestock and grew food for the West Indian trade. The Narragansett Country, as we have seen, was home to the highest concentration of enslaved people in New England throughout most of the eighteenth century.[35] The size of slaveholdings in the Narragansett Country has been long contested among historians. One has claimed that a few planters had as many as forty to sixty slaves, while another has asserted that some planters had twenty but no more than fifty; another still has contended that slaveholders rarely had fifty and that most had no more than five. Such disparities are most likely a result of poor record keeping and confusion over terminology—Narragansett Country farmers have been referred to as planters (slaveholders who own large tracts of land and twenty or more enslaved people), which is misleading, since they were farmers who held four or five enslaved people on large tracts of land. Despite these contentions, historians have more recently asserted, and I agree, that whatever the real patterns of slaveholding, there were enough enslaved people in the Narragansett Country to make it the wealthiest region of the colony and "to constitute a viable community" with a distinctive black northern culture.[36] This large concentration allowed enslaved people to form multigenerational families who often lived together; however, these relationships were not legally recognized. And like their southern counterparts, northern slaveholders rarely included the names of fathers when they recorded the births of enslaved infants.[37]

In the Narragansett Country, the slave population increased naturally. Records show that generations of enslaved families lived and labored there. For example, "Negro woman named Mary—had several children one call Moll" and "Negro Moll had several children"; Moll and her children and grandchildren all lived in North Kingstown.[38] This multigenerational concentration of blacks allowed enslaved people to pass on family and communal traditions.[39]

Most enslaved people in the Narragansett Country were involved in tending livestock and cultivating small amounts of Indian corn, rye, hemp, flax, and tobacco. Though most of the enslaved were involved in caring for animals and agricultural labor, they also worked as skilled tradesmen and domestic servants. They made routine carpentry repairs, cut firewood, and accompanied their masters to market, while enslaved women labored in the domestic economy—cooking, cleaning, nursing the sick, caring for children, and storing food. Enslaved women also milked cows and manufactured cheese and butter.[40] On Reverend James MacSparran's farm enslaved men and women were kept busy hoeing, walling, ditching, fencing, mowing, haying, and milking. MacSparran also recorded additional odd jobs and errands run by his enslaved people: "Harry Hilling Corn, My Negro's digging potatoes, Harry split 120 Stakes, Harry salted meat, Harry carted the hogs and then he and Emblo bro't ye corn and Stalks from Boston Neck."[41]

Enslaved people in the Narragansett Country, like their counterparts throughout history, experienced the common brutalities of slavery. The most common physical punishment was whipping or flogging, while the threat of sale was used as a psychological control. Enslavers also commissioned and purchased devices such as pot hooks, muzzles, and balls and chains to restrain their human property. Chronic runaways were branded and maimed—fingers, toes, and even feet and hands removed. The enslaved in the Narragansett Country were also under near-constant surveillance. Like most enslaved northerners they lived in the homes of their masters; few farms were large enough to warrant separate slave quarters. So while slaves on large southern plantations could retreat and temporarily escape white surveillance, enslaved people in Narragansett Country lived just on the periphery of their enslavers' lives. Moreover, physical proximity further emphasized the drastic differences between the enslaved and their enslaver. For example, slaves often had access to their masters' personal space, such as bedrooms and bathing chambers, and many enslaved people helped their masters dress and bathe; however, rituals such as meals, church, and burial were segregated in order to teach slaves their place, and slaves were relegated to sleep in kitchens, storage areas, barns, garrets, and attics.[42]

Challenging and Resisting the Institution of Slavery

In 1673, "negro servants" Maria and George were indicted for fornicating; they both were found guilty and sentenced to "fifteen stripes."[43] In 1707, an unnamed "negro" man reportedly murdered his master, ran away, and drowned himself rather than be captured by officials. The General Assembly ordered "that his head, legs, and arms be cut from his body, and hung up in some public place, near the town [Newport], to public view: and his body be burnt to ashes, that it may, if it please God, be something of a terror to others from perpetrating of the like barbarity for the future."[44] In 1714, a "mulatto" man ran away from the city of Newport.[45] In 1728, Jethro, an enslaved "negro," stole a canoe from his master Robert Wilcox, a yeoman of Kingstown, and paddled to Martha's Vineyard, and "hid among the Indians."[46] In 1734, Hezekiah Gorton's "negro man" was found guilty of poisoning two white women—Ann Markham and Rebecca French—with contaminated "apples and milk" and was ordered "tied or bound to the publick whipping post in s'd Town and stripped naked from his waist upwards receiving twenty five lashes on his naked body."[47] Maria and George acted outside the control of their masters when they had sex; they were willing to risk severe punishment for companionship. Both the "mulatto man" and Jethro robbed their enslavers of their human property. The poisoner embarrassed his enslaver by poisoning his guests; moreover, he could have killed them. These individual acts of resistance were as varied in motivation as they were in execution. Some were in search of autonomous relationships. Others may have sought revenge or found themselves caught in a moment of anger that led them to kill or plan to kill or cause illness. Some were seeking temporary or permanent escape from slavery. And although these acts of resistance were not aimed at destroying the business of slavery their actions did interrupt the business of their enslavers. Moreover, the actions of the enslaved defied the racial ideology of their masters—these people were anything but simple property.

Enslaved Rhode Islanders transformed local rivers and water-ways from avenues of economic opportunity, for the enslaver class, to avenues of escape. Flight via water was such a concern that in 1714 the General Assembly forbade enslaved people from boarding ferries alone, even under the directives of their enslavers; they had be accompanied by their owner or some white person in author-ity.[48] They also interrupted the business of slavery by stowing away on ships, which were plentiful in the port cities of Newport, Providence, and Bristol. It was in response to this that the Gen-eral Assembly passed a 1757 law allowing slaveholders to search private vessels where they suspected their human property was stowed, entitled them to double damages if a privateer or captain was found guilty of stealing an inhabitant's slave, and made cap-tains responsible for ensuring that no slaves were hidden on their vessels.[49] These laws reveal the determination and resourcefulness of enslaved people who refused to accept their legal status as chat-tel. However, the General Assembly was responding to needs of the individual slaveholders who were contending with defiance.

James MacSparran, the prominent Narragansett Country farmer and minister, recorded such insubordinate behavior in his diary; "I got up this morning early, and finding Hannibal had been out . . . I stript and gave him a few lashes till he begged. As Harry was untying him, my poor passionate dear [MacSparran's wife] saying I had not given him enough, gave him a lash or two, upon which he ran."[50] Hannibal was recovered and MacSparran put "pothooks about his neck." A few days later Hannibal was whipped again, after which he again ran away. He was returned by one of MacSpar-ran's parishioners, who pled with his minister to be more lenient with his slave.[51] Hannibal not was alone in his defiant behavior. In the colonial period Rhode Island slaveholders placed one hundred (ninety-two men and eight women) runaway slave advertisements in local and regional papers.[52] Over 20 percent of the runaways were identifiable by scars. Twenty of them had scars on their faces, while twenty-three were marked somewhere on their bodies. The evidence suggests that these scars were most likely a result of work accidents, punishments, neglect, or illness, rather than willingly inflicted cultural scars, which were typically identified as "country marks or guinea marks" in these advertisements. Quako, who was "short and thickset," had letters branded on his shoulders. Robert, who was born in Jamaica, had a burn scar between his cheek and his mouth. London, who ran away from Newport, had "lost" all his toes on both feet. Prime, a fourteen-year-old who stood only four feet four inches, had whipping scars on his arms and back. Sias, a "bold and impudent" twenty-four-year-old, had "several marks left by the King's evil on his neck," a reference to scrofula or tuberculous swelling of the lymph gland. Prince had "small crooked legs." Seven runaway slaves had survived smallpox and were left with lifelong scars. These physical descriptions suggest that enslaved Rhode Islanders, like their counterparts throughout the Americas, were physically punished, were employed in dangerous labor, were inadequately clothed, and received minimal medical attention.

The vast majority of the runaways were young men who absconded from Newport, Providence, and the Narragansett Country. More than 70 percent of the runaways were described as "Negroes," 15 percent as "Mulattoes," 8 percent as "Indians," and 6 percent as "Mustees."[53] In all, 72 percent of the runaways were younger than thirty, and 53 percent were between the ages of eighteen and twenty-five; 16 percent were under eighteen. Over a quarter (28.5 percent) of Rhode Island runaways escaped from the Narragansett Country, while 19 percent and 11 percent ran away from Newport and Providence, respectively. This trend mirrored the patterns of slaveholding in Rhode Island generally: Narragansett Country residents held the highest proportion of slaves in Rhode Island, followed by the cities of Newport and Providence. Runaway advertisements offer a glimpse into the diverse motivations for slave flight. While undoubtedly most fled to gain their freedom or to temporarily escape work, circumstances made each person's incentives different. Sarah Thompson, a teenager with "large eyes," fled to find her mother, who she believed lived in Providence. Richard, a "pocked marked" twenty-five-year-old, reportedly ran away to reunite with his wife.[54] Others resisted bondage through sabotage.

Four incidents of slave arson appeared in colonial Rhode Island newspapers. In 1762, Fortune, an "abandoned Negro," set fire to the Long Wharf, the city of Newport's major port, causing £80,000 of damage. Fortune was summarily executed, "hanged by the neck."[55] Fortune's actions suggest intent to disrupt or even destroy the economic heart of the city, since the Long Wharf was where Rhode Islanders launched their slave ships filled with locally grown food and distilled rum. The other arsons appear to be, not threats against the business of slavery, but personal acts of revenge. In 1773, Thomas Randall's "black servant boy," tired of tending animals, confessed to setting the barn on fire.[56] In 1772 and 1774, two disgruntled enslaved men reportedly set their respective masters' homes afire.[57] These enslaved arsonists used fire to punish their enslavers and express their dissatisfactions with their captivity.

Enslaved people also pushed back against the isolation and solitude of slavery. In 1673 "Negro Jobba" was indicted for having "carnal copulation with James Gray"; Jobba pled not guilty and the jury agreed.[58] That same year, Hope, "a Negro woman," was found guilty of fornication with James Pass and was sentenced to either fifteen stripes or a fine of forty shillings to the treasury.[59] James Gray and James Pass were most likely white men: the court record gives their surnames, and nonwhites were usually identified in court records as "Negros, Mulattoes or Indians." Maroca, a slave on James MacSparran's Narragansett Country farm, was involved in a consensual relationship with another slave named Mingo, who lived on a neighboring farm, and they had two children together, despite MacSparran's order to end the relationship. When the two continued to see one another, he sold their youngest child.[60] Indeed, such efforts to curtail the behavior of enslaved people were not restricted to individual masters. As we have seen, the colonial government tried to do the same several times, passing laws in 1703, 1708, and 1750 that attempted to control the social lives of the enslaved.[61] Enslaved people resisted the isolation of northern slaveholding, and some paid a high price for love and companionship.

Enslaved Rhode Islanders, like their counterparts throughout the Americas, also resisted the institution of slavery through recreation; they took time for themselves. Despite their many burdens, enslaved people found pleasure in and uses for their bodies that were independent of, and not beneficial to, their owners.[62] Caesar Lyndon, the enslaved business agent of Rhode Island Governor Josiah Lyndon, recorded the contents of a rather elaborate cookout held by several enslaved people. On August 12, 1766, "Boston Vose, Lingo Stephens, Phyllis Lyndon, Nepton Sispson and Wife, Prince Thurston, Caesar Lyndon, and Sarah Searing" left Newport and went out to Portsmouth for a day in the country. They took "a pigg to roast, wine, bread, rum, green corn, limes for punch, sugar, butter, tea and coffee." Two months after their outing Caesar Lyndon and Sarah Searing married; a year later, Lingo Stephens and Phyllis Lyndon became man and wife.[63] These friends were asserting their humanity amid inhumane conditions. Yes, they legally belonged to someone, but they also took time for themselves.

In fact, the enslaved attempted to institutionalize leisure and recreation. Starting as early as the late seventeenth century, enslaved communities in the North began to gather annually to feast, dance, play games, drink, gamble, and sometimes "elect" an honorary governor or king to rule for the duration of these festivities. For a day or two, enslaved people gathered to reconnect and rejuvenate. These annual festivals, which typically took place in the spring, were known as "Negro" Election Days throughout New England and Pinkster Days elsewhere in the Northeast, especially in New York and New Jersey. Similar festivals had a long history in medieval Europe, where holidays were regarded as important "safety valves" in a world of oppression and exploitation. Although these celebrations were initially organized by slave masters, enslaved people gradually appropriated them for themselves.[64]

Dancing was a key part of what made these celebrations distinctly black—both a reflection of African and African American culture—because dancing and music were sacred for people of African descent. Moreover, dance "can be an extremely subtle means of perpetuating values," particularly since "the oppressor had no handle on its meaning."[65] In the northern and southern colonies dance and music were "the most important forms of self-expression available to ordinary black men and women; however, these festivals were a northern phenomenon."[66] A Salem clergyman noted "most fatiguing dances and the never ceasing sound of the violin" that were typical at such celebrations.[67] These festivities allowed enslaved people to temporarily escape the drudgery of slavery. As cultural historian Shane White contends, the festivals were "one of the most important and revealing cultural phenomena in the history of the black experience in America."[68]

Such celebrations by enslaved people in South Kingstown, the largest and wealthiest town in the Narragansett Country, met resistance. Attempts to suppress such activities were most likely a reaction to the relatively large numbers of enslaved people in the region. Historian Sterling Stuckey has argued that Pinkster Days were "allowed" because of the "supreme confidence" of the northern enslaver class, who took comfort in the fact that enslaved people never constituted more than a tiny minority in the region.[69] However, the enslaved population in the Narragansett Country constituted a large minority; as we have seen, by midcentury the 1,306 enslaved people accounted for one-fifth of the region's population.[70] Narragansett farmers were most likely uncomfortable with any sort of public display of autonomy by enslaved people.[71]

In 1723, town councilmen in South Kingstown attempted to criminalize the gatherings that enslaved people had been having for a number of years:

> Whereas it hath bin a Custom for several years past for Indians and Negroes Servants and others to meet to Gather on the Third week in June Annually in this Town under a pretense of Keeping a sort of Fare, Which hath proved very suspicious to the Owners of such servants as well as other people It is therefore voted and Enacted that this Town Meeting that it shall be lawful for any Constable to leash such offenders and carry them before authority for order that such offenses shall be publickly whipt and any one Justice of the Peace May Order Such offenders to be Whipt at his discretion not exceeding twenty stripes, and the offender to Pay Lawfully charge if free persons and if slaves then their master to pay charge.[72]

It is difficult to discern from the record whether this annual celebration was indeed a "Negro" Election Day, but the brief description of the event and its occurrence in June suggest that it was.[73] The rebuke of the town council is puzzling considering that in other Rhode Island towns, and later in the century in the Narragansett

Country, there is evidence that the enslaver class condoned such festivities.

Enslaved people dressed for the occasion. Cyrus Bruce, enslaved by Governor Langdon of New Hampshire, wore "a massive gold chain, cherry colored smallclothes, silk stockings, ruffles, and silver shoe buckles." In 1847, Wilkin Updike, a white Narragansett Country resident, recalled, "It was degrading to the reputation of the owner if his slave appeared in inferior apparel." In fact, some enslaved people even wore their masters' swords and arrived on their owners' best Narragansett Pacers (prized horses).[74] Whether or not enslaved people had the "permission" of their masters or the approval of the local town council, for a few days out of the year they abandoned work in exchange for communal revelry.

These annual festivals were not just about recreation; they were a "rare and valued opportunity for African Americans to socialize."[75] These marginalized peoples were exercising freedom for themselves, albeit momentary, and the freedom to nurture relationships. This was especially important in the rural Narragansett Country, where enslaved people, especially women, had little opportunity to leave the farms where they labored. These celebrations allowed them to stay connected to friends and family on neighboring farms and to retain and pass on their culture, primarily through music and dance. In New England, "Negro" Election Day remained a critical part of African American social and cultural life during and after the breakdown of slavery and was celebrated well into the 1830s.[76]

Whether they gathered for festivals, had sex without the approval of their owners, ran away, stole, or set their enslavers' barns, homes, or ports afire, enslaved Rhode Islanders, like their counterparts throughout the Americas, resisted the institution of slavery and in turn the business of slavery. Their actions as individuals and as a community disrupted the business of their enslavers. And while the vast majority of those who resisted their bondage were most likely in search of personal autonomy and freedom, their defiance challenged the false claims and assertions of their owners—that enslaved people were chattel.

Slavery flourished in colonial Rhode Island, especially as the business of slavery became increasingly important to the survival and success of the colony. However, enslaved Rhode Islanders resisted the efforts of their enslavers to turn them into commodities. And although many of the enslaved labored in the business of slavery as sailors, carpenters, and distillers, their lives held meaning beyond enriching the owners. Enslaved Rhode Islanders formed families, friendships, and created communities; they ran away, they stole, they damaged property. So while the business of slavery may have defined the strictures of their lives, it did not define their lives.

3 /   Emancipation in Black and White

In October 1783, Richard Gardner, a yeoman farmer from South Kingston, sold a twenty-two-month-old baby girl, who was a "Slave for Life," to Freelove Gardner, a black woman, for "six pence."[1] Other than ownership, the deed of sale does not specify the relationship between Richard Gardner, the unnamed infant, and Freelove Gardner. However, it is reasonable to assume that Richard Gardner or another member of his family at one time owned Freelove Gardner; enslaved people commonly took on the surnames of their former owners. It is also reasonable to assume that the unnamed baby was related to Freelove, most likely her daughter. The baby might have also been related to Richard Gardner, hence his willingness to sell his "Slave for Life" to a free black woman who shared his name. This baby girl would join the growing free black population in Revolutionary and post-Revolutionary Rhode Island as enslaved people pushed for freedom and the state divested in slaveholding.

Unlike the end of slavery in the South during and following the American Civil War (1861–65), northern emancipation was uneven and protracted and spanned several decades. Revolutionary rhetoric, the conditions of war (the American Revolution), and the actions of enslaved people ultimately led to the destruction of northern slavery; however, the fight to end chattel slavery was different in each state. In Rhode Island, the breakdown of slavery began with Quaker manumissions in 1773, followed by the enlistment of enslaved men in the Revolutionary War in 1778, the passing of the Act for the Gradual Abolition of Slavery in 1784, which ended hereditary slavery, and finally the 1787 slave trade ban, which forbade residents to participate in the slave trade. Slaveholding as it existed in the colonial era came to an end in Rhode Island between 1773 and 1787, though the General Assembly would not abolish slavery until 1842. Two parallel and sometimes overlapping histories reveal how and why slaveholding was dismantled in a place that had been and continued to be so wedded to the business of slavery. Enslaved people initiated the process through many modes of resistance and were responsible for the actual collapse of slaveholding, while black and white abolitionists pushed for a legal end to slaveholding.

War and the Business of Slavery

In the colonial period, the business of slavery, as we have seen, was in many ways the only business in Rhode Island. Any threats to it were thus seen as threats to the colony itself. When the British passed the American Revenue Act of 1764 (Sugar Act), an attempt to restrict trade with the French-ruled West Indian islands, Rhode Island merchants were greatly alarmed. They considered the act "highly injurious and detrimental to all His Majesty's North American colonies in general, and to this colony in particular," because most of the West Indian trade was with non-British colonies. The governor and other colonial officials offered arguments against renewing the act. First they explained that the colony's forty-eight thousand residents could not live off the land itself—a territory of "about thirty miles square," the majority of which "is a barren soil, not worth the expense of cultivation." Furthermore, they claimed that "the colony hath no staple commodity for exportation, and does not raise provisions sufficient for its own consumption; yet, the goodness of its harbors, and its convenient situation for trade agreeing with the spirit and industry of the people, hath in some measure supplied the deficiency of its natural produce, and provided the means of subsistence to its inhabitants."[2] Economic survival lay in trade—a refrain echoed by most Rhode Islanders—and the West Indian trade in particular. They recognized that the goods they exported, everything from lumber, to cheese, to horses, were in demand in the West Indies but not in England. In fact, they argued that the West Indian market was the foundation of all their commerce: "As there is no commodity raised in the colony suitable for the European market, but the few articles aforementioned; and as the other goods raised for exportation will answer at no market but in the West Indies, it necessarily follows that the trade thither must be the foundation of all our commerce."[3]

Between January of 1763 and January of 1764, 484 trading vessels left Rhode Island. Three hundred of those vessels engaged in coastal trading along the eastern seaboard, everywhere from Newfoundland to Georgia. Their primary trading good was rum, a product made from molasses. And that molasses, as we know, came from the West Indies. Of the remaining 184 vessels that left Rhode Island that year, 150 went to the West Indies. Those ships brought back about 14,000 large casks of molasses (and only 2,500 casks came from British islands, underscoring the importance of the French islands in particular), which was distilled into rum. In other words, the West Indian trade with non-British islands was the most important piece of Rhode Island's trade-based economy. The Rhode Island Assembly declared, "Without this trade, it would have been and always will be, utterly impossible for the inhabitants of this colony to subsist themselves."[4] Rhode Islanders perceived the introduction of taxes imposed by the British (from the Sugar Act to the Townsend Revenue Acts) and the enforcement of trade regulation as a threat to their economy and an affront to their liberty. Consequently, Rhode Island joined the fight against British tyranny with their fellow colonists up and down the North American seaboard. On the eve of the American Revolution, in 1774, nearly 66 percent of Newport slaveholders were also directly involved in the West Indian and Atlantic slave trades. They owned slaving vessels, imported molasses and rum, and supplied the West Indies with basic necessities such as candles, timber, and foodstuffs.[5] Moreover, Rhode Island slave traders, who purchased African slaves with locally distilled rum, were responsible for more than 60 percent of all the North American traffic in slaves.

During the American Revolution (1775–83), Rhode Island's economy ground to a near halt as British blockades effectively shut down the ports. No slave ships sailed. The rum distilleries sat idle. The Narragansett farmers had no way to ship out their slave-produced goods. By the end of the war, the newly formed state was nearly bankrupt. After the war, Rhode Islanders returned to what they knew best—the business of slavery; they were the first American citizens to resume slave trading.[6] In 1783, within months of the cease-fire with the British, Rhode Island merchants sailed five slave ships to Africa.[7]

Yet despite the abundant and profitable exploitation of slave labor and traffic in slave bodies, before and after the war, less than a year after the hostilities ended in 1784 the Rhode Island General Assembly ended hereditary slavery in the state.[8] And just three years later, in 1787, the Assembly forbade Rhode Islanders to participate in the Atlantic slave trade; all citizens and residents of the state were restricted from directly or indirectly importing or transporting any African slaves.[9] Perpetual, hereditary bondage was over in the state of Rhode Island, and the business of slavery had been dealt a devastating blow. It seemed that black emancipation would destroy slaveholding and the business of slavery. However, the business of slavery would not only survive emancipation—it would thrive in the free state of Rhode Island.

Reckoning with Emancipation

Between Quakers' rejections of slaveholding in 1773 and the 1787 slave trade ban, Rhode Island slaveholders incrementally lost their ability to hold human property. The Quakers were the first European-descended religious group in the Americas to publicly question and eventually prohibit slaveholding among their members; they were also the driving political force behind legal restrictions placed on slaveholding. In 1774, when the town of Providence inherited Jacob Shoemaker's six slaves, the town councilmen declared that it was "unbecoming to the character of freedom to enslave the said Negroes, and set them free.[10] That same year, the Rhode Island General Assembly forbade residents to import slaves. In 1779, the Assembly forbade slaveholders to sell their slaves out of the state. And then, five years later, in 1784, state legislators passed a gradual emancipation law ending hereditary slavery. The same legislative body that had legitimized and legalized slaveholding in the colonial period eroded the ability of slaveholders to purchase, sell, and keep slaves during and after the American Revolution. This seemingly abrupt turnaround was not a rejection of the institution of slavery but instead an incremental disassociation with slaveholding as a result of Revolutionary rhetoric, an emergent abolitionist movement, and the actions of enslaved people in Revolutionary Rhode Island.

Though the white experience of emancipation was different in nearly every aspect from that of black Americans, it was just as transformative. All white people in the North, over the space of a generation or two, depending on what state they lived in, lost their claim—or potential claim—to mastery. That shift had very different consequences—from the emotional to the psychological to the financial—depending on their existing relationship to slavery. The vast majority of whites were laborers or tradesmen or farmers who did not own slaves at all; however, many of their jobs were dependent on the business of slavery. They were primarily observers in this ongoing shift, although the decline of an institution built on the innate superiority of whites surely influenced how these men and women perceived themselves. Nevertheless, the conflict over emancipation among whites was primarily between abolitionists and proslavery farmers tradesmen and merchants. Slaveholders and their supporters viewed the way things were as the way things should be; and especially as the eighteenth century progressed and slavery become more entrenched, these men, and their children and grandchildren, inherited a world in which slavery was taken for granted and ever more essential. Thus they responded to anti-slavery advocacy typically with indignation, and then more and more furious protection of their institution. On the other hand, white advocates of black freedom, starting as early as 1775, proposed, lobbied, and supported legislation that chipped away at the institution of slavery in the state. Their words were bolstered by their actions as they had relinquished their own slave property, helping create an environment in which slaveholding was no longer taken for granted.

The first Quakers came to North America in the 1650s, fleeing religious persecution in England and hoping to find economic opportunities in the colonies. Quaker colonists settled primarily in Pennsylvania, Rhode Island, and New Jersey. By the end of the seventeenth century, the Society of Friends was one of the five major denominations in British North America.[11] While the history of Quakers in Pennsylvania, where they established their first and most successful colony, is well known, their existence in Rhode Island is much more obscure.[12] Rhode Island Quakers, unlike their counterparts in neighboring states, were, for the most part, accepted into mainstream society. They settled in Rhode Island as early as 1650, and by the 1660s several prominent Newport families were Quakers. Within two decades they made up a significant minority in the General Assembly, and a Quaker, William Coddington, was elected governor in 1674, 1675, and 1678. They were politically strong enough to pass a legal provision allowing for religious conscientious objector release from militia duty. Many of the Quakers were voted out of office during Metacom's War in 1675–76, and their conscientious objector status was repealed; nevertheless, they remained politically engaged. There were several Quaker governors in the eighteenth century, and Quakers soon regained a significant minority in the General Assembly. The religion continued to grow, both in the state and in the region, and by 1772 there were forty-seven congregations in New England.[13]

The basic tenets of Quakers made them the Christians mostly likely to question slavery. Then, as now, Quakers believed in spiritual equality—that every person is capable of receiving what they refer to as the inner light or a direct awareness of God and spiritual truth that allows one to know God's will for oneself.[14] Despite that radical vision of the spiritual capacity of each individual, regardless of race (not to mention gender), their objection to slavery evolved over time. During most of the colonial period, they said little about slavery and were just as complicit in slavery as their white peers. Throughout the British colonies in North America and the West Indies, Quakers held slaves. Like the Puritans and Anglicans, they saw no conflict between their faith and slaveholding.[15] In fact, from the seventeenth century through the first half of the eighteenth century there was no outright public objection to slaveholding from any group or organization except the enslaved themselves. With very few exceptions, the institution was accepted by white colonists as a social and economic necessity.[16]

From the beginning of their time in the British colonies, Quakers believed that they could stay in good standing with God as long as they treated their slaves well. They believed they could be "good" masters as long as they made sure their slaves were adequately clothed and fed. Many Quakers educated their slaves and brought them to meetings.[17] Quakers first critiqued the trafficking of slaves, arguing, as early as the 1750s, that the cruelty of transporting humans across the Atlantic as cargo was an affront to God; as that critique of trafficking became more widely accepted by the community, Quakers eventually acknowledged that all slaveholding supported that traffic.[18] Consequently, most Quakers came to the conclusion that no Christian could in good conscience support or participate in such a horrendous trade. In the Revolutionary period, New England Quakers melded their beliefs in spiritual equality to their support of social and civic equality.[19] It is no coincidence that these ideas emerged in the 1770s, since the growing political rhetoric of independence from Britain bolstered their protest.

In 1769, Rhode Island Quakers, at a meeting held in Greenwich, Rhode Island, appointed a committee to arrange manumissions. The committee supported a new "query," or question used to challenge members to reflect on the spirituality of their actions, that proposed forbidding the transfer of slaves in any manner except to free them. At a meeting in Smithfield, Rhode Island, Stephen Hopkins, former Rhode Island governor and a signer of the Declaration of Independence, was expelled from meetings for refusing to manumit his "old negro servant, the one remaining slave who was suitable for freedom."[20] Quakers manumitted their slaves because they believed slaveholding was "contrary to true Christianity."[21] Rhode Island Quakers manumitted forty-nine enslaved people between 1773 and 1803.

The process of freeing another human being was surprisingly simple. The slave owner was required to write or fill out a manumission document in the presence of free witnesses. The manumission documents (also known as freedom papers) of the Rhode Island Quakers were quite similar to each other; one read:

To all Christian people to whom these present shall come, know you that I Robert Lawton of Newport in the county of Newport and Colony of Rhode Island, have in my possession a Negro Boy called Samuel, who according to the law and custom of said colony is deemed a slave and as my property but believing it to be contrary to true Christianity, and the divine injunction of the author thereof to hold mankind as my property or continue them in a state whereby they may be subjected to slavery after my decease, and in consideration thereof and together causes met thereunto moving, I do for my self and my heirs executive administrator and Assigns Manumit Release and Discharge, him the said Negro from a state of slavery and hereby declare him to be henceforth free as amply and fully so, as if he had been Born of free parents.[22]

The authors of these documents were careful and deliberate. They made sure that their heirs had no claims to the slaves they manumitted, a facet of these documents that is so common as to suggest that they did not necessarily trust their heirs to fulfill their wishes. They wanted to make sure that the slaves they manumitted were recognized as completely free persons—persons who owed service to no one and whose children would also be free.

Many Rhode Island Quakers, along with their counterparts in Pennsylvania and New Jersey, were also active abolitionists. The fact that they had manumitted their slaves gave them credibility in the abolitionist movement, which sought to end slavery through legislative action: they asked of others only what they had done themselves. They published broadsides, religious reflections, and homilies excoriating the horrors of slaveholding; they also sent petitions to town councilmen and state legislators calling for an end to slavery. They claimed that the Atlantic slave trade and slaveholding in the New World were "the most barbarous" institutions in history.[23] They asserted that both history and the Bible declared that the entire nation would be punished for supporting and accepting such immoral practices.[24] For these Quakers, abolition concerned not only personal salvation but the rescue of a nation from divine damnation.

Some Congregationalists were also deeply concerned about the sin of slavery. Samuel Hopkins, a Congregational minister, was an unlikely abolitionist. In fact, he probably would not have taken up the cause had he not been transferred from his church in Great Barrington, Massachusetts, and sent to a post in Newport.[25] Prior to his moving to Newport, Hopkins had been unconcerned with the institution of slavery. He had been comfortable with his mentor's slaveholding and had enslaved people working in his home, even though he did not personally own any of them. Slaves were often put at the disposal of ministers as part of their compensation. It was fellow Congregationalist Sarah Osborn, who ran a school for free and enslaved blacks in her home, who introduced Hopkins to the abolitionist movement; the commonality and brutality of slave trading in Newport made conversion rather easy.[26] Hopkins's transformation took place during the first few years he lived in Newport. As historian Joseph Conforti writes, "For the first time in his life, the backcountry minister confronted the slave trade's grim reality. Chained Africans were sometimes unloaded in Newport and sold before his eyes."[27]

Hopkins served as pastor of Newport's First Congregational Church from 1770 to 1803, where he became one of the most renowned abolitionists in New England. Hopkins came to believe that British tyranny was a result of the colonists' sins: slaveholding and slave trading.

In Newport, Hopkins privately tutored both free and enslaved blacks; he wanted to train them as missionaries for congregations in Africa. He not only trained them free of charge but was directly responsible for helping at least one of them gain his freedom.[28] In the 1770s, Hopkins began to preach against slavery, which was fairly safe to do among a congregation too poor to own slaves, but in addition he began to lobby wealthy slaveholders and other ministers to join his cause. He was successful with at least one local slaveholder, Dr. Bellmay, who released his bondsmen after conversations with Hopkins.[29]

Abolitionist sentiment was also manifested in law as the Rhode Island General Assembly began to pass legislation that hindered would-be and existing slaveholders. The supporters of the 1774 importation law claimed that "those who are desirous of enjoying all the advantages of liberty themselves, should be willing to extend personal liberty to others." According to the law any slave brought in the colony after June 1774 would be "rendered immediately free, so far as respects personal freedom, and the enjoyment of private property, in the same manner as the native Indian." Those who violated the law would receive a hundred-pound fine.[30] At the same time, the law protected the right of visitors to bring their human property into the colony for any period of time, provided they took them with them when they left. The law did not extend to slaves brought into the colony on locally owned vessels, whose captains were unable to sell them in the West Indies. The law stipulated that under such circumstances "the owner of such negro or mulatto slave give bond to the general treasure of the said, with ten days in the sum of £100 for each and every such negro or mulatto slave so brought in, that such negro or mulatto slave shall be exported out of the colony, within one year from the date of such bond; if such negro or mulatto be alive, and in a condition to be removed."[31] The prohibition was the first law to limit the right of slaveholders to acquire more slaves. The members of the Assembly were sending a clear message. They did not want any more slaves in the colony. However, they also wanted to make sure they did not damage the businesses of slave traders—hence the year reprieve afforded to them. Two years after legislators banned slave imports, they further undermined the rights of slaveholders.

In 1778 the Rhode Island General Assembly authorized slave enlistments in return for freedom. An estimated twenty thousand blacks fought in the Revolutionary War (fifteen thousand for the British and five thousand for the Patriots). In the South the majority of blacks fought on the side of the British, while in the North most blacks aligned with the Patriots. North and South alike, most enslaved African Americans were motivated by the promise of freedom, not political alliances. It was the British who first offered freedom in exchange for military service; the British reasoned they could bolster their ranks and subvert the colonists in one step. Out of fear and desperation the northern states eventually offered the same.[32]

In 1775, recruiting officers for the Continental Army were ordered not to enlist "any stroller, negro, or vagabond."[33] This order did not dismiss those black men already enlisted in the Continental Army or restrict state militias from mustering black men. Still, it sent a very clear message. Military and political leaders of the rebellion, such as George Washington and John Adams, envisioned the war as a fight for white freedom fought by white men. Many white revolutionaries feared arming an oppressed and potentially vengeful class. They were also apprehensive about sending the wrong message to slaveholding Patriots. More importantly, African Americans' unrestricted service in the Revolutionary cause would ultimately raise the issue of their incorporation into the new nation. Despite this ban, thousands of African Americans served in the Continental Army and state militias.[34]

In 1777, after a winter of devastating losses and desertions, Congress called for eighty-eight new battalions. States north and south scrambled to find enough men to enlist, and some began enlisting slaves. The southern states were, not surprisingly, quite cautious about enlisting black men, fearing the potential impact on the institution of slavery. Despite their fears, the border states of Virginia and Maryland began enlisting African Americans in 1780. While Maryland accepted the services of both slaves and free men, Virginia enlisted only free blacks.[35] Officials in South Carolina and Georgia refused to enlist any black men at all.[36] The northern states, which had a much smaller enslaved population and were less dependent on slave labor, enlisted enslaved men.[37] Slaveholders in Connecticut had the option of freeing their slaves and sending them as replacements for themselves or their sons. Massachusetts not only allowed black men to enlist but made them eligible for the draft. In New Hampshire, both slaves and free blacks were enlisted. Slaves received their freedom in exchange for service, and free blacks were granted the same bounties as white soldiers. In New Jersey, all able-bodied free men were recruited regardless of race. New York, in 1781, was among the last of the northern states to legally sanction black enlistment.[38] The New England states, with the smallest black populations, provided the largest number of black soldiers. Connecticut raised an all-black company of seven hundred.[39] Most of its members were freed slave substitutes and served as a separate unit until 1782.[40] Rhode Island, the region's smallest and least populous state, raised a nearly all-black regiment—the Rhode Island First.[41] Slave enlistments severely undermined the authority of the slaveholders. The mustering of slaves posed a direct challenge to mastery and racial ideology. Black men were no longer enslaved dependents but soldiers and freedom fighters. The need for man-power superseded the authority of masters.[42]

Rhode Island slaveholders lost control over enslaved men with the formation of the Rhode Island First. An enslaved man who wanted to enlist needed only to "present" himself and pass muster; his master was compensated but not consulted.[43] Slave enlistments were the first, albeit unintended, step in the legal dismantling of the institution of slavery. The 1778 Slave Enlistment Act declared, "That every slave so enlisting shall, upon his passing muster by Col. Christopher Greene, be immediately discharged from the service of his master or mistress, and be absolutely FREE." A committee of five men from the state's counties was created to evaluate the worth of slave soldiers. Slaveholders were paid up to £120 for the most valuable slaves.[44]

There were, undoubtedly, cases in which slaves who wanted to enlist were prevented from doing so by their masters. Slaveholders used force, trickery, or threats of retaliation to prevent their slaves from enlisting. Hazard Potter, a slave owner from South Kings-town, tried to convince his slaves not to enlist by telling them that they were only going to be used as manual laborers, put on the front lines, or sold to the West Indies.[45] Rhode Island slaveholders also petitioned the General Assembly to try to keep their slave property. John Northup, James Babcok Jr., Othneil Gorton, George Pierce, Sylvester Gardiner, and Samuel Babcock sent an official letter of protest to the General Assembly. They argued that not enough slaves "would have an inclination to enlist, and would pass mus-ter, to constitute a regiment."[46] They also doubted the willingness and ability of slaves to fight in exchange for freedom. Furthermore, they thought that enlisting slaves was insulting, embarrassing, and hypocritical. They claimed it was wrong to use "a band of slaves" to defend "the rights and liberties" of American citizens, whom they understood to be white. Moreover, they did not want to be subjected to "the same kind of ridicule we so liberally bestowed upon them [the British], on account of Dunmore's regiment of blacks." Finally, they objected to the cost of purchasing the slaves, not to mention the resistance of hostile slaveholders, who they claimed had no desire to relinquish their property. They predicted that "great dif-ficulties and uneasiness will arise in purchasing the negroes from their masters; and many of the masters will not be satisfied with any prices allowed."[47] Their opposition was both nonsensical and contradictory. If there were not enough willing and capable slaves to serve as soldiers, then they would not pass muster and their masters would not have to be compensated. Moreover, it was just as contradictory to fight a war for liberty and freedom while holding slaves as it was to enlist slaves in the fight for freedom and liberty. While opponents of the Slave Enlistment Act were unable to stop the law from passing, they were successful in limiting its scope. On June 10, 1778, just five months after slave enlistments began, they legally ended.[48] However, in defiance of the law, enslaved men kept presenting themselves and were mustered into the Rhode Island First until the close of the war. A year after the last enlistments began, in 1779, slaveholders lost the right to sell their slave property out of the state.[49]

The 1779 law was indicative of the shifts in the legal landscape, which were slow but significant. Slaveholders were losing control over what they were allowed to do with their human property. By banning out-of-state slave sales, the General Assembly prevented enslavers from fully profiting from their slave property. They were also hinting that Rhode Island's slaves would eventually be free. Crucial to that shift were the Quakers. Starting several years prior to the 1779 ban on out-of-state slave sales, Moses Brown, a former slaveholder and Quaker convert, drafted a bill calling for the end of slavery in the state. The 1775 bill was the first emancipation bill that he would write. It was rejected outright. The second bill that Brown presented, following the American Revolution in December of 1783, had signatures from town council members across the state; it called not only for an immediate end to slavery but also for a fine levied against anyone involved in the Atlantic slave trade. It too was rejected. Three months later, in February of 1784, a revised version of Brown's bill won the support of the Providence Town Council by a vote of 108 to 58. The revised bill, jointly sponsored by black veterans and white Quakers, called for a gradual end to slavery and did not mention the Atlantic slave trade. It was passed by the General Assembly; children born to enslaved mothers after March 1, 1784, would not be slaves for life.[50] There is no evidence of debates, letters, or petitions sent to the General Assembly in opposition of the law. The fight over gradual emancipation was fought in the individual towns and homes of Rhode Island. Once the Quakers had gathered enough signatures in support of emancipation, the General Assembly passed the measure. This version of the bill passed the General Assembly in spite of the opposition of some Assembly members and from Moses Brown's brother, John Brown, in particular.[51] John was a successful merchant, and although he invested in only a few slave voyages during his career he was intimately involved in the business of slavery as supplier to plantations in the West Indies.

The 1784 Act for the Gradual Abolition of Slavery was a turning point in the fight for emancipation because it brought a legal end to inheritable slavery in the state. All children born to slave mothers after the first of March were declared free; however, they were indentured to the town of their birth until eighteen years old for women and twenty-one years old for men.[52] The act immediately freed no one, and those born before March 1, 1784, were to remain slaves for life. Furthermore, town governments were encouraged to "bind out such children [those freed by the 1784 law] as apprentices" to cover the costs of their upbringing.[53] Less than a year later, the Assembly amended the law and declared that masters, not towns, were responsible for supporting and educating freed children. This change was intended to protect nonslaveholding whites from the potential public burden of supporting a population that legislators assumed would probably be dependent on public aid. In addition, the age of "service" was extended to twenty-one for women, which meant three more years of uncompensated labor. Finally, if the child's mother was emancipated before the child's twenty-first birthday, the owner was not to be held responsible for the education or support of the child.[54] Like other northern gradual emancipation laws, Rhode Island's law was designed not to help freed people transition into a free life but to protect the white public from potential black dependency.

The law also lacked enforcement.[55] No committee or organization was appointed to keep track of those children who were to be indentured rather than enslaved. No funds were set aside to ensure that masters followed the law. Legislators depended on the integrity and honesty of the enslaver class to police themselves. The burden of proof rested on freed persons. Other than personal integrity, the threat of a lawsuit, and informal public accountability, there was no deterrent to simply ignoring the law.

Despite the lack of enforcement or oversight, some enslavers took the law seriously and fully embraced its principles. On the day the gradual emancipation law went into effect, Nab, an enslaved woman "aged about thirty years," was manumitted by Henry Reynolds of South Kingstown. In the manumission, Reynolds specifically referred to the gradual emancipation law and aligned himself with the broader intentions of the law—to dismantle the institution of slavery.[56] Reynolds manumitted Nab in the name of the law even though the law did not require freedom for those born before 1784. Reynolds's action was an exception rather than the rule; Nab's manumission was representative of the larger acquiescence of the master class—the law would no longer condone or protect their rights to hold humans as chattel.

Working toward Emancipation

The actions taken by African Americans during and following the Revolutionary War were essential to the breakdown of slaveholding in the North. Enslaved northerners ran away in unprecedented numbers, volunteered for military service, and sued for, bargained for, and bought their freedom. For runaways and soldiers, freedom came rather abruptly; by contrast, those who bought their freedom or sued, bargained, or lobbied for it waited months, years, or even decades. Other northern slaves escaped slavery only in death. Like their counterparts throughout the North, enslaved Rhode Islanders employed various strategies to gain their freedom.

It is difficult to establish an accurate population of slaves and free people of color in Rhode Island in the years before, during, and following the Revolutionary War. However, there are census records from before and after the war. In 1755, there were roughly 4,697 blacks in Rhode Island, most of whom lived in the Narragansett Country, Newport, and Providence.[57] Unfortunately, colonial census returns did not specify the status of blacks; instead, the words *negro*, *black*, and *slave* were used interchangeably. However, this practice in and of itself is telling, and we can assume the vast majority of blacks were enslaved. In 1790, there were 4,355 blacks in Rhode Island, of whom 3,407 or 78 percent were free.[58] Prior to the Revolution in Rhode Island, nearly all blacks were enslaved; just seven years after the end of the war, most were free. The 1784 Act for the Gradual Abolition of Slavery would not have freed a single person until 1805. Black Rhode Islanders, like their counterparts throughout the North, did not wait on the implementation of gradual emancipation laws to set them free.

Encouraged by Revolutionary rhetoric and emboldened by the disorder of war, enslaved people dealt a major blow to the institution of slavery in the North and South—they fled. An estimated one hundred thousand slaves, one out of every five, in British North America escaped during the American Revolution.[59] Although the number of reported runaways in Rhode Island was small, it spiked in the years leading up to, during, and after the Revolutionary War. It is important to note that the following numbers represent only enslaved people whose enslavers who placed ads in Rhode Island publications; undoubtedly other Rhode Island slaves ran away, but no public documentation remains. Between 1732 and 1772, seventy runaway slave ads were placed in Rhode Island newspapers. Between 1773 and 1787, the fourteen years spanning the breakdown of slaveholding in Rhode Island, slaveholders placed forty-seven runaway ads. Eighty-two runaway ads were placed in the aftermath of the breakdown of slavery, between 1788 and 1800.[60] Nearly twice as many enslaved Rhode Islanders ran away in the Revolutionary and post-Revolutionary period (1773–1800) as in the half century preceding it. Notably, "All five of John Brown's, of the famed Brown family, slaves absconded" during the Revolutionary period; they settled in Boston.[61]

The 1770s were also a transformative decade for enslaved Rhode Islanders owned by Quakers. Beginning in 1773, Rhode Island Quakers began to manumit their slaves.[62] While most Quakers manumitted their slaves for religious reasons, some enslaved people had to convince their enslavers to release them from bondage in return for loyal service, as a death request, or in exchange for payment.[63] These reluctant manumissions suggest a more complex manumission process in which enslaved people did not simply receive but also advocated for their freedom. Such was the case for Cato Rivera, who was manumitted by Abraham Rivera in 1794 for faithful service. Then nearly a decade later, Cato purchased his mother, Phyllis, for one hundred dollars, from Hannah Rivera in 1803. Why this purchase was indexed by church officials as a manumission is puzzling. Phyllis was not manumitted; rather, she was sold. Rivera wrote, "Know all men by these present that I Hannah Rivera for and in consideration of one hundred dollars well and truly paid to me by Cato Rivera, a free man and do by these present sell set over and deliver to him the said Cato Rivera my negro woman named Phyllis mother to the said Cato hereby releasing up all my rights property claim."[64]

Nearly one-third (sixteen out of forty-nine) of those manumitted were children. A few children were freed outright, but most of them were apprenticed into adulthood. Most boys were kept as servants until they were twenty-one, while girls served until they were eighteen. For example, Daniel Weeden manumitted ten slaves; however, the one child he freed was apprenticed until adulthood, "to myself and my heirs and assigns the service of him the said negro [Ceasar] until the fourth day of the ninth month one thousand seven hundred and eighty four when he will (if living) have filled up and arrive to twenty one years of age until which period I do myself my heirs and assigns engage that he shall be clothed, victualed and educated in manner suitable for an apprentice of his age station and capacity."[65] Was Ceasar an orphan? Were his parents enslaved and thereby incapable of supporting him? The evidence suggests that former slaveholders believed these children would be a burden to newly free parents. For example, John Bowen manumitted a "negro" named Experience but apprenticed three minors, Benjamin, Daniel, and Freelove.[66] Such practices suggest that these Quakers assumed that whites were more capable parents or that they believed newly free parents were in no position to provide for their children. In either case, black children were separated from their parents. This practice, whether a result of paternalism or "compassion," split black families. Such Quaker manumissions were imperfect but still important to the emancipation process. The willingness of Quakers to free their slaves created an atmosphere in which enslaved people who were not owned by Quakers could challenge their masters with the assistance of white allies.

Military service was also a crucial component of the emancipation effort for all enslaved people because African Americans who served their country undermined the premise of race-based slavery. How could Patriot soldiers be unfit for freedom? This was especially true in Rhode Island, where a nearly all-black regiment was raised and fought in key battles.

On February 14, 1778, the Rhode Island General Assembly declared "that every able-bodied negro, mulatto, or Indian man slave in this State may enlist into either of the said two battalions, to serve during the continuance of the present war with Great Britain."[67] Enslaved Rhode Islanders immediately took advantage of the opportunity to enlist in return for their freedom. According to incomplete returns from the General Treasurer's Accounts, there were 74 enrollees between February and October 1778. This was a relatively good start, considering that the entire enslaved male population was less than 2,500; moreover, some enslaved people may have been unaware of the recruitment, some enslavers may have prevented their bondsmen from joining, and some enslaved men were at sea. The General Treasurer's Account lists 93 payments made to masters for 110 slaves.[68] The battalion mustered in on July 6, 1778. The unit included four companies with 19 commissioned officers and 144 non-commissioned officers and privates. Another company was added to the battalion later in the year, increasing its numerical strength to 226 enlisted men and officers.[69] The Rhode Island First was predominantly black but not exclusively so. The officers of the Rhode Island First were white, as with all regiments in the new country, but both whites and Native Americans served alongside blacks as soldiers in the regiment.[70]

Unlike their counterparts, black Rhode Island soldiers served as foot soldiers rather than servants, cooks, manual laborers, or foragers. The Rhode Island First fought for nearly five years in Rhode Island, New Jersey, and New York. They were one of the few units that enlisted for the duration of the war. At their first engagement, the Battle of Rhode Island, in August 1778, the soldiers were commended for their tenacity and courage against an experienced Hessian (German troops hired by the British) regiment that was reinforced by British regulars. Dr. Harris, a white Revolutionary soldier, observed that "Had they been unfaithful, or even given way

before the enemy all would have been lost. Three times in suc-
cession they were attacked, with most desperate valor and fury,
by well disciplined and veteran troops, and three times did they
successfully repel, the assault and thus preserved our Army from
capture." The Rhode Island First went on to fight in battles at Red
Bank, Yorktown, and Fort Oswego.[71] At the close of the war, the
weary soldiers of the Rhode Island First walked home. Some were
ill and most were poor, as they were paid in depreciated continental currency. Moreover, although they were veterans of the
American Revolution, they were not recognized as citizens of the
nation.[72]

The denial of citizenship, however, did not mean a lack of progress. The actions of the enslaved—running away, joining the military, and lobbying for freedom—in conjunction with an emerging
abolition movement had torn at the fabric of slavery and challenged
the morality and legitimacy of slaveholding in the new democracy.
Moreover, in the northern states, slave labor, though important,
was not the center of the economy as it was in the cash crop (tobacco
and rice) dependent economies of the South that relied wholly on
slave labor. Consequently, most northern states passed gradual
emancipation laws during and following American independence
that reflected the regional breakdown of the institution. Only two
states abolished slaveholding in the eighteenth century. Vermont's
1777 constitution freed enslaved men at twenty-one and women
at eighteen. A series of court cases brought by enslaved people,
most famously Elizabeth Freeman, previously known as Mum Bett
(1780) and Quock Walker (1781), led to the collapse of slaveholding in Massachusetts. The rest of the northern states, Pennsylvania
(1780), Connecticut (1784), Rhode Island (1784), New York (1799),
and New Jersey (1804), passed gradual emancipation laws.[73] In
other words, wholesale black freedom was postponed.

But these laws, though ideologically momentous, were curiously
inconsequential for most enslaved people. Historian John Wood
Sweet has demonstrated that most northern slaves gained their freedom long before gradual emancipation laws could take effect.[74] In
Pennsylvania, Rhode Island, and Connecticut gradual emancipation laws would not have freed a single person until 1808, 1805, and
1802, respectively. Yet by 1810 the majority of African Americans

in Pennsylvania (97 percent), Rhode Island (97 percent), and Connecticut (95 percent) were free. The gradual emancipation laws in New York and New Jersey would not have freed anyone until 1824 and 1825. Nevertheless, by 1820, 74 percent of black New Yorkers and 62 percent of black people in New Jersey were free. Gradual emancipation laws reflected the actual breakdown of slavery in the North; they were not the catalyst for the disintegration of the institution. Instead, these laws further contributed to an environment in which enslaved people could better negotiate for their freedom; some enslaved people appealed to the consciences of the enslavers, others offered loyal service for a specific number of years in return for freedom, while still others offered to buy themselves.[75]

Emancipation and the Business of Slavery

Three years after passing the gradual emancipation law, in 1787, Rhode Island forbade its citizens to participate in the Atlantic slave trade altogether.[76] As historian Jay Coughtry explains, "The merchants involved in it [slave trade] did everything they could to save it. They fought the state abolition society, violated state and federal laws passed to prohibit their commerce in slaves, defended their position on the floor of the House of Representatives, and finally enlisted the aid of a United States president to salvage their cause."[77] The authors of the 1787 Act to Prevent, and to Encourage the Abolition of Slavery and Slave Trade explicitly connected slave trading and slaveholding and insisted that emancipation would be completed only if the slave trade as a whole was ended. The condemnation of slavery led to the condemnation of the slave trade itself, even though it was a crucial component of the economy. This was the first time Rhode Island legislators had passed legislation that directly impeded a slave-related business. The majority of Assembly members saw trafficking in Africans as "inconsistent with justice, and the principles of humanity, as well as the laws of nature and that more enlightened and civilized sense of freedom which has of late prevailed." Legislators further declared that "no citizen of this state, or other person residing within the same, shall, for himself or any other person whatsoever, either as master, factor, or owner of any vessel, directly or indirectly import or transport, buy or sell, or receive on board their vessel with intent to cause to be imported or transported from their native country, any of the natives or inhabitants of any state or kingdom in that part of the world called Africa, as slaves, or without their voluntary consent." The 1787 act had stiff penalties. Any resident convicted of importing, or more importantly, transporting, African slaves was fined £100, and those found guilty of smuggling a vessel of slaves were fined £1,000.[78] The law reveals that those with antislavery sentiments had considerable power in the General Assembly. This legislation was possible because the Revolutionary War had severely hurt the local slave-trading economy: "Many merchants abandoned their businesses and left, some for good."[79] Between 1775 and 1783 there are no records of any slaving voyages, and between 1784 and 1787 only twenty-nine slaving voyages left the state, only four more than the number of voyages sent in 1774 alone.[80] The ideals and rhetoric of the Revolution in conjunction with the disruption of the slave trade, as a result of the war and British occupation of Newport, had contributed to a shift in public opinion concerning the slave trade.

In 1789, James Tallmadge, a student at Rhode Island College, later renamed Brown University, echoed the sentiments of the General Assembly when he delivered a scathing indictment of slaveholding and trading at his commencement exercises. Tallmadge asserted that any US citizen who participated in the slave trade made a mockery of the American Revolution and the new Republic. He referred to slave traders as "enemies of liberty."[81] He declared that slaveholders and slave traders should be regarded as dangerous criminals: "If capital punishment is inflicted upon the villain who attacks and robs a man of his property upon the highway, what punishment can be devised sufficiently great for those who trace the wide Atlantic and spread death and desolation on the African shore, who not only rob its unoffending peoples of their property, but of their liberty and lives and chain them down in ignominious servitude."[82] Tallmadge argued that slavery debased all men; through it, "mankind would be at once resolved into a universal monarch with some weak puny white faced creation for their sovereign, and those whose colour was farthest removed from white though a Newton, or Franklin, an Adams, or a Washington would be reduced to the most abject slavery."[83] What made his commencement speech particularly surprising was the college's connection to slave trading. The college's first president, Reverend James Manning, was a slaveholder, and approximately thirty members of the Brown Corporation, nearly half of the seventy-nine signatories who endowed the university, either owned or traded slaves. Slaveholders and slave traders, most notably the Brown, Lopez, and Rivera families, donated the land, money, and buildings for the college.[84] However, abolitionists like Moses Brown had also contributed to the founding of the school, which explains why abolitionist rhetoric was tolerated.[85]

The law and public opinion were increasingly critical of slave trading, yet in the new nation slave traders plied their trade with gusto and little regard for the law. Between 1783 and 1790, only forty-seven slaving voyages left from Rhode Island ports. However, in 1795 alone, slave traders went on thirty-two slaving voyages, a number surpassing the previous annual high of twenty-nine slaving voyages (set in 1772).[86] This blatant disregard for the 1787 slave trade ban is telling—the state was unwilling to enforce the law. In post-Revolutionary Rhode Island, the slave trade, instead of shrinking, expanded and shifted locations. And for the most part, slave traders operated with impunity. Slave trading resumed in Newport, but the city would not regain its pre-Revolutionary stature as the slave-trading center of North America or as a major export point for Narragansett goods; instead, Providence emerged as the post-Revolutionary economic center of the state. The British occupation of Newport led to depopulation that lasted decades after the war. But for merchants adept at transporting human beings across an ocean, changing ports was easy. And that just what Rhode Island's slave traders, led by the DeWolf family, did, putting Bristol on the map as the state's and North America's new slave-trading center.[87] Between 1789 and 1793, the slave trade grew by 30 percent in the state, and, the city of Bristol saw tremendous growth as the DeWolfs along with other local businessmen sponsored seventeen slaving voyages in just four years.[88] There was so much traffic in Bristol Bay that Representative John Brown, who was also a slave trader, lobbied for a local customhouse in Bristol so that merchants who sailed out of the bay would not have register in Newport.

The DeWolfs were latecomers to the American trade in African slaves; however, they "made up for their tardiness by sheer numbers." Between 1784 and 1807, members of the DeWolf family underwrote eighty-eight African slave-trading voyages. Moreover, the DeWolf family was the major employer in the growing city. They owned and operated a bank, insurance companies, textile mills, and distilleries.[89] James DeWolf and his brothers, who were among the most active slave traders in Rhode Island, received detailed advice from their uncle, Simeon Potter, on how to get around slave-trading laws, including what ports to avoid and which collectors were open to bribes or willing to turn a blind eye. Another tactic for avoiding the prohibition was to register slaving vessels with fraudulent foreign papers, indicating that the ships were owned by non–Rhode Island residents. James DeWolf went as far as lobbying to have the abolitionist customhouse collector at Bristol, Jonathon Russell, replaced with his business partner and brother-in-law Charles Collins.[90]

Dissatisfied with the limitations of the gradual emancipation law and enforcement of slave-trading laws, local abolitionists established the secular Providence Abolition Society in 1789. Moses Brown played a key role in the creation and mission of the society. Quakers dominated the society's leadership; however, the organization was open to all who opposed the institution of slavery and the slave trade in particular. In their incorporation papers, society members declared, "And as by the African Slave trade a system of slavery replete with human misery is erected and carried on it is incumbent on them to endeavor the suppression of the unrighteous commerce."[91] The group formally incorporated in June of 1790 as the Providence Society for Promoting the Abolition of Slavery, for the Relief of Persons Unlawfully Held in Bondage, and for Improving the Condition of the African Race. There were over one hundred members from Rhode Island, sixty-eight from Massachusetts, and three from Connecticut; there is no evidence to suggest that any of the members were African Americans.[92]

The society was determined to be active, not simply ideological. They wanted to end the slave trade, abolish slaveholding, and address racial oppression. For the members of this abolition society, slave traders and slaveholders were not evil men critiqued from a distance but rather neighbors, friends, and family. The members of the society wanted to prosecute state residents who continued to participate in the slave trade and those who held or sold slaves illegally. Society members brought "suit, action, plaint, or information, before any justice, judge, or court within this state, upon any law or penalty statute relative to the subject of slavery, or the slave trade," in their name.[93] The society was doing the investigative work that the state would not as profit overrode law.

In 1795, the society pursued the legal prosecution of John Brown, again for violating a 1794 federal ban restricting anyone "from carrying on the slave trade from the U.S. to any foreign place or country." John was not alone in violating the law. Disregard for the law was an understood necessity for many prominent businesses in the community.[94] In other words, ignoring the law was just a part of business. The case was both a victory and a defeat for the society. While John Brown was the first American slave trader prosecuted in federal court, he was ultimately acquitted, and the Providence Abolition Society was held responsible for the court costs.[95] Neither the 1787 law prohibiting the slave trade in Rhode Island, nor the 1794 restriction, nor the vigilance of the Providence Abolition Society halted participation in the slave trade. While abolitionist whites were powerful enough to pass a gradual emancipation law, they were not powerful enough to enforce a ban on slave trading. The desire for profit trumped the power of the law.

The business of slavery remained alive and well in Rhode Island even though the numbers of slaveholders and enslaved people dwindled; the slave trade thrived even as state and federal laws were passed to restrict American involvement in it. In other words, the number of people who owned slaves or were enslaved sharply decreased; however, the number of people involved in the business of slavery increased. In fact, in just twenty years, from 1787 to 1807, Rhode Island slave traders transported an estimated 45,230 Africans to bondage in the Americas, only about 10,000 fewer than they had transported in the previous seventy-seven years.[96] All of the other New England slave traders combined transported just 6,409 African slaves in the same time frame.[97] And many slave traders, including the DeWolfs, remained engaged in illegal slave smuggling throughout the antebellum era.[98] Emancipation had done nothing to deter the expansion of the business of slavery in Rhode Island, and slave trading actually grew tremendously after the slave trade ban was passed. This level of engagement strongly suggests that the state was not invested in preventing its residents from participating in the Atlantic slave trade.

White Rhode Islanders were willing to accept the gradual elimination of slaveholding in their region, but they were not interested in eliminating the institution itself, especially the slave trade. Rather, they remained complicit in slaveholding outside of their state; in fact, in the first decades of the nineteenth century they would further invest in the business of slavery by becoming the leading manufacturers of "negro cloth," a coarse cotton-wool material made especially to minimize the cost of clothing enslaved African Americans in the South. Their privileging of the business of slavery over slaveholding itself allowed just enough social and political space for African Americans and white abolitionists to dismantle the institution of slavery. Rhode Island, as a result, embodied two seemingly contradictory historical trajectories: the victory of black emancipation, slow but successful, was accompanied by a bolstered commitment to the business of slavery.

Cato Pearce was born in the Narragansett Country three years after the slave trade ban and six years after the Gradual Emancipation Law was implemented. While Pearce was born free, as the 1784 gradual emancipation law dictated, his parents were enslaved; thus he was to remain in the service of his mother's master until his twenty-first birthday.[1] He was a statutory slave.[2] When Pearce was just five or six years old his mother ran away. Her owner placed the following ad in the *United States Chronicle* in 1796:

> Ran-away from the Subscriber, in North Kingstown, County of Washington, on the 5th Instant, A NEGRO WOMAN, about 27 years of Age, 5 feet 4 Inches high, as walks with her Head very upright, had on when she went away, a dark Flannel Short Gown, and a Petticoat, a white Petticoat, a Man's Gray Gown, and a napped Felt Hat partly worn. Whoever will return said Negro to her Master, shall receive the above Reward, and all necessary Charges, paid by JOSHUA PEARCE, in North Kingstown, near the Devil's Foot.[3]

Pearce reminisced, "I 'member she told me to be a good boy and should bring me somethin' when she came back. She left three children behind; I was the oldest, and the youngest was only ten months old." He never saw her again. Pearce was left, effectively, parentless; his father lived on a neighboring farm and would have been unable to see to his children's daily needs.[4]

By the time Pearce was ten, only 124 of the 1,013 black people in Washington County were slaves for life, yet, for all intents and purposes, Pearce and other statutory slaves lived like lifelong slaves. They toiled for the benefit of their temporary masters, suffered corporal punishment, and did not direct their own labor. Unlike white indentured servants, Pearce would not receive land, seed, or clothing at the end of his servitude. Pearce fled bondage in 1808 when he was eighteen years old, three years short of his legal emancipation. He absconded to Providence and, like many black men, signed onto a merchant vessel as a sailor. An unexpected stop in Warwick on the return voyage led to his capture. His master, out fishing, recognized him. Pearce recalled that his enslaver "took all my wages and gave me a flogging." Two years later he fled again, this time for Massachusetts, where several court cases brought by enslaved people had led to rulings that slavery was incompatible with the state constitution. He worked for a couple of years as a farmhand and then went back to sea. In 1815, he returned to Providence and worked as a laborer; there were few enslaved people left in the state, and Pearce felt it safe enough to return, even though he still legally owed three years of service. After undergoing a religious conversion, Pearce found his calling as an itinerant Baptist preacher. However, he continued to support himself as a farm laborer.

Preaching kept him away from farmwork from Saturday night until Monday morning, which did not sit well with his employer, Elisha Potter. Potter, a longtime state senator and then US congressman, grew weary of these weekend absences and had Pearce jailed after he returned one Monday morning, sometime in 1820. According to Pearce, Potter stood with his horsewhip in hand and asked, "Why wa'nt you here last night to do the chores. . . . I won't have no nigger preachers—I'll horse-whip you." Pearce told Potter not to "strike" him. Potter then went and got the local "officer—the jailer" and had Pearce put into jail. He stayed there for two nights. Potter, a politically connected large landholder and former member of the enslaver class, felt entitled to Pearce's labor and obedience; moreover, he had significant sway in the community. In fact, he had enough social power to have Cato Pearce illegally arrested and jailed.[5] Fortunately for Pearce, county court was in session and some of the more enlightened members of the court convinced Potter to release Pearce, who, after all, had done nothing illegal. Pearce had been "jailed for preaching." Really, he was jailed for like acting a free man, something Potter and many other white northerners could not come to grips with following the collapse of perpetual, hereditary slavery in the North. Pearce returned to farm labor and preaching after his release, and throughout the 1820s and 1830s he lived and worked in rural Rhode Island saving lost souls.[6]

Cato Pearce was born, came of age, was jailed for preaching, and forged a life for himself as a preacher during the final decline of slaveholding in Rhode Island. In the year he was born, 1790, there were 958 slaves in the state; thirty years later, in 1820, when he was arrested for preaching, there were just 48 slaves left in the state; ten years later, in 1830, only 17 Rhode Islanders remained in bondage; and by 1840 just 5 slaves were counted in the Rhode Island census.[7] In the year that Pearce's memoir was published, 1842, the Rhode Island General Assembly finally abolished slavery. In Cato Pearce's lifetime, three changes created conflict between whites and blacks in the "free" northern states: northern whites lost their legal claim to mastery, the free black population grew, and black people challenged white supremacy. In Boston, New York, and Providence between 1800 and 1840, the free black population more than doubled. The growth of the free black population was both real and imagined. It was real in the sense that the absolute number of free blacks increased as more and more blacks were released from slavery and as more and more black children were born free. However, the percentage of free blacks in relation to the total population in northern cities actually dropped across the first half of the nineteenth century. In fact, free blacks rarely made up more than 10 percent of the total population of any northern state.[8] Many whites resented the growing free black population, even though the percentage of northerners who were black decreased every decade. Yet it was free black people's challenges to the racial ideology of white supremacy that created fear and panic among many white northerners.

From the last decade of the eighteenth century through the first three decades of the nineteenth century, black Rhode Islanders struggled to build lives as free individuals, while the former enslaver class grappled with the loss of mastery and attempted to maintain economic and social control over the sons and daughters of their former slaves. The attempts to control black people were evident in discriminatory laws, the exclusion of blacks from factory work, and the destruction of black neighborhoods in racially motivated riots. Moreover, black emancipation was at odds with the expanding business of slavery—the growth of the Atlantic trade and the entry into the textile industry, which was dependent on slave-grown cotton.

The Business of Slavery and Free People of Color

In 1791, just a year after Cato Pearce was born, a warrant was issued for the arrest of James DeWolf, the seventh son of the powerful slave-trading DeWolf-Potter family.[9] He was accused of murdering a slave woman by throwing her overboard on the *Polly*, one of his ships. The woman allegedly had smallpox and was tossed into the ocean to avoid further contamination of the crew and valuable "human cargo." The historical record has left little information about this captive, who is referred to as a "middle-aged Negro Wench," but her murder at sea is a stark reminder of the "realities of ill-health, trauma and death in the middle passage." The captive woman was tied to a chair, gagged, and blindfolded; confined, blind, and rendered speechless, she was then thrown into the Atlantic.[10]

DeWolf avoided a trial by absconding to the Caribbean island of St. Eustatius, where he continued to run his slave-trading business through correspondence with his brother. Isaac Manchester, a Rhode Island slave ship captain, became "aware" of DeWolf's hiding place, traveled to St. Eustatius, and gave a deposition to the governor regarding the alleged murder aboard the *Polly*. DeWolf was put on trial in St. Eustatius in 1794 and was acquitted; the judge determined that he had acted to save his men from the threat of infection. Sick slaves were routinely thrown overboard, and captains were rarely held accountable; however, it was technically illegal to willfully murder a captive. DeWolf was most likely charged because post-Revolutionary antislavery sentiment had increased public awareness about the horrors of the slave trade. Consequently, when sailors from the *Polly* reported the captive woman's death, the authorities acted. Nevertheless, after a four-year absence, in 1795, the marshal of Rhode Island dropped the arrest warrant against DeWolf, who immediately returned home to Bristol.

DeWolf, who most likely orchestrated the murder of a slave woman, went on to great wealth and prominence. He served seventeen years as a state senator and then was a US senator from 1821 to 1825. His investments in human trafficking made him Rhode Island's wealthiest man: he owned sugar and coffee plantations in Havana as well as a rum distillery, a mill, and a slave ship insurance company in Rhode Island.[11] While black Rhode Islanders strove to build free lives, white Rhode Island businessmen remained committed to and invested in the businesses of slavery.

White Rhode Islanders in the post-Revolutionary period did not confine their investments in the business of slavery to the slave trade, which the US Congress abolished in 1808; they also invested in the "negro cloth" industry. Made in part from cotton picked by enslaved people, "negro cloth"—also known as kersey— was a cheap, coarse, blended cotton-wool material manufactured especially to reduce the cost of clothing slaves in the American South. The Narragansett Country transitioned from agricultural center of the state to its industrial base as large farms were replaced with large mills. The region had been in decline since the 1770s as Narragansett farmers divided land between their sons rather than bequeathing it all to the eldest son; the parcels were increasingly diminished, thereby making it much more difficult "to produce a surplus sufficient for commercial farming so that slaves could be profitably employed."[12] Once dependent on slave labor, the Narragansett Country became increasing dependent on slave-grown cotton and the southern slave clothing market. Between 1800 and 1860, more than eighty "negro cloth" mills opened in Rhode Island, most of them located in the Narragansett Country. Twenty-two Rhode Island towns and cities manufactured kersey for over sixty years; more than eighty Rhode Island families owned part of a "negro cloth" mill at some point in the nineteenth century.[13] By midcentury, 79 percent of all Rhode Island textile mills manufactured slave clothing. In comparison, only about one-third of all the cloth produced at the famed Lowell mills in Massachusetts was destined for southern plantations.[14]

Throughout the first half of the nineteenth century, commodities traders, insurers, bankers, and manufacturers linked southern slaveholding to northern industry. Northern industry thrived because of slave labor, not as an alternative to it: free labor in the North relied on slave labor in the South.[15] Abolitionists described the business relationship between northern industrialists and southern planters as the union of "the Lords of the Lash and the Lords of the Loom."[16] This was particularly true in Rhode Island, where local industrialists operated the highest concentration of "negro cloth" mills in New England.

One of the most successful mills in Rhode Island was the Peace Dale Manufacturing Company (figure 2). In 1802, Rowland Hazard Sr. purchased a half interest in a mill on the Saugatuck River in the Narragansett Country. During its first decade of operation, the mill produced hand-spun gingham and linen; however, he had a difficult time competing against other regional factories and abandoned gingham and linen for "negro cloth." In 1819, Hazard Sr. turned the mill over to his sons Isaac and Rowland. Seven years later the brothers bought out the last investors, and in 1828 the youngest Hazard, Jonathan, joined the family business. They renamed the mill Peace Dale Manufacturing Company in honor of their mother, Mary Peace, who was southern by birth. The Hazard brothers transformed their father's modest manufacturing establishment into a major operation that supplied slaveholders throughout the South. They manufactured clothing, blankets, and shoes for enslaved African Americans in the South for twenty-seven years until a fire destroyed their equipment in 1855.[17]

Located in the heart of the Narragansett Country, the Peace Dale mill was the lifeblood of the village of Peace Dale, Rhode Island, near where their ancestors had previously held slaves and cultivated foodstuffs for the West Indian trade. In 1823, Peace Dale had just thirty residents, five houses, and one store, and the mill was worth $6,000. By 1830, the Peace Dale mill employed eighty-one people. In 1847 the mill was worth $140,000, and by 1860 there were one hundred employees. After the 1855 fire, the brothers began to manufacture shawls and cashmere, which they had been

Figure 2. Peace Dale Mills, South Kingstown, Rhode Island. Source: Peace Dale Mill, RIHS Collection (RHi X17 1429), Rhode Island Historical Society.

producing in small amounts since 1844.[18] The brothers did not try to rebuild their kersey business, most likely because of the abundance of kersey mills in the state and the growing regional divide over slavery.

For the Hazard brothers slavery was not a distant institution. Aside from manufacturing clothing, blankets, and shoes, they procured other necessities for their regular customers. In 1830, Isaac Hazard ordered two dozen axes for one of "his friends from the South"; he made sure they were "of the very best description of warranted goods."[19] The Hazards counted southern slaveholders as friends as well as business acquaintances. This was especially true for Rowland G. Hazard, who, acting as the mill's southern agent, spent twenty-three winters in the South visiting plantations and courting the business of slaveholders—his only clients. In the course of doing business, Rowland G. Hazard witnessed firsthand the workings of the southern slave system. He did not like what he saw.

In 1850, Rowland G. Hazard, while still selling slave cloth, decided to take a public stand against slavery. As a member of the Rhode

Island House of Representatives, opposing the 1850 Fugitive Slave Law, he stood in the House chambers and said: "My own convictions are that it [slavery] is the worst existing form of society for all concerned." Hazard argued for an immediate repeal of the law: "I am convinced that the slave laws are so repugnant to the moral sentiments of this section [i.e., the North] and the religious convictions of this section, that there can be no peace until they are repealed, or suffered by common consent to become a dead letter." He also acknowledged in his statement that he had a special relationship with southern slaveholding states when he asserted: "I am by descent, by the interest of business and the ties of friendship, more closely allied with the South than any other man in this House or perhaps the state." He reconciled his tolerance of the existence of slavery in the southern states and his own investments in it by clinging to an ideology of state's rights: "It is generally conceded that we must not interfere with this institution in the States by enactments of the general government, and it seems hardly fair that they should ask us not only to let them alone, but to insist we shall become what they themselves most heartily despise, *slave-hunters*."[20]

Rowland G. Hazard was a part of a generation of northerners who were increasingly critical of slavery and the political influence of the slaveholding states, despite the interdependence of northern industry and southern agriculture and raw materials.[21] He was comfortable condemning the capture and return of fugitive slaves in his own state; however, he was not willing to denounce the existence of slavery outside his region. Distance from the institution mattered for Hazard's proclaimed antislavery sentiments, yet his business did not allow him to maintain a physical separation from the institution of slavery. Regardless of his personal condemnation of slaveholding, he respected the right of white southerners to practice race-based slavery, and in return he expected slaveholders to respect the right of northerners to criticize and disregard the congressional imperative to return formerly enslaved people to bondage. Rowland G. Hazard's simultaneous support of and opposition to southern slaveholding exemplifies the situation of a group of northern businessmen who opposed slavery on moral grounds but supported and profited from slavery through their business dealings.[22]

Northern manufacturers and wage laborers in the "negro cloth" industry were key participants in the culture and the economy of slavery. In addition to profiting from and helping to perpetuate slavery in the South, they shaped race relations in the North. African Americans were largely shut out of the textile industry, as white employers preferred to hire whites and white workers often refused to work alongside black people. In the North, industrial work was the purview of whites; it was associated with free labor, and even though most blacks in the antebellum North were free their race marked them as slavelike. Northern kersey mills thus manufactured class and race in antebellum America both figuratively and literally, shaping the lives of free blacks in the North and enslaved African Americans in the South.

The vast majority of black and mixed-raced Rhode Islanders, as we know, were free by the turn of the nineteenth century; however, *free* was a terribly relative term. People of color still had to contend with slavery on multiple levels.[23] The practice of slavery still continued, as did statutory slavery. Free blacks also had to cope with the legacies of slavery—most urgently the poverty that came with nothing but freedom. Moreover, being free did not mean having rights. Free blacks had ambiguous legal protections because they were not universally recognized as citizens. Though the legal victories that led to emancipation were real, they were accompanied by the reverse—legal losses that retracted these newfound gains. Interracial marriages were banned in 1789, and African American men were barred from voting in 1822.[24] The ban on interracial marriages reflected the desire of the public officials to prevent racial mixing—at least mixing that was not forced by a white master. Black disenfranchisement was most likely triggered by increasing numbers of black property holders. Economic discrimination was also abundant; in fact, most free people of color found themselves performing the same work they had done as slaves. These attacks on recently freed people suggest more than economic and social discrimination. Black independence, in any form, was a threat to the state's the economy because black independence called into question the institution of slavery and the businesses that supported it. So while black people could be free they could not be equal. Many white Rhode Islanders feared a black population who, at least in theory, were free to work and move where they pleased.[25] Free blacks had to contend with a white citizenry that did not view them as citizens or, as we'll see, even legitimate residents of the new nation.[26] So although some white northerners had committed to ending slavery in their own region, free people of color were to remain on the margins of society, especially in employment.[27]

The vast majority of free women of color labored in the domestic trades, including cleaning, washing, weaving, sewing, child care, papermaking, and soap making. These jobs changed little with the disintegration of slavery, since perception of what was appropriate work for women and men was unaffected by emancipation. Black women, like all poor women, had to work to supplement the meager, often irregular income of their husbands, sons, and fathers. While the wages of black women were much lower than those of black men, their income was steady, as domestic work was in demand year round. What changed most for women of color, in freedom, was living outside the control of a master or mistress. They were no longer confined to the household; they had mobility and independence. Moreover, they no longer had to perform all the domestic labor in a household. Freedom allowed them to specialize and even refuse to do some menial tasks. Their ability to quit and find other employment radically changed domestic work and drew bitter complaints from whites seeking domestic help. For the first time, women of color could prioritize their needs and the needs of their families over the needs of whites.[28] A few black women even went into business for themselves. Mary Caesar, for example, sold cakes, while other black women peddled vegetables, fruits, candy, and bread; others hawked liquor on the streets.[29] Elleanor Eldridge, a landlord, became the largest black property holder in the state.[30]

Free men of color also performed many of the same tasks they had done as slaves; however, they were increasingly shut out of the skilled trades. Enslaved tradesmen enriched their white masters, while free black tradesmen were in competition with white men who barred them from their apprenticeships and trade organizations. Consequently, the majority of free men of color worked primarily as "unskilled" day laborers: porters, grooms, handymen, ditch diggers, servants, wagon team drivers, painters, cooks, and stevedores (loading and unloading ships). According to the 1825

Providence City Directory, 60 percent of free black men were classified as laborers. Most laborers spent just as much time looking
for work as working, since unskilled labor was seasonal and white
workers got preference. A few men of color found success as small
businessmen in the service sector. There were a small number of
black shoemakers, grocers, barbers, gardeners, and retailers. With
a few exceptions, black men were absent from the professional
classes—lawyers, doctors, merchants, newspaper editors, and the
like. Unlike many of their northern neighbors, free people of color
in Rhode Island lacked the population density necessary for significant self-sufficiency; blacks made up less than 5 percent of Rhode
Island's population, and most freed people were poor. On the other
hand, free black artisans, professionals, and storekeepers in New
York, Philadelphia, and Boston depended on the patronage of their
city's sizable free black population. By 1810, those cities boasted
several thousand free blacks, while Providence and Newport had
just several hundred.[31]

Despite their small numbers, black Rhode Islanders made small
but significant gains. In 1822, black Rhode Islanders, collectively,
only owned about $10,000 in property; however, by 1820 and 1840
they owned $18,000 and $46,000 respectively. Further, the number of African American heads of household, which was a marker
of financial stability and independence, increased by 121 percent
between 1832 and 1844. The number of property holders (real
estate) increased by 305 percent between 1829 and 1860.[32]

Wealth varied wildly among African Americans in Rhode
Island. A forty-year-old coachman owned just $30 of personal
property, while a fifty-six-year-old horse farrier and veterinarian
owned $5,000 of real estate and had $500 of personal wealth. Nevertheless, the vast majority of black households, 88 percent, "were
without appreciable amounts of property." Yet according to the
1860 census all the major black property holders in Rhode Island
(those owning property in excess of $500) were laborers except
Manuel Fenner (the aforementioned horse farrier and veterinarian). Historian Robert Cottrol argued that Providence "seems to
have been a difficult place for black professionals," as they rarely
stayed more than a few years, most likely because there were so few
blacks to pay for professional services. Black professionals' short

residence in Providence may explain why they did not amass much property. Unlike black barbers, small businessmen, and laborers, black professionals could not cultivate white clientele.[33] For black Rhode Islanders, education and a respected profession were not always avenues to economic success. What is surprising is that "no blacks were among the general factory operatives."[34] The typical factory job did not require special skills, training, or advanced education. Racism kept blacks off the factory floor.

Men of color, did however, find a significant niche as merchant marines—sailors on commercial ships. Throughout the Northeast, men of color sought work at sea; in fact, they were vastly overrepresented in merchant marine work. For example, between 1800 and 1820, nonwhites held about 20 percent of all seafaring jobs, although they represented just 5 percent of the total population of the region.[35] According to customhouse records, Rhode Island was the birthplace, or primary home, for well over a thousand merchant seamen of color. These men were described on seamen certificates as "African, sable, colored, Indian, black, mulatto, yellow, copper, dark copper, darkish, inclining to brown, and brown and ruddy."[36] With the exception of whaling vessels, which remained as white as northern factories, there was at least one nonwhite crewmember aboard 90 percent of trading vessels that left Newport between 1803 and 1865; and between 1824 and 1831 several merchant ships had majority-black crews.[37] Most labored aboard commodity-trading vessels rather than whalers and slave ships; in fact, members of a local black self-help organization formally agreed to not serve aboard slave ships. This prohibition did not prevent all black men from working on slave ships; however, it does suggest that the black community frowned on labor that undergirded the institution of slavery.

Black men were attracted to seafaring for a variety of reasons. Seafaring culture had strong egalitarian tendencies—racial boundaries often came second to ship hierarchy; crew members were paid according to rank rather than race, which allowed for some upward mobility; and, unlike day labor, seafaring work was more consistent and better paying. There were, however, significant drawbacks. Sailors were away from their families for long periods of time, usually months and sometimes years. Nonwhite sailors very rarely rose above the rank of cook, steward, or seaman. Racism kept them out of the officer ranks: with very few exceptions, nonwhites could not hope to attain the title of captain regardless of their skills and knowledge. Moreover, the work was dangerous, especially for black sailors, who had to contend with southern "Negro Seamen Acts" that called for black sailors to be imprisoned during their stays in southern ports, imprisonments that sometimes resulted in illegal enslavement. Finally, discipline on the ship was harsh and punitive; as historian W. Jeffrey Bolster has argued, "Black men suffered disproportionately the capricious nature of shipboard punishments."[38]

After a few generations of free black workers, the demographics of the industry changed. In the antebellum era, the number of nonwhite seamen steadily declined as white immigrant laborers replaced men of color; moreover, large port cities like Providence devoted more resources to industry and increasingly outsourced commerce shipping to states like Maine, which had even smaller populations of color.[39]

Poverty, Race, and Poor Laws

Even as people of color in Rhode Island, like their counterparts throughout the northern states, became exempt from the laws of slavery, their lives were still shaped by institution of slavery. The stranglehold of the institution is seen mostly clearly when we examine the material resources, or lack thereof, of the newly freed. In fact, the emancipation process itself often impoverished them further, separating them from the few resources they might have had.[40] Runaways, by necessity, began their free lives with little more than the clothes on their backs. Black soldiers were paid in continental currency that quickly depreciated after the Revolution. Those who were privately manumitted or received their freedom as a result of the gradual emancipation law were not legally entitled to any assistance; indentured white servants, in contrast, received clothing and seed and sometimes even land at the end of their servitude. By not allotting any resources to newly freed people, the state was effectively setting up an economically dependent population, whom they would later blame for their own poverty. Consequently, most free people of color were poor; they joined the ranks of the working poor—the majority of the population. Moreover, most free people of color remained poor because, as we have seen, they were relegated to the margins of the economy.

In the seventeenth and eighteenth centuries, two-thirds of all white immigrants arrived as indentured servants, and when enslaved people are counted among those migrants to North America, nearly 90 percent of all migrants were impoverished. The working poor were dependent on each day's labor to subsist and were usually only one disaster away from requiring private or public aid. Only two out of ten white indentured servants survived their terms and escaped poverty. Seasonal and cyclical unemployment, illness, insufficient wages, mental illness, a large pool of migrants, low pay for women (often half the pay of men), abandonment, and high mortality rates all contributed to poverty.[41] Among the poor, the newly freed faced even more hardship and obstacles than poor whites.

The poor, especially people of color, were heavily regulated in the new nation. The poor were effectively barred from moving out of the communities in which they were born or bound, because receiving assistance—food, clothing, shelter, and burials—required that one be a legal resident of the town, city, or county. And legal residency required that an individual be born, be bound, or own property within town limits. People who were not legal residents could be "warned out of town," ordered to leave and return to the place of their birth or their last servitude.[42] Town councilmen usually gave no reason for warning people out of town or simply stated that the applicant would "likely be chargeable" to the town. The implication seems clear: towns were worried about having to take care of too many poor people, and enforcing residency requirements was an effective way to weed out excess dependents. That bureaucratic fear of a dependent population, however, was inseparable from racism. Just as free people of color were heavily regulated and deemed likely dependents in the decades before the Revolution, so too were they disproportionately targeted after the Revolution. In 1800, half of those warned out of towns were people of color, although they made up just 5 percent of the total population.[43]

Free people of color who attempted to settle in towns outside their birthplace or their most recent place of servitude faced serious challenges from town authorities.[44] This was especially true as the poor fled economically depressed Newport for Providence in search of work.[45] The British blockade had decimated the city economy, which was slow to recover, and the city of Providence emerged as the economic center of the state. After the war, the black population in Newport decreased by 50 percent, from 1,200 to 600.[46] Freed people, it is clear from these drastic population shifts, ignored and defied poor laws by moving at will. They refused to stay in economically depressed places and believed that their freedom gave them new mobility. The government, however, did not share that belief, and their migrations were met with hostility and removal orders.[47] In 1787, the city council ordered Jane Whipple, a "negro" or "mulatto" who was born in Providence and had lived in the city for a total of twenty years, removed to Cumberland, where she had served as an indentured servant from the age of five to eighteen.[48] The council allowed her one week to move.[49] That same year, they rejected Huldah Abbey's application for legal residence. She was born in North Providence but had lived in Providence "nearly" all of her twenty years.[50]

Even Revolutionary War veterans were restricted from "legally" relocating. On September 9, 1794, Bristol Rhodes was ordered by the Providence town council to leave town and return to Cranston, his last place of legal residency. Rhodes, a former slave, had earned his freedom fighting in the Continental Army and had lived in Providence for five years.[51] Neither his freedom nor his service to country shielded him from the legal disabilities of his race.[52] In 1793, Prince Thurston, "a poor black adjudged by the Hon. Town Council to belong to Newport," was ordered removed and turned over to the Newport overseer of the poor when he failed to pay his bill at a local boardinghouse in Providence.[53] Watty Greene, a "mulatto" girl, Cato Gardner, a "negro" man, Mary Ceasar, a "mulatto woman," and several families of color were all removed from Providence for illegal settlement after complaints from "honorable" white men.[54] Removals also served as a tool to control free people of color. In 1816, Mary Cooper, a "woman of color," was banished to her birthplace (Rehoboth) after her white employer complained of her bad behavior. According to her employer, Mary was a thief and a drunk. She also reportedly neglected his children and threatened to burn his home and kill his family.[55] Mary's employer used her illegal settlement to punish her.

Legal residency did not protect free people of color from scrutiny and harassment. Patience Ingraham, a "mulatto or Indian" woman who ran an informal boardinghouse, was charged with "keeping a common, ill governed, and disorderly house and of permitting to reside there, persons of Evil Name and Fame, and of dishonest con-servation, drinking, tipling, whoring and misbehaving themselves to the Damage and Nusance of the Town."[56] Ishmael Brown, John Hix, Jack Grene, and Samuel Strange, all black boarders in Ingra-ham's house, were ordered to appear before the town council, who turned them over to Henry Bowen, a white man, for workhouse duties as punishment.[57]

Many free people of color who legally lived in Providence resided in white households. Prior to 1810, most free people of color in the city lived in white-headed households. After 1810, a substan-tial number of them remained in white households (see table 4).[58] This is largely attributable to the fact that many freed people left slavery and entered servitude in the same motion and sometimes remained in the same household. It is particularly notable that the number of blacks in white households increased between 1810 and 1820, after two decades of decline. This suggests that living in white households may have been a financial necessity—since free-dom did not ameliorate the burdens of poverty—and may also have been a strategy to avoid contests over legal residency. However, the decline in Narragansett agriculture and the expansion in trading and industry pulled many people of color from the countryside to the city just as Newport's post-Revolutionary economic decline spurred many to migrate to Providence.

The Snowtown and Hardscrabble Riots

The growth of the free black population in the North, however proscribed, was accompanied by a growth of violence against free people of color. Race riots—any group of twelve or more people, motivated by racial hatred, engaged in extralegal violence—during the antebellum period was neither commonplace nor rare in the North.[59] Race riots usually fell into two categories. The first

Table 4. Free Blacks in White-Headed Households in Rhode
Island, 1774–1820

Year	Percentage of blacks (free and enslaved) living in white-headed households
1774	82%
1790	73.2 %
1800	62%
1810	34.2%
1820	39.3%

Source: Based on census data in Robert J. Cottrol, *The Afro-Yankees: Providence's Black Community in the Antebellum Era* (Westport, CT: Greenwood Press, 1982), 48.

involved blacks who protected themselves, their friends, and their families from slavery. The second, which was the more common, involved violent assaults by whites when black people challenged white supremacy.[60] These riots became larger and increasingly violent across the first half of the nineteenth century, often with hundreds of participants. There were distinct regional differences in the targets of rioters. Northern white rioters usually targeted the property of blacks—homes, churches, and businesses—while southern white rioters most often targeted black bodies. However, white northerners also physically attacked blacks; a race riot in Philadelphia included rape and castration.[61]

Most race riots took place in black or mixed-race neighborhoods and were prompted by an array of grievances and anxieties. Blacks who refused to show social deference to whites prompted the two discussed here, as we will see. These racially mixed enclaves were home to poor and working-class whites and blacks, fugitives, and criminals. Fringe businesses like dance halls, brothels, and gambling houses were commonly located in these neighborhoods, often in private homes.[62] Hardscrabble and Snowtown were two such enclaves in Providence, Rhode Island. And like their counterparts across the North, these two neighborhoods were home to several fringe entertainment establishments; Providence had a large transient population of sailors who were looking for not only temporary lodging but access to prostitutes, liquor, and gambling. In fact, the behavior and demands of sailors were so notorious that barring them from one's boardinghouse was a sign of gentility.[63]

On October 18, 1824, white Rhode Islanders destroyed nearly all the homes in the predominantly African American neighborhood of Hardscrabble. Seven years later, white Rhode Islanders rioters wreaked havoc for four days in Snowtown, another predominantly black community. It was the first time the state militia had been called to put down a public disturbance.[64] Both of these riots occurred in Providence, where many of the state's African Americans lived, and began when blacks refused to show public deference to whites. Both riots culminated in the destruction of black property. The white residents of Providence, like whites throughout the North, were uncomfortable with and resentful of the ever increasing population of free and increasingly independent blacks.

Hardscrabble was "situated in the north-west part of the town of Providence, in a romantic glen, and consisted, previous to its destruction, of about twenty buildings inhabited by people of colour."[65] Hardscrabble was named for its residents—those who provided "maximum labor for minimal remuneration," as they were often employed in the most difficult labor for the lowest pay.[66] The cheap rents in Hardscrabble attracted not only the working poor but also criminals and fugitives of every race. Dance halls were common in Hardscrabble, such as the home of Henry T. Wheeler, a black man, who ran his business on the first floor of his two-story home. Near Wheeler's home, on the evening of October 18, 1824, several black Hardscrabble residents refused to step off the sidewalk to let a group of whites pass. Their refusal to move aside set the stage for violence; Wheeler's home was the first target. Forty whites, carrying clubs and axes, gathered in front of the Wheeler residence and began destroying it. The rioters literally took the home apart, tearing it down to its studs. The rioters were so systematic in their efforts that they took breaks in order to catch their breath. Their success encouraged more destruction. The rioters grew to fifty or sixty strong. They destroyed twenty structures—nearly all of the black-owned homes and businesses in Hardscrabble.[67]

The next day, ten white men—Oliver Cummins, Joseph Butler, Nathaniel Metcalf, Amos Chaffee, John Sherman, Gilbert Humes, Arthur Farrier, James Gibbs, Ezra Hubbard, and William Taylor— were indicted for disturbing the peace and destroying private property. All the men were residents of Providence employed as laborers or tradesmen. Butler, Sherman, and Taylor were not tried, because the sheriff could not locate them. All of the other men pled not guilty. They argued that there was no conclusive evidence that any of the defendants were involved in the riot, and they claimed that the rioters had performed a public service. The state called dozens of witnesses, who identified Farrier, Metcalf, Humes, and Cummins as agitators and participants in the riot.[68] However, the defense countered with witnesses who testified that Cummins and Humes were not involved; no such claims were made on behalf or Metcalf and Farrier.

The defense not only claimed that the defendants were not involved but also defended the actions of the rioters. Mr. Tilling-hast, the defense lawyer, repeatedly asked the state's witnesses, "What business was usually carried on in this house [Henry Wheeler's home]?" All the witnesses denied ever frequenting the house and testified they did not know. The state's attorney objected to the line of questioning, stating, "The character of the house was not on trial." The defense attorney replied, "They had a right to inquire what sort of a building it was, whether it was a house or a pig-stye." He then asked if the defendant could be "indicted for tearing down a pig stye."[69] In his closing remarks, Tillinghast stated: "Like the ancient Babylon it has fallen with all its graven images, its tables of impure oblation, its idolatrous rites and sacrifices, and my client stands here charged with having invaded this classic ground and torn down its altars and its beautiful temples!" The people of Hardscrabble had brought it on themselves, Tillinghast suggested, because their immoral behavior had provoked the "good" citizens of Providence to destroy their neighborhood.

The defendants were not alone in their opinion of Hardscrabble and its residents. The report released by the court read:

> Among this number [upwards of 1,200 black persons living in Providence] there are a great many industrious and honest individuals who in their departments render themselves

useful members of society; but the mass, as might be inferred, can hardly be considered a valuable acquisition to any community, and their return to the respective places from whence they came, probably would not be considered a public calamity. Between this class and the whites bickerings and antipathies would naturally arise. This has long been partially the case, until on the evening previous to the Riot, a sort of battle royal took place between considerable parties of whites and blacks, in consequence of an attempt of the latter to maintain the inside walk in their peregrinations through the town. If such has been the case heretofore, the moral and orderly town of Providence would not have been disgraced by the existence of a Hard-Scrabble, or of a mob to demolish it.[70]

Cummins and Humes were declared not guilty because there was conflicting testimony concerning their involvement. Metcalf and Farrier were found factually guilty but not legally guilty; while the court acknowledged that Metcalf and Farrier were among the rioters, it claimed that it could not determine what damage, if any, the two men were responsible for. This finding was absurd: if they had participated in the riot then they were responsible for the damage it caused. Ultimately, no one was punished for the rioting in Hardscrabble, and the residents received no compensation for the loss of their property.[71] Following the riot, "a large number of coloured people" left Providence for the black republic of Saint Domingue—the independent black republic in the West Indies.[72] Christopher Hill, a widower with three children who worked a series of odd jobs—gardening, woodcutting, and farming—emigrated to Liberia with his family after his home was destroyed in the riot.[73] Black Rhode Islanders were fleeing the state in search of liberty.

Seven years later, in 1831, an evening dispute between several black Olney Lane residents and several white steamboat workers in Snowtown developed into the most violent and deadly riot the city had ever seen.[74] It is difficult to fully understand the Snowtown riot because the primary evidence remaining from the riot, *The Committee's Report*, which was compiled by prominent white men in the community, is fundamentally flawed. The committee members themselves noted that:

the testimony upon which this statement rests, was not given under oath, nor in the presence of the blacks, and the most material of the witnesses were parties to the affray [a noisy fight between two or more people in a public place]. How far a close cross-examination of the sailors would qualify the account here given, we are unable to say. Nor can we state what proof, contracting material parts of this narrative, can be furnished by the blacks. Until that proof is produced before the proper tribunal, no opinion as to the comparative guilt of the whites and blacks, ought to be formed.

The accounts of the Snowtown Riot were entirely from the point of view of whites—white rioters and white government officials. According to these authorities, Snowtown was home to "idle blacks, of the lowest stamp" who "have constituted a continuing nuisance of the most offensive manner."[75]

On a Wednesday evening late in September several white steamboat workers armed with sticks and clubs approached five white sailors on Olney Lane. The steamboat workers told the sailors that they had been involved in fight with the "darkies" and asked the sailors for their help. The group continued up the lane and joined a white crowd of about one hundred people. According to the committee's report, it was not clear whether a shot was fired from a home of a Snowtown resident or if stones were thrown from the crowd toward a black-occupied home on Olney Lane. Whether it was a stone or a gunshot, the offense served as a catalyst for the riot. Another shot was fired from an Olney Lane home, and William Henry, one of the white sailors, cried out that he had been wounded. George Erickson and William Hull, two white rioters, continued up the street and encountered a black man standing on the steps of his home holding a gun. He warned the men to "keep their distance." One of the white men—Hull suspected it was Erickson—cried, "Fire and be damned." The man fired. Erickson was shot and mortally wounded. Hull and another rioter sustained non-life-threatening injuries.[76] Thus began four nights of violence and destruction.

On the first night of the riot, the rioters were so numerous and out of control that the sheriff and his men were unable to pacify the crowd, so they retreated and left the rioters to their destruction. The mob reassembled the next evening on Olney Street. The news that a black man had shot and killed a white man had spread through the city, outraging the white residents of Providence. Anticipating another night of violence, the sheriff and his men arrested seven white agitators from the crowd, but they were unable to control the rioters as their numbers increased throughout the night. In fact, the rioters threw stones and bricks at the sheriff and his men. The sheriff asked the governor for assistance. The First Light Infantry, consisting of twenty-five men, marched onto Prospect Street toward Olney's Lane between nine and ten o'clock at night. The mob attacked them and they retreated. The sheriff and the military were convinced that "nothing short of firing would produce any other effect than increased irritation and ferocity in the mob."[77] The rioters followed the retreating soldiers, throwing stones. Several soldiers sustained injuries, from minor bruises to head wounds. That night, the rioters tore down several more black homes, broke windows, and assaulted at least two black residents. The crowd did not disperse until four o'clock in the morning.[78]

On the third day of unrest, the rioters planned to break into the jail and release the seven men who had been arrested the day before. In a preemptive move, the local magistrates processed the accused men on the same day. Four were released because of insufficient evidence, and the remaining three were transferred over to another court and released. Even so, thirty to fifty rioters gathered in front of the jail on Friday evening to call for the release of their fellow rioters. After considerable persuasion the sheriff was able to convince the rioters that the prisoners had already been released.[79]

On the fourth evening of the riot, the state was better prepared. By six o'clock, 130 soldiers had been mustered. Under the authority of the governor, the militia men were marched over to Smith's Bridge, in Snowtown, where a white mob had gathered. One rioter disarmed a soldier, which led to a brief clash between rioters and soldiers. Requests from the governor and the sheriff for the crowd to disperse and return home were met with angry chants of "Fire and be damned."[80] The militia men, seemingly out of options, finally fired on the crowd. Their actions ended four days of terror and destruction. When all was said and done, four homes had been completely destroyed, eight homes had been severely damaged, four men (one white, three black) had lost their lives, and thirteen had been seriously wounded.

The town council condemned the mob for their "lawless attack upon private property, provoking insults and aggravated assaults," but they ultimately blamed the victims.[81] The council put together a committee to investigate the riot. The fourteen members consisted of bankers, lawyers, clergymen, and businessmen—all "respected" white citizens of Providence. At least one of the committee members, Richard Arnold, was a slaveholder, a prominent local businessman who also owned and operated a plantation in Georgia.[82] According to the committee's report, the rioters targeted "houses of suspicious reputation"; their targeted rioting was used to justify the destruction of black property. Committee members asserted that respectable black residents of Snowtown did not stop the rioters because they too were tired of the "ordinary evils of the houses of ill fame."[83] The committee failed to consider that the residents of Snowtown were in no position to defend themselves or their neighbors. They were busy fleeing their homes, carrying beds, bedding, chairs, tables, and other personal property.[84] None of the perpetrators were held accountable for the Snowtown riot, and no compensation was offered to its victims. In less than a decade, two black neighborhoods had been attacked in Providence, and in both instances the victims had been blamed. According to the authorities, black Rhode Islanders had brought it on themselves.

Free blacks did indeed engage in extralegal businesses such as gaming houses, dance halls, and brothels, as they were often denied access to legitimate business opportunities. However, many of their clients, as noted by the civil authorities, were the white citizens of Providence. Some of the rioters may have been customers of the businesses they destroyed. Even the white authorities condemned whites who frequented the businesses and residences of the Snowtown neighborhood:

> The blacks of this town have been unusually bold for the last few weeks and have repeatedly defied the civil authority. But in this case, we must go higher, and let the blame fall upon those who encouraged and countenance their dissolute habits and mode of living. If these huts and brothels which have caused the town so much expense and trouble were not let out in the

manner they are the number of disorderly blacks would be less and their characters generally improved. But as long as they can hire one room, and get money sufficient to purchase fish and rum, we can never look for improvement.[85]

According to the officials, the problem was not only the existence of quasi-legal black-owned businesses, which were patronized by both whites and blacks, but also the white landlords who rented out the properties to them.

The Hardscrabble and Snowtown riots, like race riots throughout the North, were about much more than a few black people refusing to publicly defer to whites, and they were about much more than white rage at black assertions of independence. These riots highlight white resentment of black freedom. From the point of view of the rioters and their supporters, black emancipation had demoted all whites, especially those whites who had never owned slaves. Their whiteness, in and of itself, was no longer a clear marker of freedom if black people were also free. And for black people freedom was not really freedom if they had to continue to defer to whites simply because they were white. These riots highlight what the breakdown of slavery looked like on the streets of northern cities. It was contentious and violent, it was fraught with anxiety and anger, and black people, abandoned by the state, were left in pursuit of full freedom.

In the new nation, in the North, most black people were free but they did not have liberty. They did not have the protections and opportunities afforded to white people because neither the law nor mainstream white society recognized them as citizens. And as the business of slavery shifted from Atlantic commerce to the textile industry, freed people found themselves shut out of the new industrial economy. They also faced serious social discrimination, as public officials and white society at large were uncomfortable with the realities of black freedom, especially as it pertained to their ability to move around and claim social space. Black people responded to this multifaceted marginalization by building their own institutions to bolster and protect their vulnerable communities.

5 /   Building a Free Community

In 1789, in a letter to "all the Africans of Providence," members of the nation's first black mutual aid society—the Free African Union Society (FAUS or the Union)—expressed their frustration with the racism they faced in the new American republic. They described their position, "being strangers and outcasts in a strange land, attended with many disadvantages and evils, with respect to living, which are like to continue on us and our children while we and they live in this country." The Union praised those who were "endeavoring to effect their return to their own country and the settlement there, where they may be more happy than they can be here."[1]

Thirty-seven years later, in 1828, New Englander Hosea Easton catalogued the continuing racism faced by black Americans in his *Address: Delivered before the Coloured Population, of Providence Rhode Island on Thanksgiving Day*:

> Now as we composed a part of the number who are said to be free, of course it becomes our duty to consider how far our liberty extends. The first inquiry is, Are we eligible to an office? No.—Are we considered subjects of the government? No.—Are we initiated into free schools for mental improvement? No— Are we patronized as salary men in any public business whatever? No—Are we taken into social compact with Society at

large? No.—Are we patronized in any branch of business which is sufficiently lucrative to raise us to any material state of honour and respectability among men, and this [sic], qualify us to demand respect from the higher order of Society?—No.—But to the contrary. Everything is withheld from us that is calculated to promote the aggrandizement and popularity of that part of the community who are said to be the descendants of Africa.[2]

This relentless assault on black liberty served to create a structural racism that was nearly impenetrable. The anxieties of the union members at the turn of the nineteenth century were indeed justified. For people of color, the struggle for freedom was often circular. There was no steady progress forward. Instead, the fight for equality was filled with fits and starts, misgivings, small victories, and disappointments.

As individuals, black Rhode Islanders could effect little change; however, as a community they could and did address the racism that relegated them to the margins of politics, the economy, and society as a whole. In the colonial period the business of slavery served to enslave black people; in the postcolonial period it served to impoverish, alienate, and disenfranchise black people. In response, like their counterparts throughout the northern states, black Rhode Islanders came together to build institutions and fight for their rights as free people. They established mutual aid societies: FAUS in 1780, the African Benevolent Society (ABS) in 1807, the Female Benevolent Society in 1809, and the African Union Meeting House in 1819. Mutual aid societies were of special value to developing communities because they helped create and institutionalize different roles, relationships, values, and ways of living outside the institution of slavery.[3] The birth of black institutions throughout the North demonstrated the desire of black people to direct their own futures.

Understanding the formation, challenges, successes, and failures of the nation's first free black associations is critical to a full accounting of how free blacks negotiated the constraints of inequality, particularly in a society ambivalent about black freedom. Historians have long noted that mutual aid societies were essential to the social development and economic survival of free black communities.[4] These organizations addressed the specific needs of newly freed blacks, who were particularly vulnerable to economic downturns and personal tragedy because they often lacked access to economic and moral support from mainstream institutions like churches. Black mutual aid and benevolent societies provided a multitude of services to the African American community, serving as schools and churches as well as informal banks and disability insurers. Perhaps more importantly, these institutions provided newly free blacks with spaces to address social, economic, and political grievances. Finally, they served as symbols of black permanency and discontent with the status quo.

The Free African Union Society

FAUS was founded in November of 1780 in Newport, Rhode Island. It is the earliest known free black association in the United States. FAUS members held their first meetings in the home of Abraham Casey, a property holder and member of a small but influential black middle class.[5] The Union provided a variety of support services such as paying for burials and providing widows and children of former members with financial aid. All members were required to pay dues and demonstrate good moral character. Union founders were not content to organize African Americans in Newport; they also reached out to blacks in Providence.

With chapters in Newport and Providence, FAUS became the public voice of Rhode Island's free black community.[6] Although the Union had a structure similar to that of contemporary white organizations, its functions and goals were unique.[7] Unlike white organizations, FAUS had no restrictions based on occupation, religion, or ethnicity.[8] The common oppression faced by all black Americans bound them together despite class differences. Most of the Union's leaders were staunchly middle class—entrepreneurs and businessmen; however, a couple of prominent members were seamen, and day laborers were counted among the general membership. Enslaved men were not restricted from joining, though there is no evidence of enslaved members taking any leadership roles. It is important to note that these voices were all male. Women were allowed to join but did not have voting rights.[9] Members sought to build a community that was morally upright, economically stable, and politically self-directed.

FAUS played an essential role in the survival and continuity of the free black community in Rhode Island. As we have seen, newly freed blacks had to contend with discriminatory poor laws and severe economic insecurity.[10] FAUS provided much-needed economic security by supporting the dependents of its members. For example, Susannah Wanton, the widow of Newport Wanton, received payments when her husband was ill; the Union also covered the cost of his burial and even paid for the tea, rum, and sugar that were served at his funeral. Genny Gardner, also a widower of a Union member, was paid one dollar for her "present relief."[11] Membership provided some sense of financial stability for black men and their families. FAUS also conducted business for out-of-town members and kept them informed about community issues. For example, Kingston Pease depended on fellow members to conduct his business and care for his family while he made arrangements to relocate to New York.[12] The Union, in other words, provided more than monetary support: it provided social support.

Membership in a mutual aid society allowed black men to do what slavery had denied them, to prioritize the care of their families. Providing for their families during sickness and death restored a sense of manhood. Historian James Horton goes so far as to argue that "for black men the ability to support and protect their women became synonymous with manhood and manhood became synonymous with freedom."[13] Ultimately, FAUS was a legitimizing organization for black men. Their habit of referring to each other as "Mr." or "Sir" suggests that they took pride in honorific titles. These titles invoked status and respect, two characteristics often denied to black men by whites in the new nation. Union membership allowed free black men to demonstrate their respectability and validated their manhood.[14] Within the Union they were leaders, men who demanded and commanded respect; they were providing for their families and protecting their communities.

Although FAUS had both working-class and middle-class members, the organization was not immune from class conflict. The protracted and ongoing demise of slavery led to intragroup conflict among free blacks. African American Rhode Islanders understood that their oppression, as free people, was linked directly to the color of their skin and legacies of slavery. Across the late eighteenth and nineteenth centuries, state laws had gradually, and grudgingly, restricted the institution of slavery, but one constant remained: the institution was centered on people of African descent. Furthermore, the laws that restricted the rights of free black people, such as the voting ban, rested on the premise that blacks were unfit for full freedom because they were racially inferior. Consequently, FAUS members were often overly critical of the "base behaviors" of working-class blacks who patronized dances halls and gaming houses: "While we are feasting and dancing, many of our complexion are starving under cruel bondage, and it is this practice of ours that enables our enemies to declare that we are not fit for freedom—and at the same time this imprudent conduct stops the mouths of our real friends who would ardently plead our cause."[15] FAUS members claimed that such behavior discouraged support for abolition and equal rights from sympathetic whites. However, as historians Leslie Alexander and Patrick Rael have argued, black leaders advocated for moral improvement as a "strategy for racial activism rather than a capitulation to White standards of respectability."[16]

It is difficult to accurately differentiate class among nineteenth-century black Americans; however, education and home ownership often distinguished middle-class blacks from their working-class counterparts. The men who dominated FAUS were usually property holders—homeowners.[17] For example, FAUS founder Abraham Casey owned a two-story home on Levin Street. Levin Street, in Newport, was home to several prosperous black families, most notably the Rice homestead, built in 1815. Isaac Rice, born in 1792 in the Narragansett Country, ran successful catering and landscaping businesses. His home was said to be a stop on the Underground Railroad. Several members were well educated—as a result of private tutoring, given that most public and private schools banned blacks. John Quamine, Bristol Yamma, and Salmar Nubia all studied theology under the Reverend Samuel Hopkins and Reverend Ezra Stiles. Caesar Lyndon, who had been owned by Rhode Island governor Josiah Lyndon, had acted as a business agent and secretary for his enslaver; he also ran a small but successful private lending practice. His loans were so successful that he was able to purchase his freedom.[18]

Prominent Union member Newport Gardner was also a home-owner, and like Abraham Casey he opened his home as a meeting place. The ABS (founded in 1807) initially met in Gardner's home.[19] According to local folklore, Gardner was the son of a prosperous African who had been sold into slavery by an unscrupulous Rhode Island slave trader whom his father had entrusted to educate him.[20] Regardless of how he came to be enslaved, his extraordinary intelligence and musical talents were noted and encouraged by his enslaver. Gardner soon became a sought-after musician and used the money he earned giving lessons to purchase his freedom.[21]

The presence and prominence of an African-born Union member, like Gardner, most likely influenced the Union's attempt to resettle their community in Africa despite many misgivings about the continent and its inhabitants. While many black Rhode Islanders were proud of their African ancestry, as evidenced by the names they gave their associations, they were also conflicted about their heritage. This conflict was primarily religious. Most late eighteenth- and nineteenth-black Americans, free and enslaved, were Christians, and many were concerned about their "heathen" brothers in Africa. FAUS members believed that black Christians, like the Israelites, were a chosen people. They expressed a desire to lift Africans from heathenism and immorality. Free black Rhode Islanders wished to return to the land of their ancestors not only to escape American oppression but also to transform a "godless" people into practicing Christians. In an open letter to the "Affricans of Providence," FAUS members wrote, "The Nations in Affrica, from which we spring, being in heathenish darkness and sunk down in barbarity, are and have been from many years, many of them, so foolish and wicked as to sell one another into slavery, by which means millions have either lost their lives or been transported to a Land of slavery."[22] This type of critique of Africa was not unique to black leaders in Rhode Island: self-conscious black communities throughout the North had similar views.[23] Despite their critiques, black Rhode Islanders remained convinced that Africans could be saved and that Africa could be a "promised land." They dreamed of a place where blacks could prosper morally, spiritually, and economically. Their desire to escape the "evils and disadvantages" of racism in the new nation, as well as their desire to save their "heathen" brethren, led FAUS members to pursue the option of emigrating back to Africa.

Returning to Africa was hardly a new idea. In 1735, a regional newspaper reported that a free black Rhode Island couple had saved "two or three thousand Pounds, having a Desire to return to their own Country."[24] However, free black Rhode Islanders wanted to return as a community, and, as we will see, they had the ardent support of local whites, who preferred to live in a society free of black people.

In the post-Revolutionary era, whites on both sides of the Atlantic sought to remove their free black populations through African colonization.[25] As early as 1772, in response to complaints about black poverty, Grandville Sharp, a British abolitionist, began making plans for a black colony in Africa. Over ten years later, he successfully petitioned the British Parliament for a self-governing province for free blacks in West Africa. In 1786, he published his settlement plan. In May 1787, a free black province, Sierra Leone, was settled near the Sierra Leone River. Within two years, settlers had deserted or succumbed to disease. The settlement was reestablished in 1791 and renamed "Freetown."[26] The new settlement was financed and governed by English businessmen who opposed slavery and the Atlantic slave trade.[27]

The African colonization movement also drew settlers from the United States, and even from as far north as Nova Scotia. The British relocated black Nova Scotians to Sierra Leone, former slaves who had fought with the British during the American Revolution. The land they had been promised in Africa was poorly suited for agriculture or was not there at all. Furthermore, when war broke out between England and France, the colony was attacked by passing French ships. In an effort to raise money, the Sierra Leone Company began charging the settlers one shilling per acre for land they had been promised free of charge.[28] As a consequence, many black Nova Scotian settlers were forced to indenture themselves or their children to survive.[29]

Free blacks in the United States were divided over African colonization.[30] In the eighteenth century, emigration was largely condemned by black communities in Pennsylvania, New York, and Connecticut but supported by blacks in Rhode Island, Massachusetts, South Carolina, and Maryland. Some opponents of African emigration felt it was wrong to abandon their enslaved brothers and sisters in the southern United States, while others believed that emigration to Canada or Haiti made more sense. Finally, some free blacks refused to yield to white racism. They insisted on their rights as American citizens. On the other hand, supporters of black colonization believed that because slavery was race based free blacks would never be truly free. They were convinced that their freedom would always be in jeopardy and severely limited. One explanation of why Rhode Islanders and Bostonians were more receptive than their northern neighbors to African colonization was New England's continued participation in the slave trade in the postcolonial period. Between 1787 and 1808, Rhode Island merchants transported nearly forty-six thousand African slaves to the Caribbean and the southern United States, as we have seen, despite a 1787 law that made it illegal for Rhode Island citizens to participate in the slave trade.[31]

Black Rhode Islanders attempted a self-directed migration to Africa. They made African colonization, first planned by whites and intended for England's free black population, their own cause.[32] They used their connections to influential whites to facilitate a return to Africa, yet they did not wholly rely upon white individuals or organizations. Their insistence on directing their own future, however, may have been their initial and fatal mistake.

Prior to the Revolutionary War, white Rhode Islanders who advocated an end to slaveholding had discussed African colonization. Samuel Hopkins and Ezra Stiles, both of whom had relationships with FAUS members, were supporters of colonization. In 1774, they had raised funds to train Bristol Yamma and John Quamine, members of Hopkins's congregation, as ministers for African congregations. They proposed a plan to send them to Africa as missionaries and settlement negotiators.[33] The Revolutionary War and Quamine's subsequent death temporarily disrupted their plans.[34] However, as the free black population increased after the war, white interest in colonization grew. In 1786, William Thornton, an ardent abolitionist, "spoke to crowds of blacks, and within a few weeks of his arrival in New England claimed that two thousand freed-men were ready to follow him to West Africa."[35] So when Thornton brought the news of Sierra Leone to black Rhode Islanders that same year, in 1786, there was existing support and interest.[36]

Many whites in the United States supported and championed black emigration because they could not envision a place for free blacks in the new nation. Free blacks posed an ideological problem for citizens of a nation that acknowledged and protected race-based slavery on the rationale that blacks were inferior and inherently unfit for freedom. For many northern whites, a free society meant a society free of blacks, so many whites supported African coloni-zation. Throughout the North, gradual emancipation laws allowed whites to claim that they had a free society while still having access to bound black labor. By the antebellum era, the northern states had almost completely eradicated their dependence on slave labor and relied instead on the inexpensive labor of newly freed people who increasingly faced economic competition from European immi-grants. Some white New Englanders wanted to remove all traces of blacks, who were living reminders of slavery, in order to claim a history as a land of freedom—white freedom. Consequently, north-ern whites emphasized slavery as a southern problem and used the popular press to characterize blacks as a threat to civility and order. Their characterization of free blacks as lazy and immoral allowed whites to blame blacks for their own poverty without acknowledg-ing the many ways that racism that contributed to black poverty.[37] It was in this environment that FAUS members embraced African colonization.

In 1787, black Rhode Islanders advocated for and began plan-ning a return to Africa.[38] With conviction the members of FAUS articulated why African colonization was their only plausible option: "We, the members of the Union Society in Newport, take-ing into consideration the calamitous state into which we are brought by the righteous hand of God, being strangers and out-casts in a strange land, attended with many disadvantages and evils, which are like to continue on us and on our children, while we and they live in this country."[39] The words of the FAUS members invoke Exodus 23:9: "Also thou shalt not oppress a stranger: for ye know the heart of a stranger, seeing ye were strangers in the land of

Egypt." FAUS member and officer Anthony Taylor expressed their
urgency to emigrate in a letter to William Thornton: "Our earnest
desire of returning to Africa and settling there has induced us
further to trouble you with these lines, in order to convey to your
mind a more particular and full idea of our proposal."[40] He wanted
to know how to procure rights to land and asked for assistance in
raising funds to purchase settlement land in Africa.

FAUS members had the support of many local whites in their
attempts to resettle in Africa. One member wrote, "Every white
person in Town seems to be forward in promoting the matter."[41]
Thornton, an intermediary between FAUS and the larger white
community, relayed news and sought funds for the Rhode Island
colonization effort. In a letter to FAUS members he wrote, "I imag-
ine you have been acquainted with my having conveyed your sentiment to the Committee on Affrican Affairs in London, whose
answer on your account I now wait, and which I mean immediately
to transmit."[42] Union members were not sure whether they could
trust Thornton and were adamantly opposed to him scouting possible settlements in Africa. Longtime FAUS member Samuel Steven
stated, "We do not approve of Mr. Thornton's going to settle a place
for us; we think it would be better if we could charter a Vessel,
and send some of our own Blacks."[43] The Union circulated letters
to several other black organizations promoting the cause of African colonization throughout the newly formed states. The African
Company of Boston was in full agreement.[44]

Black communities that supported African colonization often
lacked the resources to execute a return to Africa.[45] To the chagrin
of the founding Newport chapter, the Providence chapter of the
Union took the lead in acquiring funds for the colonization effort;
they petitioned the Rhode Island General Assembly in January
1794 for assistance in their endeavor to settle in Sierra Leone.[46] The
Newport chapter sent a sharp retort; they reminded the Providence
chapter that they did not speak for the entire FAUS. They also
asserted that such a petition should have been approved and carried out by both chapters, especially considering that the Newport
chapter was responsible for the formation of the Providence chapter. The Newport chapter appointed one of their most influential
members, Newport Gardner, to accompany James Mackenzie, a

seaman and FAUS officer, to represent the Union in Sierra Leone.[47] In November of 1794, Mackenzie set sail aboard the *Charlotte* to obtain information about settlement in Sierra Leone.[48] Newport Gardner was not on the ship.

Mackenzie arrived safely in Africa and submitted a letter to the Sierra Leone Board of Directors on behalf of FAUS of Rhode Island. The council members decided they would accept up to twelve families. Each family would receive ten acres and a communal town lot. There were, however, some conditions. Potential colonists had to obtain recommendations attesting to their moral character, agree to follow the laws of the colony, provide their own transport, and clear a third of their granted land by the end of their second year. The Council of the Sierra Leone Company wrote directly to local abolitionist Samuel Hopkins, not to the FAUS president and officers, asking him to vouch for the potential colonists.[49] The leading officials in the Sierra Leone Company were white men, who depended on other white men to vouch for the characters of potential black settlers. Sierra Leone, clearly, was not the black utopia that FAUS members had hoped for. Black Rhode Islanders were appealing, not to a self-governed free black colony, but to a colony that was financed and governed by white men in London.

Samuel Hopkins thwarted the Union's emigration effort by writing a "negative evaluation of the Providence leadership."[50] It is unclear why Hopkins did this, considering he worked closely with several members of the Union. Maybe it was because his friend, Bristol Yamma, had died and he no longer had personal relationships with the union leadership, or maybe he resented that the Union had not sought his permission or advice before sending Mackenzie to enquire about settlement. This second explanation is likely, given that white abolitionists often butted heads with black leaders who attempted to direct their own destinies. Many white abolitionists held paternalistic attitudes toward blacks and resented black Americans who took charge of their own affairs.[51] Despite the desire of some black Rhode Islanders to emigrate to Africa, the power to do so was out of their hands. They needed white patronage, and ultimately they needed the approval and support of Samuel Hopkins. When Hopkins refused to vouch for the character of Union members, their plans were ruined.

The success or failure of the colonization project is not as historically significant as the social context that inspired some free blacks to want to flee Rhode Island. Black aspirations to leave the "free" state of Rhode Island for an unknown land speak volumes about the difficulties of everyday life for free African Americans in Rhode Island. The fact that they organized and planned an escape from racial oppression so soon after the Revolution is noteworthy. While white Americans were exercising their newfound freedoms and liberties, free black Americans were searching for a glimmer of freedom and liberty an ocean away.

FAUS dissolved in 1797, but its remaining members reorganized in 1802 as the African Humane Society. By 1805, the society had only 36 members, a far cry from the 108 members FAUS had boasted in 1785. Seventy-two members had died since the Union's founding.[52] In 1807, free black Rhode Islanders organized a new mutual aid society—the ABS. The desire of the free black community to repeatedly reconstitute their institutions speaks to the importance of these types of organizations. Despite setbacks and disappointments they refused to give up on institution building; they were determined to maintain organizations that catered to their needs and to create spaces where they could gather and help one another, especially increasing access to education.

Black Rhode Islanders, like their counterparts throughout the North, were increasingly committing to uplift ideology, the belief that blacks could obtain social and political equality through education and good behavior. They believed that individual self-improvement would help undermine racism. Many advocates of uplift ideology also shunned public displays of their African identity; they characterized such displays as common or unpatriotic and felt that blacks could demonstrate their patriotism and worthiness for full inclusion in American society by living frugal and virtuous lives. This argument was not uncontested: leaders in black communities throughout the North cautioned against a sole focus on moral improvement, asserting that racial progress also demanded the inclusion of African identity through burial practices, dance, and public celebration.[53]

The African Benevolent Society and the African Female Benevolent Society

In 1807, during a general meeting of blacks in Newport, someone proposed establishing a school for blacks. All in attendance supported the proposal.[54] The ABS sought to raise black Rhode Islanders "out of that state of ignorance and depression, into which the injustice, Pride and avarice of others have attempted to sink your color."[55] They declared, "Our Object shall be the establishment and continuance of a free school for any person of colour of this Town."[56] The ABS had neither sex nor race restrictions, and, unlike FAUS it had white members. Initially, members had to pay a membership fee of fifty cents. However, membership was extended in 1810 to "all that are willing to promote the means of education for the African Race"; however, dues were collected from those who could afford to pay.[57]

Education was the single most discussed, and lamented, aspect of black life that the ABS worked on. State law did not bar African American children from attending public schools; however, schools in Providence, Newport, and Bristol, where the majority of black Rhode Islanders lived, were segregated through local ordinances.[58] Rural school districts had integrated schools because the small number of African American children in these areas did not warrant separate facilities.[59] However, Rhode Island did not establish a public school system until 1830. There had been other schools for free people of color—abolitionists like Sarah Osborn and Samuel Hopkins had run small private schools for blacks out of their homes. However, the ABS was the first autonomous black institution to focus exclusively on educating black Rhode Islanders; moreover, it was the first black-funded school in the United States supervised and administered by black Americans. Perhaps more importantly, it offered a free education. Seventy-eight students attended the ABS school during the first year of operation, in 1808.[60] By 1810, just three years after its founding, the society had nearly fifty members.[61] The school was open during the day and in the evening. However, financial difficulties forced the society to offer evening-only classes just a year after the school opened. The directors thought an evening school was more practical because it allowed for adult attendance.

Three men dominated ABS leadership: Arthur Flagg Jr., Newport Gardner, and Reverend William Patten. Flagg served as society president from 1807 to 1810 and as secretary from 1813 to 1820.[62] His father, born in 1739 and freed in 1801, worked as a rope maker, owned property in Newport, and had been active in FAUS, where he served as a judge and treasurer. Flagg grew up in the midst of black Newport's social and political leaders, and FAUS meetings had often been held in his childhood home. Gardner, perhaps the most politically active black American in post-Revolutionary Rhode Island, acted as ABS president from 1811 to 1820. Patten, a local white abolitionist and minister of the Second Congregational Church of Newport, served as society treasurer from 1810 to 1824.[63] These men were experienced in institution building and were among the handful who were granted the coveted position of "director" within the society; society directors, elected by members, wielded considerable power and influence in the institution. They were charged with managing money, planning the academic schedule, and finding and retaining instructors.

African American Rhode Islanders, having learned a valuable lesson from the failed colonization effort, were now faced with the unavoidable reality of their need for white patronage. While the ABS had no racial restrictions concerning membership or officer status, there were racial concessions. Four of the eleven director positions were set aside for white men, and four black directors and two white directors needed to be present to transact any business. Although whites had a place within the society, black Rhode Islanders made sure to maintain their autonomy; all decisions required the approval of the "coloured" majority.[64] Men in the society were as concerned with black autonomy as they were with male hegemony.

Women were not restricted from joining the society, but they did not occupy positions of power within the school, and a quorum of the male membership was required to conduct any society business. Not surprisingly, women appeared to favor membership in the African Female Benevolent Society (AFBS). The AFBS was established in 1809, a couple of years after the ABS. One of the founding members, Obour Tanner, was a former slave who corresponded regularly with famed black poet Phyllis Wheatley. Women like Tanner understood the freedom of thought and expression that literacy could bring to free blacks.[65] AFBS members had reportedly "habitually taught and partially clothed twenty-five or thirty children."[66] Records mention the AFBS school but do not indicate exactly what happened to it. The evidence suggests that the AFBS school merged at some point with the ABS school.[67] Although the women no longer ran a school, the AFBS remained an autonomous organization. The two organizations appeared to be very dedicated to one another; they corresponded regularly, and the female society regularly contributed to the ABS school with funds from their treasury. In 1809, for example, they allotted ten dollars for the men's society to support the school, no small amount considering that in its best years the ABS collected just over seventy dollars in membership dues.[68] The black women of Newport were as concerned about access to education as their male counterparts. It appears that the AFBS was a little more stable than the ABS. In 1810, they reported having forty members with meetings "regularly attended" and payments that were "tolerable punctual."[69] The larger ABS encompassed men from the middle class to the working class. The AFBS, on the other hand, was most likely almost exclusively middle class; at a time when the majority of black families were living day to day, women who could afford membership dues and had the time to devote to charitable work were most likely from financially secure families.

Staffing and financial problems plagued the ABS School. The directors could not maintain a regular schedule or retain a permanent teaching staff. The school was often open only for a few months at a time, and instructors changed frequently. As a result of delinquent membership payments the school was closed during the summer and winter of 1813.[70] In 1819, the school was so late in opening that the society thought it was better to use their money to help support children already enrolled in other private schools or receiving tutoring; that year the ABS provided funds for thirty-two children of color to attend other schools.[71]

Finding and keeping instructors was particularly difficult for ABS directors. The society preferred to hire black female instructors; many of the students were young or female. Moreover, employing black women was in accordance with uplift ideology.

However, because black female instructors were in short supply, the directors were often forced to compromise. They hired black men and white women but not white men.[72] Black society members were concerned about white male hegemony; they did not want a white man in a position of authority within the school. Their ideological conviction was made easier by the fact that most white men would not accept employment at a "colored" school. In 1809, the mere rumor of hiring a white male instructor created a stir and led to the formation of a committee of society members. The committee assessed the opinions of society members and found that they indeed disapproved of hiring a white male instructor. Despite the assertions from the directors that a white instructor might improve enrollment, a black man was hired.[73]

The society, continually plagued with money shortages and low meeting attendance, commissioned another committee to suggest ways to improve.[74] In 1816, to make the meetings more congenial and orderly, the leadership of the society decided to issue fines to address inappropriate conduct. Interrupting someone while he or she was speaking cost the offender twenty-five cents; failure to rise and address the moderator when wishing to speak led to a fine of one shilling and six pence. These fines, though most likely initiated to promote proper manners and encourage uplift, probably punished those least able to afford them. Members were also given the option of paying their dues in weekly installments instead of annually, probably in the hopes of attracting a broader swath of black Rhode Islanders, especially the working classes, who were less likely to have enough disposable income to pay for an entire year of dues.[75]

The society school fared best in what would be its last years. In addition to receiving money from the Quaker Society of Friends, it was able to operate below budget for two consecutive years. In 1821, it had a full school year, fall through spring, and money left over in the treasury.[76] As a result, the school opened early in 1822. That same year, it collected $71.29 in membership dues and operated at a cost of $52.50, which left a surplus of nearly $20.00.[77] That brief financial success, however, was an anomaly. Two years later, sometime in 1824, the African Benevolent Society, like many nineteenth-century black mutual aid societies, dissolved. Despite money troubles, the society had managed to educate hundreds of free people of color during its seventeen years (1807–24) of existence. Its story is not one of steady progress or decline but one of perseverance in the face of adversity. Moreover, the financial struggles of the ABS and its eventual dissolution did not deter black Rhode Islanders from continuing to build institutions. During the last years of the ABS in Newport, blacks in Providence were busy constructing another institution—this time a physical one—the African Union Meeting House.

The African Union Meeting House

The African Union Meeting House (AUMH) was not only the first black church in Providence; it also housed an autonomous school.[78] In March of 1819, blacks in Providence gathered at the First Baptist Church to discuss arrangements for establishing a "regular" school.[79] A committee was formed that sent the following message to the pastors of churches with black congregants: "The active zeal evinced by many of the people of colour, in the town of Providence, to provide a place for the education of their children, and the public worship of GOD, is, in our opinion exceedingly laudable, and worthy of the liberal encouragement of all the good people."[80] It took three years for black people in Providence to construct their school. They raised $800 among themselves and $600 through donations from white residents. Moses Brown, a prominent local abolitionist, donated the land, which was valued at $200, for the building site. Local blacks constructed the building.[81] They laid the foundation in April of 1819; by December they had raised the roof, and in May of 1820 they finished the framing. Finally, in June of 1821, the clapboard on the exterior was finished. On August 31, 1821, the AUMH was furnished with pews, which had been sold to members to offset the cost. Although black men and money built and furnished the building, the deed remained in the hands of the famed Brown family.[82] Here as elsewhere, black autonomy was tenuous.

Though black Rhode Islanders did not legally own the land on which the AUMH stood, they appropriated the space and displayed their pride in their African heritage through their celebration and dedication of the meetinghouse. The building dedication included a parade and a performance by an African choir, which was under the direction of a Brown University music student; they made their debut at the dedication.[83] Black Rhode Islander William J. Brown, who attended the AUMH school, reminisced about the dedication in his autobiography:

> The young colored men formed a military company [called the African Greys] to escort the African societies to their new house of worship. The African societies wore their regalias. The president of the societies, who was their commander, was dressed to represent an African chief, having on a red pointed cap, and carried an elephant's tusk in each hand; each end was tipped with gilt. The other officers carrying emblems, decked with lemons and oranges, representing the fruits of Africa, and other emblems. The military company wore black belts and carried muskets, and officers with their side arms.[84]

The African Greys, led by Commander George Barrett, who fought in the War of 1812, were the black military company of Providence, although they were ceremonial and not recognized by the state.[85] This display of military power, if only honorific, must have been disconcerting to the pacifist Quaker sponsors who were escorted by the company to the meetinghouse; Brown was able to convince them to leave their firearms outside the church. Moreover, the presence and pageantry of the company suggest that black Rhode Islanders were not attempting to conform or fit into white mainstream society. Instead, they publicly displayed their difference in the streets of Providence. The men in the company dressed as they thought their African ancestors dressed; and however inaccurate their attempt may have been they were creating culture—African American culture.[86] Like their counterparts throughout the North, free black Rhode Islanders used parades at such occasions to declare both their freedom and their place in the country.[87]

The AUMH school was not free; students were charged $1.50 per quarter. However, despite the cost, many black families found the resources needed. In the fall of 1821, one hundred and twenty-five students enrolled.[88] But, like their counterparts in Newport, blacks in Providence had difficulty keeping teachers. William Brown, a former student, wrote, "After keeping the school for one year his [Mr. Ormsbee's] labors came to a close, and for a year and a half the school was suspended, not being able to procure a teacher. Colored teachers were very rarely to be found, and it was difficult to procure a white teacher, as it was considered a disgraceful employment to be a teacher of colored children and still more disgraceful to have colored children in white schools."[89] After decades of inconsistent schooling, black Rhode Islanders raised a permanent structure dedicated to educating the black community. Yet their difficulties in staffing their school only underscore their marginal position within the community, state, and nation. The AUMH also served as a church open to all denominations. The various ministers who preached in the pulpit also taught in the school when needed.[90]

Like their counterparts throughout the North, black Rhode Islanders' faithful commitment to institution building was an early precursor to a burgeoning black nationalism, decades before that sense of racial pride was articulated as an ideology.[91] Between 1780 and 1820, black Rhode Islanders created four institutions to specifically address the economic, political, educational, and spiritual needs of the black community. They could have called these institutions black, negro, or colored, but instead they chose to refer to themselves as African.[92] They referred to themselves as "strangers and outcasts in strange land": though most of their parents and grandparents had been born in North America and though many of them had fought for this "strange land," they nevertheless felt like outsiders.[93] When they dedicated their churches, schools, and meetinghouses, they proudly paraded their cultural heritage—a syncretized mixture of inherited traditions and imagined projections about life in Africa—through the streets.

They dressed as "African" chiefs and celebrated the "fruits" of the African continent. FAUS members clearly felt an affinity to their African "brethren" and believed the condition of black Americans was dire enough to warrant emigration. The Union warned black Rhode Islanders that the same problems they faced would also limit their children. Furthermore, African American leaders understood that blacks throughout the Americas faced serious problems: they could observe "the yet more wretched state of many hundreds of thousands of our brethren who are in abject slavery in the West Indies and the American states, many of who, are treated in the most inhumane cruel manner and are sunk down in ignorance, stupidity and vice." The sense of being an outsider, with little hope of ever being accepted or treated equally by white society, encouraged black separatist thought. Black Rhode Islanders lived in a white-dominated nation where blackness was associated with dependence, immorality, inferiority, and—most damningly— slavery. The idea of a prosperous, morally upright black nation helped black Rhode Islanders cope with the constant assaults on their character. Black nationalist sentiment was in many ways a social and political necessity.[94] Free blacks had to create their own institutions because they were barred from mainstream institutions. They clearly understood they were apart from, not a part of, this nation that claimed equality for all. They sought to better themselves by establishing unions, schools, meetinghouses, and churches. The economic and social disabilities they faced led the free black community to turn inward. Their relentless pursuit of institution building demonstrated their perseverance. Out of uncertainty and insecurity, they formed organizations to secure their futures in a racially hostile state and nation.

FAUS, the ABS, the AFBS, and the AUMH were all expressions of what the black community of the time would have called "uplift ideology," but they can also be considered to be nascent expressions of black nationalism. The same applies to black Rhode Islanders' self-directed attempt to emigrate to Africa. As Sterling Stuckey wrote, "It is small wonder that a certain tension, with creative potential for the promotion of nationalist sentiment, was set up in the minds of some blacks," considering the oppression that black people faced, as slaves and noncitizens, in a nation that called itself into being on the basis of liberty for all. In other words, the fact that the vast majority of blacks in the United States remained enslaved, and that free blacks were socially, economically, and politically marginalized in the new American republic, was "the seed ground for black nationalist organization and sentiment."[95]

In January 1826, twenty-nine years after the dissolution of FAUS, two years after the disbanding of the ABS, and five years after the dedication of the AUMH, thirty-two black Rhode Islanders finally managed to find their way to Africa. They were members of the legendary voyage headed by Paul Cuffe, a successful black businessman, sea captain, and abolitionist, who chartered a ship to Sierra Leone. Seventy-year-old Salmar Nubia and eighty-year-old Newport Gardner were among the settlers. Their dream of returning to Africa was realized late in life and briefly. Later in that same year, Nubia and Gardner died free men on the continent on which they had been born.[96] Their tenacity was remarkable; they helped establish free black communities on two continents.

Black Rhode Islanders worked hard to build and establish black institutions in the decades following the American Revolution. They established an autonomous and permanent free black presence in the state of Rhode Island. They did so even as the state's white residents continued to invest in slavery—first through the reinvigoration of the Atlantic slave trade and then through the manufacture of "negro cloth."

Black Rhode Islanders remained committed to fostering community through institution building well into the antebellum era. By the 1830s, there were several black improvement associations such as Harmony Lodge No. 1, a Female Literacy Society, and a Female Tract Society. In the 1840s, five all-black churches were established in Providence—Zion, Meeting Street, Pond Street, Christ Church, and Second Freewill; there were also two black churches in the Narragansett Country, one in Wakefield and one in Morresfield.[97] These churches provided an important place of leadership for black men as well as a place of worship and dignity for the larger black community that had previously been segregated within white churches. William Brown remembered, "Many attended no church at all because they said they were opposed to going to churches and sitting in pigeon holes, as all the churches at the time had some obscure place for the colored people to sit in."[98] These churches provided a physical space, just like their schools and association meetings, for African Americans to meet and discuss social and political issues. Thus these formal places for gathering relieved individual blacks of some of the burdens of their everyday lives and created a multilayered community that could act in black people's interests. Black Rhode Islanders used these places to fight for access to the ballot box in the 1840s and to campaign for desegregated schools in the 1850s and 1860s.

6 / Building a Free State and Nation

On May 17, 1864, the members of the Fourteenth Regiment Rhode Island Heavy Artillery (Colored) published an editorial in their self-published newspaper, *Black Warriors*. It read:

> It is the aim of this paper to promote discipline and good order in the camps, to incite the soldier to that efficiency which is the result of a thorough knowledge of his duty; to raise the status of colored troops by proving their capability of appreciating, preserving and defending the principles of the Liberty either by pen or sword; to sustain our government under whose banner we have enlisted by moral as well as physical force, and to war against Copperheads and Traitors. The people of Louisiana have crowned themselves with honor in the revision of the State constitution so that slavery and involuntary servitude shall forever be abolished, and the suffering thousands of this State be constitutionally free from the great tyrant.[1]

Assigned to protect a fort and citizens in the heart of slave country, these black soldiers wanted to make clear that they were anything but dependent or servile. They sought to claim both citizenship and masculinity through fighting for the Union. They called themselves "Black Warriors."

Black Rhode Islanders not only built their own institutions but attached themselves to state and federal institutions—the state militia, public schools, and the federal army. During the Dorr Rebellion—a constitutional crisis centered on the expansion of the vote to men who did not own property—black men enlisted with the local militia to restore order; they hoped their service would be rewarded with a restoration of their right to vote. Black Rhode Islanders also successfully integrated the state's public school system. And when the southern states began to secede from the Union they volunteered to fight to keep the United States of America whole and to free their enslaved brothers and sisters.

When the Dorr Rebellion broke out in 1841, Rhode Island, as we have seen, was the leading producer of slave clothing and was home to over eighty textile mills. Antebellum Rhode Islanders were just as dependent on the business of slavery as their colonial and post-colonial forebears had been. They shifted from the West Indian and Atlantic slave trades to the kersey mills; the "negro cloth" industry was doubly dependent on slave labor, as slave-grown cotton was used to make the cloth that was then sold to southern slaveholders. Moreover, the shift from trading slaves and exporting agricultural goods to making and exporting slave clothing directly contributed to the Dorr Rebellion. At the turn of the nineteenth century, as factory laborers populated the cities, fewer and fewer white men worked as farmers or shop-owning tradesmen, and thus fewer and fewer owned land. The rise of wage labor, a consequence of the emergence of the "negro cloth" industry, created a large class of propertyless whites who were not eligible to vote. Ironically, many of those who literally made slave clothing sought a more democratic state; their bosses, the mill owners, however, resisted the expansion of suffrage.

The Dorr Rebellion

Rhode Island's constitutional crisis, the Dorr Rebellion, created an unlikely opportunity for African Americans in Rhode Island to reclaim and expand the right to vote. By this point, in the 1840s, African Americans in Rhode Island had been building institutions for decades, cultivating a race-based political identity and, even more important, leaders who could mobilize the community. And like the generation of black postrevolutionaries who had bought, bargained, or stolen themselves to gain freedom, antebellum blacks sought access to the ballot box. They built on traditions of resistance and self-determination to regain and expand their voting rights. First, as we shall see, they aligned themselves with progressives and advocated for universal male suffrage. When progressives failed, in 1841, to achieve unrestricted male suffrage, black Rhode Islanders switched sides and lent their military services to the state in hopes of persuading lawmakers to remove race-based voting restrictions.

In 1841, the only people who could vote in Rhode Island were white men who held at least $134 worth of real estate. Free black men who held the requisite amount of property could, and did, vote in the state before an 1822 law barred all black men from voting. Once again, the gains of emancipation seemed illusory.

These now disenfranchised black men, and the growing numbers of landless white men, did not join forces in their campaign for the vote. As historian Robert Cottrol asserts: "Blacks and poor whites pled their separate cases for enfranchisement."[2] That gap between the communities prevented what would have been an increasingly powerful alliance. In the last two decades of the eighteenth century, 75 percent of white men had met the voting property qualification for voting; however, by 1840, only 40 percent of white men were eligible to vote.[3] In the late 1830s, black property holders in Providence nearly regained access to the ballot when town officials levied a tax on them. They took their grievance of taxation with no representation to the General Assembly, and several members "said it was perfectly right: if the colored people were to be taxed they should be represented." But at least one General Assembly member could not conceive of black voting: "Shall a Nigger be allowed to go to the polls and tie my vote? No, Mr. Speaker, it can't be. The taxes don't amount to more than forty or fifty dollars; let them be taken off" the tax rolls.[4] The tax for black property holders was rescinded, as was the possibility of voting. The fear of a black vote canceling out a white vote was not completely unfounded, even though the potential number of black voters was very small. In 1840 there were 3,238 blacks in the state of Rhode Island, compared to 108,837 whites, and while nearly half of them lived in Providence only 668 were of voting age. Yet elections were close in Providence and were often determined by just a few hundred votes. The small size of the state's electorate meant that in a statewide contest "blacks could account for as much as 4 to 6 percent of the electorate" if they were allowed to vote.[5]

In 1841, Thomas Dorr mobilized the state's disenfranchised masses, black and white alike, to push for radical reform and to eliminate the constitutional provision requiring property for voting. Although Dorr was a member of Rhode Island's property-holding class, he rejected traditionalist views in favor of universal male suffrage, including the vote for blacks. Under the leadership of Dorr, white working-class men (who were referred to as Dorrites) established the Suffrage Association and advocated an overhaul of the state's constitution. The People's Constitution, written by Dorr, called for universal white male suffrage and a bill of rights—a renovation and moderation of the conservative 1663 charter that governed the state's General Assembly. Dorr was following in the footsteps of local tradesmen. In 1833 a group of white skilled laborers began holding weekly meetings to discuss ways to advocate for suffrage expansion. Their document, *An Address on the Right of Free Suffrage*, asserted that the vote should be extended to those men who served in the militia or paid taxes of any kind. They also compared the condition of propertyless white men in Rhode Island to that of slaves in the American South.[6]

Black men played a tenuous, and short-lived, role in these activities. The attack on the property qualification intrinsically raised questions about the validity of the racial restriction for voting. Furthermore, black men participated in the first part of the Dorrite campaign and voted in the Suffrage Association activities despite efforts of those in the movement to restrict their involvement. A petition signed by leading African American Rhode Island businessmen, tradesmen, and common laborers professed,

> We have long and with but little aid been working our way up
> to respectability and competence—we have, nevertheless, been
> enabled to possess ourselves of the means and advantages of
> religion, intelligence and property—we unhesitantly assert
> that the United States has been founded on the principle that
> all men were created free and equal and that exclusion would

violate that principle—the annals of nations clearly teach that there is always danger in departing from clearly defined and universal truths, and resorting to unjustifiable and invidious partialities.[7]

Yet their arguments fell on deaf ears. Most whites within the Dorr campaign, in 1841, even the abolitionists, were either opposed to or ambivalent about black suffrage; Frederick Douglass led a rally in the state in 1841 to protest the exclusion of black men in the Dorrite fight for the extension of the vote, but even his powers of persuasion were unsuccessful.[8] The members of the Dorrite convention voted 46 to 18 to retain the whites-only clause in the People's Constitution.

The middle- and upper-class whites who opposed the Dorrites, known as the Charterites or the Law and Order Party, also opposed black suffrage. Many were mill owners and landowners from the Narragansett Country. They responded to Dorr's campaign with repression and fear. The Law and Order Party played on class, ethnic, religious, and sectional divisions in the state and characterized the Dorrites as foreign-born, anti-capitalist Catholics—and thus a threat to native-born Protestants farmers and industrialists. They also proposed a counter to the People's Constitution, the Freeman's Constitution, which called for an extension of the franchise to all native-born white males, guaranteed individual liberties, and planned moderate improvements to House apportionment. Foreign-born white men would be required to hold $134 worth of property; black men were excluded altogether. Voters at the Rhode Island constitutional convention of 1842 rejected the Freeman's Constitution by a narrow margin, 8,686 to 8,013.[9]

In the wake of the Charterites' failed constitution, the Dorrites held an unsanctioned election and elected Thomas Dorr "governor" of Rhode Island; the members of the General Assembly did not recognize him. Dorr and his supporters began establishing a government. He also attempted to gain the support of President John Tyler, but Tyler refused, stating that he would support the Charterites if the conflict could not be solved though peaceable means. On his way back from Washington, advocates of universal male suffrage showered Dorr with praise and promises of military support. In Rhode Island, a crowd of 1,200 supporters met Dorr; some of them were armed.[10]

On May 17, 1842, Dorrites took command of two old Revolutionary War cannons at the Mall in Providence; the existing and legally recognized governor Samuel King, who allied himself with the Charterites, summoned the citizenry to take arms at the state arsenal. Dorr decided to attack the arsenal despite the warning of some of his advisers. Under the command of John Weber, Dorr and about 230 supporters demanded the surrender of the armory in the name of the people's governor—Thomas Dorr. Colonel Blodjett of the Charterite militia refused; Dorr ordered a cannon fired, but the relic misfired and the Dorrites retreated in disarray. That very first foray into fighting was also the end of the reformers' movement. Several of Dorr's legislators defected in protest of his use of violence. Dorr went into hiding, reemerging several days later with a very small band of New York volunteers, who engaged in small skirmishes that resulted in no casualties. Dorr again retreated into exile. The Freeman's Constitution was ratified in November 1842. It included universal suffrage for all native-born men and a property qualification of $134 for naturalized citizens; the property requirement would remain in place until 1888. Dorr finally surrendered in October of 1843 after the citizens of Rhode Island had accepted the constitution: in 1844 he was found guilty of treason and sentenced to hard labor in solitary confinement for the rest of his life.[11]

Black men were among the members of the Providence militia that put down the rebellion. Some two hundred armed black men threw their support behind the Charterites; they patrolled the streets and protected the armory. Initially, blacks had supported the Dorrite cause for expanded suffrage; however, once the People's Constitution explicitly excluded black men, black people were left with few options and ultimately chose to ally themselves with the Charterites.[12] They anticipated that their service would lead to the extension of the suffrage to black men. They understood their precarious position in the new republic and were able to come together to decide which road would lead to the best possibility of gaining access to the ballot box. Their calculated gamble paid off, since the 1842 Constitution extended the vote to all native-born men, black and white.[13] Moreover, the new state constitution abolished slavery.

The Rhode Island General Assembly waited until there were just a few slaves left in the state to abolish the institution; there were five slaves listed in the 1840 census.[14] It was no coincidence that the General Assembly extended the vote to black men and abolished slavery in the same document. If black men could vote, how could they too be slaves? The decision of black Rhode Islanders to avail themselves to the local militia and became part of the state's most visible and tangible institution led to the final destruction of race-based slavery in Rhode Island. Black Rhode Islanders were finally free; furthermore, black men had unequivocally gained one of the most basic treasures of citizenship—the vote.

But their legal victory did not shield them from voter intimidation. Some Dorrites boycotted the next statewide election and "threatened to mob any black who dared enter the polls." In an attempt to discourage black voting, poll officials were known to single out black voters by publicly asking whether they could sign their names. These tactics had the effect of decreasing the number of black men who registered to vote, in Providence, from 363 to 244 in Providence between 1844 and 1848. Nevertheless, black men never again legally lost the right to vote in Rhode Island.[15]

Throughout the antebellum era black Rhode Islanders continued to assert their rights. They incorporated fugitive slaves into their communities and repudiated the 1850 Fugitive Slave Law, which made aiding a runaway slave a federal offense. Six days after the passage of the law the black community held a mass meeting pledging to "sacrifice our lives and our all upon the altar of protection to our wives, our children, and our fellow sufferers in common with us." African Americans in Newport established a neighborhood watch "to be on the lookout, both for the panting fugitive and also for the oppressor when he shall make his approach."[16] Black people used their homes and churches to hide and assist fugitive slaves. The *Providence Journal* estimated that several hundred fugitive slaves were residing in the city.[17] Like their counterparts throughout the mostly free North, black Rhode Islanders wanted much more than freedom—not being held a property; they wanted full inclusion in the nation.[18] For many black Rhode Islanders, full inclusion in the state and nation meant equal access to the public school system.

"Will the General Assembly Put Down Caste Schools?"

Segregated public schools—the embodiment of state-sanctioned, systematic discrimination—were another legacy of race-based slavery. Segregated schools were among the most visible, salient barriers to social equality. And although the state of Rhode Island did not directly segregate public education, state legislators did not prevent local segregation ordnances. Consequently, in Providence, Newport, and Bristol, where the majority of black people lived, black children were not allowed to attend public schools with white children.

Spanning the last years of the antebellum period and the Civil War, the fight to integrate all of Rhode Island's public schools made it clear that even after the enfranchisement of black men and the abolition of slavery in 1842, African Americans continued to face substantial, daily barriers to civic equality. And like their forebears who organized the nation's first free black mutual aid society, the Free African Union Society, in 1780, and the black men who took up arms in the 1842 Dorr Rebellion, antebellum black community leaders organized and fought to integrate Rhode Island schools in an attempt to further black equality.

George Thomas Downing, a prominent local businessman, spearheaded the campaign to integrate Rhode Island's public schools. In 1857, he began circulating pamphlets, holding public forums, and writing editorials denouncing separate education for blacks and whites.[19] He asserted that black schools were inferior "in their threadbare facilities, mediocre teachers, and stunted curricula."[20] The school integration campaign was most strongly supported by middle-class blacks—property holders, businessmen, and entrepreneurs.[21] For example, George Henry, an affluent black gardener, wrote: "I find myself paying a heavy tax, and my children debarred from attending the schools, for which I was taxed. So a few of us got together and resolved to defend ourselves against such an outrage."[22] As taxpayers black Rhode Islanders felt entitled to fair and equal access to public schools.

On the other hand, some poor and working-class black Rhode Islanders wanted to retain control of their children's education because they did not trust that black children would be treated fairly in schools with white majorities.[23] These less well-off blacks were much more reluctant to give up the small gains and autonomy of separate schools for their children, even if those schools were inferior. Many blacks, including some middle-class members of the community, were particularly concerned about losing the Pond and Meeting Street schools that employed black teachers and had sound reputations.[24] Downing had no qualms about losing the Pond and Meeting Street schools or black teachers. He acknowledged "that if this change takes place, colored teachers will be thrown out of employ. It should not be; they should not be thrown out if most competent, because they are colored." However, he insisted, the potential loss of those jobs was not a sufficient reason to maintain segregation: "Then, again, a whole class should not be proscribed, inconvenienced, denied their rights, that one or two families of a town may receive two or three hundred dollars a year."[25] Downing did not address or acknowledge the strong objections of many white parents and school administrators to the idea of black teachers instructing white students regardless of their competence or ability. And while two teaching positions seemed rather paltry to Downing, the respect and steady income those two jobs generated were important to a small black community marred by poverty.

In 1857, Downing, along with several other middle-class black men from Newport, Providence, and Bristol, formed a committee on school integration. Named chairman, Downing was the primary author of the committee's petition—*Will the General Assembly Put Down Caste Schools?*—which called on the Rhode Island legislature to ban separate schools and override the local ordinances in Providence, Newport, and Bristol. The committee used legal, patriotic, and moral arguments to denounce segregation. They pointed out that the 1842 state constitution did not mention race in the public school system: "It is the duty of the General Assembly to promote Public Schools; not caste schools—not schools set apart for particular classes, to the exclusion of others, as are these schools which we are opposed to." The committee claimed to speak for most of the black community, and in some ways they did. Reportedly, "a large and enthusiastic meeting" of African Americans at the Zion Church endorsed the arguments and positions taken by the committee on integration.[26]

In the petition, the committee laid out their primary reason for advocating for an integrated public school system:

> Our grievance is, that the local school powers of the three places above mentioned [Providence, Newport, and Bristol] have given us indifferent school houses, with but partial accommodations as compared with the other school houses; that they have given us indifferent teachers: but aside from all this, even had these parties given us all the accommodations they give others—as good school houses, as good teachers and the like, still would we complain and deny the right of these parties to select out—set us apart, make us a proscribed class, and thereby cause us to feel that we have separate interests not alike concerned and interested in whatever pertain to the interest of the State; and thereby cause us to be regarded in the eyes of the community as inferior, a despised class to be looked down upon; and thus blunt our patriotism—thus impair those noble and manly aspirations that induce a man to strive to be something; to labor on and upward with other men; that induce a parent to say to his child, "strive my son, an inviting and honorable field of promotion is before you."[27]

The committee asserted that African Americans deserved the same education as whites, not just an equivalent education. Moreover, black Rhode Islanders wanted their children to be inspired by a great education; they wanted their children to dream of greater possibilities. The committee further charged that the segregated system impeded the ability of black children to attend school because it forced them to go to designated "colored schools" outside of their wards and districts instead of attending the common school in their own neighborhood. Out of the forty-eight public schools in Providence, only three admitted black children.[28]

In addition, the committee sought equal enforcement of truancy law and access to the public high schools, which barred black children; this, they claimed would send a message to the entire community that education was just as important for black children as it was for white children. Finally, they argued that blacks had more than earned their right to an integrated public education because of their services from the American Revolution to the Dorr Rebellion and because they were citizens entitled to rights of citizenship: "Have we refused to pay taxes? Have we done anything to forfeit our rights as citizens? Have we not stood ready to defend? Yes! Has not our blood been freely spilt in defense of the State? Then why in the name of the constitution—in the name of justice and honor between men—are we proscribed and refused our just rights?"[29] The committee went on to caution that the exclusion of blacks was also breeding the exclusion of other classes or people: "This proscriptive policy is dangerous . . . it is growing to an alarming extent; nor is it directed alone against colored men; by and by we may see schools established 'exclusively' for the working man's son, for the farmer and mechanic's son, then another school for the rich man's son, each to be supported by the public fund—this spirit manifests itself already in the High School of that city [Providence]; that poor men's children are snubbed, that they cannot fully hold up their head under what they have to endure in school, because poor."[30] Downing and other committee members clearly understood that racism also bred classism and that both were intertwined and particularly damaging to the black community, which was also predominantly poor.

The committee members knew that public protests and boycotts had ended race-based segregation in Worcester, Cambridge, New Bedford, Nantucket, and Boston. Letters from these nearby school districts accompanied the petition and remarked on the success of integration.[31] They pointed to nearby Boston as a model of racial progress; white parents had not withdrawn their children from school, and there were no reports of major animosity between black and white students in the classroom.[32]

After laying out the legal and moral arguments, as well as refuting the contention that white parents would pull their children out of school, the committee demanded that the General Assembly pass a law stating "that in no City, Town or District of the State shall any scholar be refused admission into any Public School thereof because of his race, color or religious opinions."[33] For the committee members, school integration was about much more than equal access to education; it was about equal access to the nation and all the opportunities it afforded those who were truly free. Although there was no specific right to education, for these black Rhode Islanders access to opportunity in the form of education was a right of citizenship:

> It is the limited, proscribed education, and no education at all on the part of many colored people, that is much of the reason why colored men have not been anything else than menials, they have not been producers, developers, leading to the development of the State's interest. Let them be educated alike, let all public institutions be alike accessible to them and some developer will be produced of whom the State will be proud. . . . It is the interest of the State to have all its inhabitants educated; for as such they become intelligent and good citizens.[34]

They argued that an integrated school system would benefit not only blacks but the state and nation as a whole. Downing and other integrationists encountered opposition from whites who claimed whites would stop supporting the school tax if the schools were integrated, which in turn would gut public education. They also claimed that the black schools were sufficient. The *Providence Journal*, although antislavery, opposed school integration and, as noted by historian Robert Cottrol, "spent a good deal of time attacking George Downing as an outsider fomenting trouble among what the *Journal* saw an essentially content black population." The publication asserted that desegregation would force interactions between white girls and black boys and that rich white parents would remove their children, destroying the class democracy of the public school system.[35]

Despite this pushback, the integration committee continued their campaign, and in 1859 debates on the floor of the General Assembly indicated that a measure banning separate schools would pass the state legislature. At the last minute, prosegregation forces presented a petition purportedly signed by forty-five African Americans opposing the ban. There were charges that most of the signatures were forged. Nevertheless, the implication that the committee did not speak for the state's black community was enough to fracture the fragile support for integrating schools. School desegregation was debated again in 1860, but the General Assembly failed to pass a law banning segregation. Public school integration was sidelined during the Civil War (1861–65) as the state focused on raising and training troops. However, as the war came to a close, in 1865, the state legislature took the issue up again. The service of African American men and the Union's new role as an army of liberation changed the tenor of the debate. Public opinion had shifted enough to slightly favor public school integration. Yet a few local politicians attempted to ambush any integration law.

Representatives from Newport, Providence, and Bristol filibustered to prevent a vote banning school segregation. In an attempt to pacify integrationists, the Providence City Council announced the construction of six new "colored" schools. In Newport and Bristol, the filibusters failed to derail integrationist momentum. The city of Newport's new chairman, Thomas Wentworth Higginson, was a friend of Downing's, an abolitionist, and a commander of black troops in the Civil War. Higginson led the fight for school integration in the city. The "colored schools" in Bristol were marked for demolition, and there were no plans to build new ones. Instead, black and white children would attend school together. Only the Providence school committee refused to consider integration, probably because integration would have the greatest effect in Providence, where the majority of black Rhode Islanders lived.[36]

Unimpressed with the plans and promises of new schools, Downing wrote another petition to the state legislature demanding an end to segregated schooling in the state. He also published an "Address to Negro Voters" that encouraged blacks to support Edward Harris and Rowland Gibson Hazard for governor and lieutenant governor in place of James Smith, who was an opponent of school integration.[37] When the issue of school integration was brought to the floor of the Rhode Island General Assembly in 1866, the state legislature "overwhelmingly voted to outlaw separate schools in the state."[38]

After a nearly ten-year campaign, black Rhode Islanders claimed unfettered access to one of the most visible public institutions in the nation—public schools. Like the long, protracted fight for freedom from slavery, the battle for integrating public schools in Rhode Island was fraught with setbacks, disappointments, and intragroup conflict, yet black Rhode Islanders continued to struggle to create an equal space for themselves in the American Republic. Amid their struggle to desegregate public schools, in 1863, black Rhode

Islanders took up arms to fight for the rights of black people outside the state of Rhode Island; they risked their lives to free their enslaved brothers and sisters in the American South.

The Black Warriors: Rhode Island's Black Civil War Regiment

The soldiers of the Rhode Island Fourteenth Heavy Artillery, like the soldiers of the nearly all-black Rhode Island First in the American Revolution, challenged race-based slavery both literally and figuratively. Black Civil War soldiers faced many of the same restrictions and prejudices that black Patriots had encountered eight decades earlier. Both groups were initially denied entrance into the nation's military, regardless of their willingness to fight, and once they were admitted they faced segregation and mistreatment. In the 1770s and in the 1860s, the courage, conviction, and fortitude of black men to face battle was widely questioned by both the military and mainstream white society. Nelson Viall, the commander of the Rhode Island Fourteenth, recalled how commonly black courage was questioned: "At this time doubts were freely expressed as to the propriety of making a soldier of the negro, while a large number of whites would not go to the front themselves they were loud in their denunciation of the colored man as a soldier."[39] In wars more than eighty years apart, black men, through their service, proved their fitness as soldiers and heroes.

From the outset of the American Civil War, black men, free and enslaved, wanted to fight; however, the Union Army turned them away, as the war for the preservation of the Union was initially envisioned as a "white man's" war. Black people recognized, long before most white northerners, that the fate of the Union was directly tied to the issue of slavery and that the future of slavery was tied to the outcome of the war.[40] As early as 1862, black men in New York formed their own military companies and began to drill. In Boston, they drew up a resolution modeled on the Declaration of Independence and appealed for permission to go to war. Black men in Philadelphia volunteered to infiltrate the South to incite slave revolts. In the South, slaves began to free themselves as soon as the war began. An estimated five hundred thousand slaves, one in every four enslaved people, absconded during the war.[41] Only after enslaved people flooded Union camps did the aim of the war change to include emancipation.[42] Runaways were a visible, literal reminder that slave labor—or the lack thereof—was one of the keys to defeating the Confederacy. The Confederacy depended heavily on the labor of enslaved people for auxiliary military services as well as for the staple crops necessary to maintain for foreign credit. To destroy the Confederacy, it was necessary to do away with slavery. And just as the actions of enslaved people undermined the Confederacy, the service of black men transformed the Union Army into an army of liberation. Former slaves first entered Union ranks in the summer of 1862, and as resistance to the draft and the body count increased, white northerners became increasingly amicable to the idea of black soldiers. Free black men enlisted in specially commissioned northern regiments after the Emancipation Proclamation took effect on January 1, 1863; and in May of that year, droves of the formerly enslaved began to join the newly established Bureau of Colored Troops. An estimated 179,000 African American men served in the army and 18,000 served in the navy; most were former slaves and all were led by white officers.[43] In the North, nearly 33,000 black men enlisted in the Union Army; nearly all were living as free men when the war began.[44] Their service demonstrated free blacks' commitment to abolition and challenged northern racism. The service of both free black and enslaved men changed the course and temperament of the war.

Although the focus is often on the role black men played in the military, historian Benjamin Quarles reminds us that black women, including Harriet Tubman, "served as nurses" during the war, while others established ladies' aid societies and "went down as teachers to work with the newly freed slaves."[45] Black women designed and made flags, sewed uniforms, and organized send-offs; perhaps more importantly, they took on the care of the entire black community when their sons, husbands, and brothers left for war. Throughout the North, free black people organized on behalf of the enslaved; they fought, not for their own, however tenuous freedom, but for the freedom of their people.[46] They acted as citizens even though most of them lacked full citizenship rights.

Racial discrimination permeated the war experience for all black soldiers. They served in segregated units, were excluded from commissioned office, and were paid less than their white counterparts. Black soldiers fought two wars—a war to end slavery and a war against racial inequality in the military. They were particularly insulted by the discrepancy in pay. White soldiers received thirteen dollars per month plus clothing, while black soldiers were paid ten dollars per month minus clothing. Some black soldiers refused their pay altogether—a significant sacrifice considering they had families to support and many had just exited slavery.[47] Yet despite the discrimination they faced, African Americans continued to enlist.

On October 23, 1861, Rhode Island governor William Sprague IV called for an all-black regiment from his state. Over one hundred black men presented themselves to the Providence armory in the days after his announcement. Because Sprague did not have the authority to override the federal government's ban on black troops, it was not until June 1863, when the War Office gave the state of Rhode Island permission to organize, that the state's black company came into official existence. Within a year and half the Rhode Island Fourteenth would expand into a full regiment.[48] Many black Rhode Islanders were eager to join the fight. William L. Humbert, a sought-after tailor, was one of the first volunteers. He was later promoted to corporal. Charles A. Jackson was so zealous in his recruitment of other black men that he lost his place in the first company and was transferred to the second, where he was promoted to sergeant. Other black men came, whether willingly or unwillingly, as the result of the draft.[49] In August 1863, a newspaper reporter marveled at the physical prowess of Rhode Island's black regiment.

> The appearance of three hundred muskets in our streets in the hands of as many sturdy, stalwart black men, was a novel sight in Providence, and we are sure it was looked upon with unusual interest. In the ranks were men well worthy of more notice than we shall be able to give them. Look, for instance, at the two Freeman boys at the right of the line of the first company. Peter the file leader is a splendidly formed man, huge, muscular, and powerfully built. Charles Freeman is his equal in

all that goes to make up the physical man. Though they are of the same name and fashioned after the same mould, they are in no other way relatives. Peter is from the border and hails from slavery. Charles is of Rhode Island stock and hails from Bristol. Jermiah Noka, who stands near the right, is also a noteworthy specimen of a Rhode Islander. He is one of the purest examples which a modern intermingling of African blood has left to us of the once all powerful tribe of Narragansetts. His fine shape, his decidedly Indian cast of features, his genial and winning smile, his generous expressions, inevitably recall the memory of the lost Narragansett. Sergeants Jenkins, Phenix, and Howland, of this city, are well known and capable men, and well drilled soldiers.[50]

The reporter was not the only one "impressed" with the regiment. After a surprise inspection, a general described his impression of the troops to the governor of Rhode Island: "I have never formed a regiment even on Sunday morning inspection in more perfect condition. Excellence is the proper term to apply to its conditions and soldierly bearing."[51] While both the reporter and the general reveal their racism in their surprise at how "soldierly" the men appeared, they also disclose a clear sense of admiration.

The Rhode Island Fourteenth Regiment Rhode Island was the first black heavy artillery regiment in the North. The regiment eventually grew to twelve companies composing three battalions; there were 1,822 men in total. The first company was almost entirely composed of Rhode Islanders. However, black men, free and enslaved, from the North, the Midwest, and the South, served in the Rhode Island Fourteenth. All three battalions served until the end of the war.[52] Within a couple weeks of the War Office's go-ahead, the men were drilling at the Dexter Training Ground in Providence. Two months later they paraded through the streets of Providence. The regiment was headquartered on Dutch Island, where the soldiers began building defense works to protect the people of Providence. They guarded the Fall River Iron Works and the Burnside Rifle Works, and they also patrolled the streets.[53] On December 9, a group of black women from Providence presented the Fourteenth Regiment with "a handsome silk flag."[54] John T. Waugh, a prominent black property holder and public school desegregation supporter, officiated at the presentation and charged the soldiers to "do your utmost to wipe out the foulest blot which stains our land. See to it that history writes that you nobly sustained the honor of the flag."[55] The regiment's First Battalion left Rhode Island on December 19, 1863, sailing from Newport to New Orleans. They removed Confederate torpedoes at Fort Esperanza (Texas) and performed garrison duty at Camp Parapet (Louisiana) and Fort Jackson (Florida).[56]

On January 8, 1864, the Second Battalion left for New Orleans. One officer, Captain John M. Addeman, remembered that the men were "packed like sheep in the hold" and that they received meager rations and water. Because both measles and mumps had been reported aboard the ship, the soldiers were quarantined at Camp Kenyon instead of joining the First Battalion in Texas.[57] The men were reportedly "dropping off rapidly from a species of putride sore throat"; the ground was so moist that the dead were buried in the levees. On March 7, 1864, the disease-weary battalion was ordered to take over guard duty at the fort in Plaquemine, Louisiana.[58] The battalion had several deadly clashes with guerrillas in the area.[59] On August 6, 1864, the battalion engaged the enemy when an estimated one hundred mounted infantry attacked Plaquemine. The rebels initially breached the fort and got into town; however, the Second Battalion troops drove them out and the rebels retreated. Three men were killed and one wounded; four others were captured and later murdered. The rebels also lost several men. The Second Battalion spent the remainder of their service at the fort completing building projects and on garrison duty.[60]

A smallpox outbreak delayed the departure of the third and final battalion, whose soldiers were interned on Dutch Island. The Third Battalion finally left Rhode Island in April 1864, but before they left, the black women of New York presented the Third with a "beautiful silk standard" as "as an expression of their gratitude for your noble response in aid of the national cause."[61] When the soldiers arrived in New Orleans they were assigned garrison duty at Fort Banks.[62] All three battalions were moved to Fort Jackson at the close of the war. Disease permeated the fort, and deaths were frequent; the "daily sound of the death march by the Drum Corps was so depressing orders were issued to discontinue music at funerals."

Of the 1,822 men that had enlisted in the Rhode Island Fourteenth, 1,452 remained by February of 1865.[63] The Fourteenth Regiment returned home in October of that year to a parade in Providence, where they marched to City Hall for a celebratory meal.[64] While the men returned to public fanfare, many of them were cheated out of "five-sixths" of their bounties. According to the 1865 Committee on Bounty Fraud, commissioned officers in the Rhode Island Fourteenth, led by "J.C. Engley the evil genius of this regiment," compelled some of the soldiers to forfeit proportions of their bounties to purchase "worthless watches and various articles of clothing." The regiment was disbanded a few days later; many of the men settled permanently in the state.[65]

The soldiers of the Rhode Island Fourteenth did more than guard military installments and protect local populations in their fight to end slavery and preserve the Union; they also struggled for equality and dignity within the military. They resolved to be treated as soldiers, not as black soldiers. As the First Battalion waited aboard ship in New Orleans for their orders, a few men weary of being confined to the ship slipped past the guard to go ashore. They encountered some white Union soldiers who attempted to "force them into subjection." They fought back until the local police intervened and returned them to their ship.[66] Although the details of the skirmish are unknown, what is clear is that the soldiers of the Fourteenth did not show the expected racial deference to their white counterparts.

Like many of their counterparts in other black regiments, the soldiers of the Fourteenth protested race-based pay. In March 1864, while on garrison duty in Fort Esperanza (Texas), companies A, C, and D of the First Battalion were put "under arrest for refusing to accept the pay at that time offered by the Government to the colored soldiers." Their commander, Nelson Viall, was sympathetic: "Enlisting as they did with the understanding that their pay was to be the same as that of white troops it is not surprising that they should be indignant—the whole Regiment chafed under the abuses of the State." Nevertheless, several of the leaders of the resistance were court-martialed and sentenced to prison at Fort Jefferson in Florida.[67] The men of the Rhode Island Fourteenth refused to be treated as second-class soldiers, and although the leaders of the protest were jailed they made their protest known.

Black Rhode Islanders attached themselves to state and national institutions in their pursuit of inclusion and equality. During the Dorr Rebellion they offered their services to the state of Rhode Island in hope of regaining and expanding access to the ballot box. They sustained a decade-long fight for full and unfettered access to the state's public schools. They risked their lives for the freedom of enslaved African Americans in the South. Black Rhode Islanders understood that their quest for citizenship was tied to their ability to become part of state and national institutions, even when they were not welcomed or invited to join.

Conclusion

In 2012, nine years after Ruth Simmons appointed a steering committee to investigate Brown's connections to slavery, the university took heed of one of the committee's recommendations and established the Center for the Study of Slavery and Justice. The center encourages scholarly research and public education concerning the impacts and legacies of race-based slavery in the Americas as well as contemporary issues surrounding human trafficking. The steering committee also suggested that the university find ways to commemorate and memorialize Rhode Island's participation in the Atlantic slave trade. Martin Puryear, a renowned sculptor and National Medal of Arts recipient, was commissioned to create a memorial on the grounds of the university. The memorial was dedicated on September 27, 2014; it has two pieces and sits on the front green near the oldest building on campus, University Hall (1770). The sculpture is a "massive ductile-iron chain" rising up from a dome measuring eight feet around; the chain is broken at eye level (see figure 3). A stone plinth with engraved text reads:

> This memorial recognizes Brown University's connection to
> the trans-Atlantic slave-trade and the work of Africans and
> African-Americans, enslaved and free, who helped build our
> university, Rhode Island, and the nation. In 2003 Brown President Ruth J. Simmons initiated a study of this aspect of the

university's history. In the eighteenth century slavery permeated every aspect of social and economic life in Rhode Island. Rhode Islanders dominated the North American share of the African slave trade, launching over a thousand slaving voyages in the century before the abolition of the trade in 1808, and scores of illegal voyages thereafter. Brown University was a beneficiary of this trade.[1]

It is the first marker of slavery on campus.

For over seventy years historians have been writing about how the institution of slavery played a critical role in the social, political, and economic development of the North, and since the 1990s a plethora of studies have investigated how northerners used slave labor and were key participants in the business of slavery.[2] The availability of this research has made it increasingly difficult to ignore the presence of black people, enslaved and free, as well as white northern participation in the slave trade, in northern public history sites. However, the responses to this "new knowledge" have been varied and complex. A few establishments and memorials have simply refused to tell the stories of black Americans and have willfully downplayed the role of slavery in the economic ascent of northern industry and capitalism. Nevertheless, most sites have put forth significant efforts to share the experiences of enslaved and free black people and to explain northern investments in slavery, especially as black history has become increasingly popular. However, these reinterpretations are often additive rather than fully incorporative. And as less and less public funding is set aside for public history, site researchers and interpreters have had to walk a fine line between hewing to historical accuracy and offending private benefactors.

In 1903, Thomas Bicknell (1834–1925), a well-known historian and educator from Barrington, Rhode Island, raised money for a memorial and dedication of enslaved people in his hometown, many of whom had been owned by his ancestors. In Princes Hill Cemetery among the elaborately carved and polished Victorian headstones sits one unpolished white stone with a black plaque that reads: "In Memory of the Negro Slaves and their Descendants Who Faithfully Served Barrington Families Erected 1903" (figure 4). The dedication included singing; a prayer by Reverend William Chapin,

Figure 3. Slavery Memorial at Brown University. Source: Photo by Warren Jagger. Artist Martin Puryear. Slavery Memorial, 2014. Brown University.

the rector of the St. Johns Episcopal Church; a scripture reading by Reverend J. Coughlin, the minister of Barrington Methodist Episcopal Church; an address by Elisha Dyer, the former Rhode Island governor; and Bicknell himself, the former commissioner of the state's public schools.[3] The ceremony ended with a poem, singing, and a benediction. Like the slavery memorial at Brown, installed 109 years later, this public monument to slavery skirts the centrality of slaveholding and the business of slavery to the development and economic rise of the colony and the state of Rhode Island. Moreover, it fails to acknowledge the horrors of human bondage and the legacies of race-based slavery.

The memorial at Brown acknowledges that free and enslaved black people contributed to the building of the university and that some of the founding benefactors were involved in the slave trade. What it does not express is that without slaveholding and the Atlantic and West Indian slave trades, Brown, like the other Ivy League universities, would not exist. As historian Craig Wilder has recently argued, "The academy never stood apart from American slavery—in fact, it stood beside the church and the state as the third pillar of a civilization built on bondage."[4] The text of the

Figure 4. A Memorial Monument to the Negro Slaves of Barrington, Rhode Island, Princes Hill Cemetery. Photo by Joanne Costanza.

Brown memorial limits Rhode Islanders' participation in slavery to the slave trade in the eighteenth century; it does not indicate how common slaveholding was, record the continued investments in the business of slavery during the nineteenth century, or trace the legacies of those practices and investments. As I have shown in these pages, the business of slavery in Rhode Island extended much further than slave trading and including feeding and clothing enslaved populations in the West Indies and the American South through the American Civil War. Moreover, the business of slavery in Rhode Island directly influenced the creation of race-based slavery, stunted the emancipation process, and restricted the freedoms of black people after the collapse of slavery. In Rhode Island, the business of slavery undergirded the entire economy: it was not just central to the economy, it *was* the economy. Also missing from the memorial are the past attempts of white Rhode Islanders to dehumanize people of African descent through their businesses, laws, and customs. Finally, the viewpoints of black people are completely absent. How did they and their descendants interact with the institution that was so intimately tied to their oppression? It is not enough to simply mention the existence of black people in

Figure 5. Historical Marker at God's Little Acre, America's Colonial African Burial Ground, Newport, Rhode Island. Photo by Joanne Costanza.

northern public history sites: we must fully engage their experiences and incorporate their lives and labors into interpretations of our past.

In Rhode Island the relics of the institution of slavery and the business of slavery are still standing—from the ports where slave ships launched, to the Colonial African Burial Ground (see figures 5 and 6), to the crumbling and restored mills that manufactured "negro cloth." Some of these historic places have plaques that hint at the history of race-based slavery, yet these stories remain at the margins of the state's extensive public history commemorations.[5] The limited interpretations of the institution of slavery at Rhode Island public history sites are symptomatic of the denial that permeates the North in general. Some examples of this denial are statements that slaveholding was rare, that slavery was mild, that emancipation was quick, that free blacks were fully incorporated into the new nation, that only a few northerners were invested in the business of slavery, or that investments in slavery were confined to the slave trade. These myths are difficult to address because

Figure 6. Gravestones at God's Little Acre, American's Colonial African Burial Ground, Newport, Rhode Island. Photo by Joanne Costanza.

most people get their history from public schools and public history sites. Public schools have few resources to address the major revisions of the past twenty years, and public history sites have just begun to incorporate new historical analyses of slavery and capitalism. These myths, however, have power, and we as a society pay a cost when they are perpetuated.

The erasure or marginalization of the black experience and the centrality of the business of slavery to the northern economy allows for a dangerous fiction—that the North has no history of racism to overcome. Consequently, there is no need to redress institutional racism or work toward reconciliation. In other words, contemporary racial disparities are not grounded in historical discrimination and instead are a reflection of poor personal choices, or even worse, innate inferiority. Without a full accounting of the role that free and enslaved black people played and the centrality of the business of slavery in the founding, maintenance, and economic ascent of United States, objections to righting the wrongs of the nation's past will remain. Whether we are addressing affirmative action at our institutions of higher education or racial disparities in mass incarceration, we must remember that our interpretations of the past shape whom we think of as worthy, contributing members of our nation. In many ways slavery, the stalled emancipation process, and circumscribed black freedom cast those of African descent as a people apart from the nation, even though their labors made the nation. A lack of public commemoration of how race-based slavery and its legacies marginalized an entire race of people for centuries serves to further ostracize people of African descent today. The ductile-iron chain memorial should be Brown University's first, not only, commemoration of slavery. Moreover, the state of Rhode Island must publicly memorialize how the business of slavery and the labors of black people were central to the survival and thriving of both the colony and the state.

Notes

The following are abbreviations used in the Notes:

JA-SC   Judicial Archives, Supreme Court Judicial Records Center, Pawtucket, RI

RIBHS   Rhode Island Black Heritage Society

RIHS   Rhode Island Historical Society

Notes to Introduction

1. Brown University Steering Committee on Slavery and Justice, "Slavery and Justice Report," 2006, 12–13, http://brown.edu/Research/Slavery_Justice/documents/SlaveryAndJustice.pdf; Robert P. Emlen, "Slave Labor at the College Edifice: Building Brown University's University Hall in 1770," *Rhode Island History* 66, no. 2 (Summer 2008): 35–43.

2. In 2002, Yale University held a conference titled "Yale, New Haven, and Slavery" to discuss local ties to slavery. The conference coincided with the release of the *Hartford Courant* special issue "Complicity: How Connecticut Chained Itself to Slavery," September 29, 2002 (www.courant.com/courant-250/moments-in-history/hc-250-complicity-story-gallery-20140603-storygallery.html), and three years later the same writers published a book on the same topic (Anne Farrow, Joel Lang, and Jennifer Frank, *Complicity: How the North Promoted, Prolonged, and Profited from Slavery* [New York: Ballantine, 2005]). In 2011, Harvard and Brown held a joint conference investigating the history of capitalism and slavery in the region. And in 2013, Princeton University launched the Princeton and Slavery Project, which will investigate direct and indirect links between the university and the intuition of slavery. See also Craig Steven Wilder, *Ebony and Ivy: Race,*

Slavery, and the Troubled History of America's Universities (New York: Blooms-bury Press, 2013); "Yale, New Haven and American Slavery Conference," *Yale News,* September 6, 2002, http://news.yale.edu/2002/09/06/yale-new-haven-and-american-slavery-conference; "Slavery's Capitalism: A New History of American Economic Development. A Conference, April 7–9, 2011," Brown University, n.d., accessed November 25, 2014, www.brown.edu/web/slavery-conf/; Catherine Duazo, "Seminar Explores U.'s Little-Known Connection to Slavery," *Daily Princetonian,* October 15, 2013, http://dailyprincetonian.com/news/2013/10/seminar-explores-u-s-little-known-connection-to-slavery/.

3. DeWolf is sometimes spelled D'Wolf, especially in historical documents. Thomas Norman DeWolf, *Inheriting the Trade: A Northern Family Confronts Its Legacy As the Largest Slave-Trading Dynasty in U.S. History* (Boston: Beacon Press, 2008); Katrina Browne, dir. and prod., "Traces of the Trade: A Story from the Deep North," *P.O.V.,* PBS, 2008.

4. See Leslie M. Harris, *In the Shadow of Slavery: African Americans in New York City, 1626–1863* (Chicago: University of Chicago Press, 2003); Graham Russell Hodges, *Root and Branch: African Americans in New York and East Jersey, 1613–1863* (Chapel Hill: University of North Carolina Press, 1999); Joanne Pope Melish, *Disowning Slavery: Gradual Emancipation and "Race" in New England, 1780–1860* (Ithaca, NY: Cornell University Press, 1998); Gary B. Nash and Jean R Soderlund, *Freedom by Degrees: Emancipation in Pennsylvania and Its Aftermath* (New York: Oxford University Press, 1991).

5. Bernard Bailyn, "Slavery and Population Growth in Colonial New England," in *Engines of Enterprise: An Economic History of New England,* ed. Peter Temin (Cambridge, MA: Harvard University Press, 2000), 254–55.

6. See Seth Rockman, *Scraping By: Wage Labor, Slavery and Survival in Early Baltimore* (Baltimore: John Hopkins University Press, 2009); Walter Johnson, *River of Dark Dreams: Slavery and Empire in the Cotton Kingdom* (Cambridge, MA: Belknap Press, 2013); Edward E. Baptist, *The Half Has Never Been Told: Slavery and the Making of American Capitalism* (New York: Basic Books, 2014).

7. Gavin Wright, *Slavery and American Economic Development* (Baton Rouge: Louisiana State University Press, 2006), 14.

8. I use the term *black* or *African American* to refer to people of African descent, including mixed-race people. I use the term *people of color* when I am referring to people of Native American and African descent; I also use this term when individuals self-identified as mixed race. I use the term *African* only when I am sure that the person or persons were born in Africa. I do this for two reasons. First, it is almost impossible to know at any given moment in colonial period which slaves were born in Africa, in the West Indies, during the Middle Passage, or in North America. Second, following the American Revolution, state officials in Rhode Island created a white/black binary in assigning a racial category to its populations. They classified "mulattoes," "mustees," Native Americans, and "negroes" as black, which makes it nearly impossible to tease out the various racial identities in postcolonial Rhode Island. In contrast, in colonial Rhode Island, *negro* referred to mixed heritage with African heritage

predominating; *mulatto* referred to a white and black mixture; *mustee* referred to a Native American and African mixture, and *Indian* referred to a predominantly American Indian heritage. As members of the Rhode Island General Assembly attempted to strip mustees and Native Americans of their land and rights, they created a separate monolithic "other" category—black. These "black" people had no claims to native ancestral lands. However, this practice of grouping all nonwhites as black was largely confined to state records. For example, runaway slave advertisements and manumission records (from the colonial period through the turn of the nineteenth century) specifically identified the ethnicity of slaves and former slaves. In other words, slaveholders continued to acknowledge the ethnicity of their bondspeople. Slaveholders, unlike state officials, were not interested in creating a single group of "others." Instead they were interested in reclaiming or manumitting their property, which necessitated an accurate description that specified ethnicity and mixed-race heritage. Joanne Pope Melish, "The Racial Vernacular: Contesting the Black/White Binary in Nineteenth-Century Rhode Island," in *Race, Nation, and Empire in American History*, ed. James T. Campbell, Matthew Pratt Guterl, and Robert G. Lee (Chapel Hill: University of North Carolina Press, 2007).

9. Philip Sheldon Foner, *Business and Slavery: The New York Merchants and the Irrepressible Conflict* (Chapel Hill: University of North Carolina Press, 1941); Bernard Bailyn, *The New England Merchants in the Seventeenth Century* (New York: Harper and Row, 1964); Stanley F. Chyet, *Lopez of Newport: Colonial American Merchant Prince* (Detroit, MI: Wayne State University Press, 1970); Jay Coughtry, *The Notorious Triangle: Rhode Island and the African Slave Trade, 1700–1807* (Philadelphia: Temple University Press, 1981); John McCusker and Russell Menard, *Economy of British America, 1607–1789* (Chapel Hill: University of North Carolina Press, 1985); Margaret Ellen Newell, *From Dependency to Independence: Economic Revolution in Colonial New England* (Ithaca, NY: Cornell University Press, 1998); Margaret Ellen Newell, "The Birth of New England in the Atlantic Economy," in Temin, *Engines of Enterprise*; John McCusker and Kenneth Morgan, *Early Modern Atlantic Economy* (New York: Cambridge Press, 2000); Wright, *Slavery*.

10. Coughtry, *Notorious Triangle*.

11. Ira Berlin, *Many Thousands Gone: The First Two Centuries of Slavery in North America* (Cambridge, MA: Harvard University Press, 1998), 222–33, 369.

12. "1842 Constitution of the State of Rhode Island and Providence Plantations," State of Rhode Island General Assembly, http://webserver.rilin.state.ri.us/RiConstitution/ConstFull.html; Kenneth S. Carlson, "Rhode Island General Assembly—Slavery Related Legislation: 1636–1863, Inclusive," September 28, 2000, and April 3, 2000, Rhode Island State Archives.

13. Myron O. Stachiw, *"For the Sake of Commerce": Rhode Island, Slavery and the Textile Industry. An Essay to Accompany the Exhibit "The Loom and the Lash: Northern Industry and Southern Slavery,"* pamphlet (Providence: RIHS, 1982).

14. Pierson argues that, "despite the strictures of bondage, the black Yankees of eighteenth-century New England created a sustaining folk culture of their own." He asserts that black colonial New Englanders retained African values and perspectives on life, which contributed not only to African American culture but also to American culture. William Dillion Piersen, *Black Yankees: The Development of an Afro-American Subculture in Eighteenth-Century New England* (Amherst: University of Massachusetts Press, 1988), ix, x.

15. Charles A. Battle, *Negroes on the Island of Rhode Island* (N.p.: n.p., 1932); Irving H. Bartlett, *From Slave to Citizen: The Story of the Negro in Rhode Island* (Providence, RI: Urban League of Greater Providence, 1954); Robert J. Cottrol, *The Afro-Yankees: Providence's Black Community in the Antebellum Era* (Westport, CT: Greenwood Press, 1982); Robert K. Fitts, *Inventing New England's Slave Paradise: Master/Slave Relations in Eighteenth-Century Narragansett, Rhode Island* (New York: Garland, 1998); Bryan Rommel-Ruiz, *Atlantic Revolutions: Slavery and Freedom in Newport, Rhode Island and Halifax, Nova Scotia in the Era of the American Revolution* (Ann Arbor: University of Michigan Press, 1999).

16. Lorenzo J. Greene, *The Negro in Colonial New England* (New York: Athenaeum, 1971); Edgar J. McManus, *Black Bondage in the North* (Syracuse, NY: Syracuse University Press, 1973); Piersen, *Black Yankees*; Melish, *Disowning Slavery*; John Wood Sweet, *Bodies Politic: Negotiating Race in the American North, 1730–1830* (Baltimore: Johns Hopkins University Press, 2003); Wendy Anne Warren, "Enslaved Africans in New England, 1638–1700" (PhD diss., Yale University, 2008); Catherine Adams and Elizabeth H. Pleck, *Love of Freedom: Black Women in Colonial and Revolutionary New England* (New York: Oxford University Press, 2010).

17. Africans were first deemed inferior because their lack of Christianity and their "assumed" cultural primitiveness indicated that they were "fit" for enslavement. African responses to slavery in the New World, which ranged from extreme defiance to submissiveness, led Europeans to conclude that slavery was the only way to manage such people. Consequently, once blacks were free they needed white oversight. See Winthrop D. Jordan, *White over Black: American Attitudes toward the Negro, 1550–1812* (New York: Norton, 1977); Melish, *Disowning Slavery*.

18. Carol Berkin, *First Generations: Women in Colonial America* (New York: Hill and Wang, 1996), 124.

19. James Horton and Lois Horton, *In Hope of Liberty: Culture, Community, and Protest among Northern Free Blacks, 1700–1860* (New York: Oxford University Press, 1997), 4–8.

20. Northerners were dedicated to bound labor because it was essential to their diversified economy. Berlin, *Many Thousands Gone*, 47–63; Melish, *Disowning Slavery*.

21. Horton and Horton, *In Hope of Liberty*, 6.

22. William M. Wiecek, "The Statutory Law of Slavery and Race in the Thirteen Mainland Colonies," *William and Mary Quarterly*, 3rd ser., 34, no. 2 (April 1977): 258–59.

23. McManus, *Black Bondage*, 62.

24. See Greene, *Negro*.

25. Berlin, *Many Thousands Gone*, 222–33.

26. Cottrol, *Afro-Yankees*, 44.

27. Ibid., 60–79.

28. McManus, *Black Bondage*; Melish, *Disowning Slavery*; Nash and Soderlund, *Freedom by Degrees*; George Fishman, *The African American Struggle for Freedom and Equality: The Development of a People's Identity, New Jersey, 1624–1850* (New York: Garland, 1997); Harris, *In the Shadow*; Graham Russell Hodges, *Slavery and Freedom in the Rural North: African Americans in Monmouth County, New Jersey, 1665–1865* (Madison, WI: Madison House, 1997); Horton and Horton, *In Hope of Liberty*; Margot Minardi, *Making Slavery History: Abolitionism and the Politics of Memory In Massachusetts* (Oxford: Oxford University Press, 2010), 7–8.

29. Rum, made from West Indian molasses, was a critical export for northern colonies. As economic historian John McCusker argued, "The export of rum contributed significantly toward righting the balance of payments of the continental colonies." He analyzed the contribution of each colony's trade toward meeting their English debts to determine rum's importance to each colony and colonists. John McCusker, "The Rum Trade and the Balance of Payments of the Thirteen Continental Colonies, 1650–1775" (PhD diss., University of Pittsburgh, 1970), 4–12.

Notes to Chapter 1

1. John Russell Bartlett, trans., *Records of the State of Rhode Island and Providence Plantations in New England*, vol. 10, *1784–1792* (New York: AMS Press, 1968), 70.

2. Ibid., 143.

3. John Russell Bartlett, trans., *Records of the Colony of Rhode Island and Providence Plantations in New England*, vol. 1, *1636–1663* (Providence, RI: AMS Press, 1968), 243.

4. John Russell Bartlett, trans., *Records of the Colony of Rhode Island and Providence Plantations in New England*, vol. 2, *1664–1677* (New York: AMS Press, 1968), 534–35.

5. Rhett S. Jones, "Plantation Slavery in the Narragansett Country of Rhode Island, 1690–1790: A Preliminary Study," *Plantation Society* 2, no. 2 (1986): 157.

6. In the North, slaves accounted for just over 2 percent of the total population in 1680 and just over 5 percent by 1750. Slaveholding remained especially small in colonial New England; most slaveholders held two or fewer slaves. Despite slaves' relatively small numbers, slave labor helped make the northern colonies viable. Northern slaves cleared the forest, built the roads, constructed the first permanent dwellings, and produced the food. Slaves labored in all aspects of the northern economy—as farmhands, domestic servants, sailors, assistants, and artisans. Ira Berlin, *Many Thousands Gone: The First Two Centuries of Slavery in North America* (Cambridge, MA: Harvard University Press, 1998), 47–63, 369.

7. Like Hodges and Nash and Soderlund, I argue that the interdependence of the city and countryside was fueled by slave labor and the business of slavery. Hodges specifically asserts that slavery was practiced in New York and East Jersey for two centuries because of the interdependence of the city and countryside: the city was the center of regional society, while the countryside supplied the city with food, fuel, and raw material for export. There was little separation between the rural and urban economies, and slave labor was present and critical at each end. Similarly, Nash and Soderlund show that slaves in Pennsylvania labored in the countryside cultivating crops as well as in the city on merchant ships and in artisan shops, tanneries, and homes. John Russell Bartlett, trans., *Records of the Colony of Rhode Island and Providence Plantations in New England*, vol. 6, *1757–1769* (New York: AMS Press, 1968), 379–83; Paul Weiler, "Rhode Island–West Indies Trade in the Eighteenth Century" (MA thesis, University of Iowa, 1947); Jay Coughtry, *The Notorious Triangle: Rhode Island and the African Slave Trade, 1700–1807* (Philadelphia: Temple University Press, 1981); Berlin, *Many Thousands Gone*, 369; Graham Russell Hodges, *Root and Branch: African Americans in New York and East Jersey, 1613–1863* (Chapel Hill: University of North Carolina Press, 1999); Gary B. Nash and Jean R. Soderlund, *Freedom by Degrees: Emancipation in Pennsylvania and Its Aftermath* (New York: Oxford University Press, 1991).

8. The first town, Providence, was established by Roger Williams in 1636. Two years later, Anne Hutchison founded Portsmouth. Within the same year, religious divisions in Portsmouth led William Coddington to establish the town of Newport. Warwick, the last of the four original towns, was founded in 1643 by Samuel Gorton. Gorton had been banished from Portsmouth and encountered frosty receptions in Providence and Newport. Sydney V. James, *Colonial Rhode Island: A History* (New York: Charles Scribner's Sons, 1975), 13–30.

9. Ibid., 106–10.

10. Ibid., 1.

11. Rhode Island Government, "Maps Rhode Island," www.ri.gov/, accessed June 29, 2009.

12. Most merchants were engaged in intercolonial trading; however, their primary trading good was rum that they made from West Indian molasses. Rhode Islanders consumed 48 percent of the rum that was distilled; 42 percent was used for intercolonial trade, and slave traders bought the remaining 10 percent. In fact, slave traders had a difficult time getting their hands on enough rum. Weiler, "Rhode Island–West Indies Trade"; J. Stanley Lemons, "Rhode Island and the Slave Trade," *Rhode Island History* 60, no. 4 (Fall 2002): 101.

13. Lynne Withey, *Urban Growth in Colonial Rhode Island: Newport and Providence in the Eighteenth Century* (Albany: State University of New York Press, 1984).

14. The continental British North American colonies, later the United States, received less than 5 percent of all the slaves transported in the Trans-Atlantic slave trade. The majority of enslaved Africans were shipped to the West Indies

and South America. John Thornton, *Africa and Africans in the Making of the Atlantic World, 1400–1680* (New York: Cambridge University Press, 1992).

15. Weiler, "Rhode Island–West Indies Trade," 5–6.

16. Ibid., 15.

17. John Russell Bartlett, trans., *Records of the Colony of Rhode Island and Providence Plantations in New England*, vol. 3, *1687–1706* (New York: AMS Press, 1968), 175, 387; Thomas Williams Bicknell, *The History of the State of Rhode Island and Providence Plantations* (New York: American Historical Society, 1920), 1048.

18. James, *Colonial Rhode Island*, 119.

19. John Russell Bartlett, trans., *Records of the Colony of Rhode Island and Providence Plantations in New England*, vol. 4, *1707–1740* (New York: AMS Press, 1968), 58.

20. Elaine Forman Crane, *A Dependent People: Newport, Rhode Island in the Revolutionary Era* (New York: Fordham University, 1985), 10; Rachel Chernos Lin, "The Rhode Island Slave Traders: Butchers, Bankers and Candlestick-Makers," *Slavery and Abolition* 23, no. 3 (December 2002): 21–38.

21. Weiler, "Rhode Island–West Indies Trade," 20–21.

22. Bernard Bailyn, *The New England Merchants in the Seventeenth Century* (New York: Harper and Row, 1964), 7.

23. The New England trade with the West Indies stimulated local economies, especially the shipping industry. Coughtry, *Notorious Triangle*, 25; Anne Farrow, Joel Lang, and Jenifer Frank, *Complicity: How the North Promoted, Prolonged, and Profited from Slavery* (New York: Ballantine Books, 2005), 53–54, 95–119.

24. Depending on the year, Rhode Island slave traders controlled between 60 percent and 90 percent of the North American trade in slaves. This assertion is based on queries done on the Slave Trade Database (www.slavevoyages.org/tast/index.faces). The online database collects the records of over thirty-five thousand slaving voyages and allows searches with the following variables: date of voyage, ship's country of origin, place where voyage ended and began, principal place of slave purchase and sale, vessel name, captain name, date, mortality rates and percentages of men, women, and children. Emory University holds the copyright (2008 and 2009).

25. "Shipping News," *Rhode Island Gazette*, October 25, 1732.

26. George Scott, "The following is a Particular account of Negroes Rising and Overcoming Capt. George Scott, in His Passage from Guinea," *Boston Gazette*, April 26, 1731.

27. Jane Fiske compiled and numbered three types of court documents—dockets, record books, and file papers—from Newport courts between 1659 and 1783. Dockets were recorded by court clerks and listed cases in the order in which they were to be heard. Court clerks who entered basic and essential data about each case also kept record books. The file papers contain depositions—the statements of people giving testimony. In most cases it was nearly impossible to discern judgments because the verdicts were not filed with the other papers and

lacked any notation to indicate dates, names or docket numbers. Samuel Vernon and William Vernon v. Thomas Rogers, Newport, Rhode Island, October 4, 1765, in Jane Fletcher Fiske, *Gleanings from Newport Court Files, 1659–1783* (Boxford: J. F. Fiske, 1998), #1070.

28. The slaves were valued at £2,470. John Channing and Walter Chaloner v. Henry Livingston, Newport, Rhode Island, October 24, 1753, in Fiske, *Gleanings*, # 845.

29. Coughtry, *Notorious Triangle*.

30. Weiler, "Rhode Island–West Indies Trade," 20.

31. Irving H. Bartlett, *From Slave to Citizen: The Story of the Negro in Rhode Island* (Providence, RI: Urban League of Greater Providence, 1954); Bartlett, *Records*, 6:381.

32. Bartlett, *From Slave to Citizen*, 5.

33. Wim Klooster and Alfred Padula, eds., *The Atlantic World: Essays on Slavery, Migration, and Imagination* (Upper Saddle River, NJ: Pearson, 2004), 34.

34. See Crane, *Dependent People*, 54.

35. Every captain, merchant, person, or persons bringing in "negro" slave(s) from other colonies was taxed three pounds per head. The 1715 law assessed duties on "negro" slaves imported into the colony. Legislation in 1717, 1719, and 1723 exclusively set aside slave duties for public works. In 1723 the 1711 duty on Negro slaves was repealed. The act did not penalize direct imports from Africa because the colonial government did not want to hinder the slave trade. Bartlett, *Records*, 4:190–93, 225, 330, 424.

36. Christopher (majority owner) and George Champlin owned the sloop. The Champlin family owned a large estate in the Narragansett, but they were also involved in commerce—slave trading in particular.

37. The article is based on the original manuscript in the library of George L. Shepley, with notes and introduction by Professor Verner W. Crane of Brown University. Verner W. Crane, "A Rhode Island Slaver: Trade Book of the Sloop *Adventure*, 1773–1774," 1922, Shepley Library, Providence, RI.

38. Herbert Klein, *The Atlantic Slave Trade: New Approaches to the Americas* (Cambridge: Cambridge University Press, 2010), 100.

39. Weiler, "Rhode Island–West Indies Trade," 20.

40. John Russell Bartlett, trans., *Records of the Colony of Rhode Island and Providence Plantations in New England*, vol. 5, *1741–1756* (New York: AMS Press, 1968), 8–14.

41. Ibid., 5–14.

42. Howard W. Preston, *Rhode Island and the Sea* (Providence: State of Rhode Island and Providence Plantations, 1859) 34.

43. James Blaine Hedges, *The Browns of Providence Plantations: The Colonial Years* (Providence, RI: Brown University Press, 1968), 1–6.

44. Ibid., 8–9.

45. Ibid., 10–20.

46. Lemons, "Rhode Island," 98.

47. Brown University Steering Committee on Slavery and Justice, "Slavery and Justice Report," 2006, 15–17, http://brown.edu/Research/Slavery_Justice/documents/SlaveryAndJustice.pdf.

48. Stanley F. Chyet, *Lopez of Newport: Colonial American Merchant Prince* (Detroit, MI: Wayne State University Press, 1970), 24–30; Crane, *Dependent People*, 77.

49. Virginia Bever Platt, "'And Don't Forget the Guinea Voyage': The Slave Trade of Aaron Lopez of Newport," *William and Mary Quarterly* 32, no. 4 (1975): 601–4.

50. Newport merchants held a disproportionate number of slaves. Platt, "'And Don't Forget,'" 607; Crane, *Dependent People*, 53–62.

51. Platt, "'And Don't Forget,'" 616.

52. Rhode Island census records taken before 1850 pose some problems as they do not indicate whether black inhabitants were enslaved; consequently, most researchers, myself included, have counted all blacks as slaves. Cherry Fletcher Bamberg has done considerable work on and in these records; please see the Rhode Island Genealogical Society website (www.rigensoc.org) for Bamberg's statement on colonial census records. I have relied on census records and statistics published by historians Edgar J. McManus, Lorenzo J. Greene, and Ira Berlin, "Some R.I. Census Returns," accessed December 11, 2014, www.rigensoc.org/index.php; Edgar J. McManus, *Black Bondage in the North* (Syracuse, NY: Syracuse University Press, 1973), 202–5; Lorenzo J. Greene, *The Negro in Colonial New England* (New York: Athenaeum, 1969), 344; Berlin, *Many Thousands Gone*, 369–72.

53. McManus, *Black Bondage*, 203.

54. Berlin, *Many Thousands Gone*, 369–72.

55. Robert K. Fitts, *Inventing New England's Slave Paradise: Master/Slave Relations in Eighteenth-Century Narragansett, Rhode Island* (New York: Garland, 1998).

56. The distinction between a slave society and a society with slaves is not static; however, the North was only ever a society with slaves. Griswold is a cultural landscape historian; her book *The Manor* is a multigenerational study of mastery, the loss of mastery, and to a lesser extent the history of slavery on Shelter Island. Griswold contends that Shelter Island was a society with slaves rather than a slave society because of the small number of slaves in comparison to the West Indies and the fact that there was no single staple crop. I on the other hand contend that the relatively high number of slaves, and the fact that enslaved people were producing foodstuffs and livestock for a distant market (West Indies), are the reasons why places like Shelter Island and the Narragansett Country were quasi-slave societies. Berlin, *Many Thousands Gone*, 8–10; Mac K. Griswold, *The Manor: Three Centuries at a Slave Plantation on Long Island* (New York: Farrar, Straus and Giroux, 2013).

57. William Davis Miller, *The Narragansett Planters* (Worcester, MA: American Antiquarian Society, 1934). Fitts, *Inventing New England's Slave Paradise*.

58. Christian M. McBurney, "The Rise and Decline of the South Kingstown Planters, 1660–1783" (BA honors thesis, Brown University, 1981), iii.

59. The Narragansett Country or South County encompasses present-day South Kingstown, North Kingstown, Wickford, Wakefield, Peace Dale, Exeter, and Charlestown. South Kingstown was the heart of the Narragansett Country; its planters were wealthier, more socially prominent. and more politically connected than their counterparts in the other towns.

60. Two land companies, the Pettaquamscutt Purchasers and the Narragansett Proprietors, fought for control of the Narragansett region between 1660 and 1700. These companies purchased tracts of land from war-ravaged and destitute Narragansett peoples. In the 1690s, settlers came primarily from Aquidneck Island. Through the 1730s they increased their wealth by buying tracts on credit and then reselling parts of them to pay off their debts. Narragansett farmers have been referred to as planters because they held relatively high numbers of slaves and ran their large farms like plantations. McBurney, "Rise and Decline," i–vi, 55. Miller, *Narragansett Planters*, 4.

61. Miller, *Narragansett Planters*, 20–41.

62. William D. Johnston, *Slavery in Rhode Island, 1755–1776* (Providence: RIHS, 1894), 126.

63. Narragansett slaveholders differed considerably from southern planters in the size and management of their slaveholdings. Southern planters typically held twenty or more enslaved people; consequently, Narragansett slaveholders are best compared to small or middling southern slaveholders—"slaveholding households with upwards of three slaves"—in historian Elizabeth Fox-Genovese's enumeration. Elizabeth Fox-Genovese, *Within the Plantation Household: Black and White Women of the Old South* (Chapel Hill: University of North Carolina Press, 1988), 32; Edmund S. Morgan, *American Slavery, American Freedom: The Ordeal of Colonial Virginia* (New York: Norton, 1975), 365.

64. McBurney, "Rise and Decline," 50–55.

65. Bartlett, *From Slave to Citizen*, 10; McBurney, "Rise and Decline," 58–59.

66. Fitts, *Inventing New England's Slave Paradise*, 121–40.

67. Most scholars of slavery in North America define a planter as someone who owned at least twenty bound laborers.

68. Fitts, *Inventing New England's Slave Paradise*.

69. Ibid., 65–75.

70. Farrow, Lang, and Frank, *Complicity*, 49–50.

71. Rhode Island's economic history offers strong support for Joanne Pope Melish's contention that slave labor allowed white men to pursue entrepreneurial businesses. Bernard Bailyn, "Slavery and Population Growth in Colonial New England," *Engines of Enterprise*, ed. Peter Temin (Cambridge, MA: Harvard University Press, 2000), 254–55; Gavin Wright, *Slavery and American Economic Development* (Baton Rouge: Louisiana State University Press, 2006), 14; Joanne Pope Melish, *Disowning Slavery: Gradual Emancipation and "Race" in New England, 1780–1860* (Ithaca, NY: Cornell University Press, 1998).

72. Crane, *Dependent People*, 24.

73. The Brown brothers grew up with enslaved people in their household. They also owned slaves as adults. The best record of slaveholding in the Brown

family was left by Moses Brown: "He had working for him several African men, including Bonno, the oldest, aged about twenty-five years; Ceasar, recently purchased at age twenty-three; and Cudjo, born in Rhode Island of African parents. In addition there was at least one woman slave in the household named Eve. She had been bequeathed by Uncle Obadiah to his daughter Mary, the sister of Moses' wife; she lived with Anna and Moses at their home on Towne Street." Charles Rappleye, *Sons of Providence: The Brown Brothers, the Slave Trade and the American Revolution* (New York: Simon and Schuster, 2006), 56.

74. By 1775 nearly 80 percent of the exports of New England went to the British West Indies. In fact the West Indian planters were so dependent on provisions from the northern colonies that famine broke out during the American Revolution when ships could not get there. An estimated fifteen thousand slaves in Jamaica died of hunger between 1780 and 1787. Farrow, Lang, and Frank, *Complicity*, 49–50.

75. McManus, *Black Bondage*, 56–60; Stanley Engerman, Seymour Drescher, and Robert Paquette, eds., *Slavery* (New York: Oxford University Press, 2001), 102.

76. *Old South Leaflets* (Boston: Directors of the Old South Work, 1896–1922), 24–26, 53–61.

77. Leslie Harris, *In the Shadow of Slavery: African Americans in New York City, 1626–1863* (Chicago: University of Chicago Press, 2003), 14–17.

78. George Fishman, *The African American Struggle for Freedom and Equality: The Development of a People's Identity, New Jersey, 1624–1850* (New York: Garland, 1997), 27–28.

79. Harris, *In the Shadow*, 26–28.

80. McManus, *Black Bondage*, 55–88.

81. Catherine Adams and Elizabeth H. Pleck, *Love of Freedom: Black Women in Colonial and Revolutionary New England* (New York: Oxford University Press, 2010), 103–48.

82. McManus, *Black Bondage*, 67.

83. Throughout British North America, colonists commonly enslaved Indians during the first decades of settlement. In fact, prior to the eighteenth century, most slaves were Native Americans, not Africans. Margaret Ellen Newell, "The Changing Nature of Indian Slavery in New England," in *Reinterpreting the Native American Past and the Colonial Experience*, ed. Colin Calloway and Neal Salisbury (Boston: Colonial Society of Massachusetts, 2003), 107.

84. Prior to European contact, the Pequot lived in semipermanent village settlements. They cultivated corn, beans, squash, and tubers; they supplemented their diet through hunting, gathering, and fishing. The Pequot lived in a patrilineal society organized by family lineages and clans and strictly adhering to social deference. The Pequot territories were adjacent to Algonquian lands; the two groups were closely related, culturally and linguistically, to the Algonquian people of southern New England. William Starna, "The Pequots in the Early Seventeenth Century," in *The Pequots in Southern New England: The Fall*

and Rise of an American Indian Nation, ed. Laurence M. Hauptman and James D. Wherry (Norman: University of Oklahoma Press, 1990), 33–40.

85. In 1646, the commissioners of the United Colonies authorized the exchange of Indians for African slaves. Historian George Moore designates this period as the beginning of the European-directed domestic slave trade in the North American colonies. The first North American slave trade overlapped the initial settlement period of Rhode Island. George Henry Moore, *Notes on the History of Slavery in Massachusetts* (New York: Negro Universities Press, 1968); Alfred A. Cave, *The Pequot War* (Amherst: University of Massachusetts Press, 1996), 1–32.

86. Metacom's War was a debilitating defeat for the Narragansett peoples. The settlers enslaved the captives and sold them to settlers in South Carolina—the first European-controlled domestic slave trade. Colonists from Massachusetts, Rhode Island, Connecticut, and New York all bought Native American slaves from South Carolina. Their number is unknown. The war transformed many New England Indians into dependents. David J. Drake, *King Philip's War: Civil War in New England, 1675–1676* (Amherst: University of Massachusetts Press, 1999).

87. Metacom was also known as Phillip or King Phillip.

88. Drake, *King Phillip's War.*

89. Metacom's War secured English hegemony in New England—it was a crushing defeat for Native Americans. Bartlett, *From Slave to Citizen,* 5.

90. John A. Sainsbury, "Indian Labor in Early Rhode Island," in *New England Encounters: Indians and Euromericans, 1600–1850,* ed. Alden T. Vaughan (Boston: Northeastern University Press, 1999), 262.

91. Ibid., 263–69; Maureen Alice Taylor and John Wood Sweet, eds., *Runaways, Deserters, and Notorious Villains: From Rhode Island Newspapers,* vol. 2, *Additional Notices from the Providence Gazette, 1762–1800 as Well as Advertisements from All Other Rhode Island Newspapers from 1732–1800* (Rockport, ME: Picton Press, 2001).

92. Edward H. West, *History of Portsmouth, 1638–1936* (Providence, RI: J. Green, 1936).

93. Bartlett, *Records,* 4:389.

94. Bartlett, *Records,* 2:535; Bartlett, *Records,* 3:193.

95. Moore, *Notes on the History,* 52–61, 123, 153, 155.

96. As historian Alan Gallay has argued, Native American and African slavery must be studied together, not separately, because not only were they part of the same system but the decline of Native slavery influenced the turn to African slavery. Alan Gallay, *The Indian Slave Trade: The Rise of the English Empire in the American South, 1670–1717* (New Haven, CT: Yale University Press, 2002).

97. Samuel Swan v. Robert Wilcox, Newport, Rhode Island, March 24, 1728/9, in Fiske, *Gleanings,* #463.

98. Tiya Miles and Sharon P. Holland, "Introduction: Crossing Waters, Crossing Worlds," in *Crossing Waters, Crossing Worlds: The African Diaspora*

in Indian Country, ed. Tiya Miles and Sharon P. Holland (Durham, NC: Duke University Press, 2006), 3–13.

99. Joanne Pope Melish, "The Racial Vernacular: Contesting the Black/White Binary in Nineteenth-Century Rhode Island," in *Race, Nation, and Empire in American History*, ed. James T. Campbell, Matthew Pratt Guterl, and Robert G. Lee (Chapel Hill: University of North Carolina Press, 2007); Tiffany M. McKinney, "Race and Federal Recognition in Native New England," in Miles and Holland, *Crossing Waters*, 57–79.

100. Johnston, *Slavery in Rhode Island*, 114.

101. Only the northern towns of Providence and Warwick passed laws banning slavery. Bartlett, *Records*, 1:243.

102. McManus, *Black Bondage*, 56–60; Engerman, Drescher, and Paquette, *Slavery*, 102.

103. Bartlett, *Records*, 2:535.

104. Bartlett, *Records*, 4:54. Thomas Windsor brought forty-seven slaves from Africa to sell in Rhode Island and Massachusetts. The first slaves in New England most likely came aboard the *Desire* into Massachusetts in 1638. Wendy Anne Warren, "'The Cause of Her Grief': The Rape of a Slave in Early New England," *Journal of American History* 93, no. 4 (March 2007): 1032.

105. Bartlett, *Records*, 3:492.

106. McManus, *Black Bondage*, 74–89.

107. Bartlett, *Records*, 3:492–93.

108. Bartlett, *Records*, 4:50.

109. Beginning in 1711 both blacks and Native Americans were commonly referred to as commodities. Bartlett, *Records*, 4:131.

110. The Rhode Island General Assembly passed a 1728 Act requiring a one-hundred-pound bond for manumitted slaves. Bartlett, *Records*, 5:415.

111. *Acts and Laws of His Majesty's Colony of Rhode Island and Providence Plantations in New England from 1745–1752* (Newport, RI: J. Franklin, 1752), 92–93; Bartlett, *Records*, 5:320.

112. Bartlett, *Records*, 6:64.

113. Louis Masur, "Slavery in Eighteenth-Century Rhode Island: Evidence from the Census of 1774," *Slavery and Abolition* 6, no. 2 (1985): 140–41.

114. Bartlett, *Records*, 3:492–93; *Providence Gazette*, September 1, 1770; Robert J. Cottrol, *The Afro-Yankees: Providence's Black Community in the Antebellum Era* (Westport, CT: Greenwood Press, 1982), 20.

115. Irene Burnham et al., *Creative Survival: The Providence Black Community in the Nineteenth Century* (Providence: RIBHS, 1985), 30–36; Adams and Pleck, *Love of Freedom*, 53.

116. Bartlett, *From Slave to Citizen*, 12.

117. Cottrol, *Afro-Yankees*, 29; Bartlett, *From Slave to Citizen*, 12.

118. Bartlett, *From Slave to Citizen*, 12; Oliver P. Fuller, *The History of Warwick, Rhode Island, from Its Settlement in 1642 to the Present Time: Including Accounts of the Early Settlement and Development of Its Several Villages;*

Sketches of the Origin and Progress of the Different Churches of the Town, and c., and c. (Providence, RI: Angell, Burlingame, 1875), 189.

119. Emanuel, a free "negro," was found guilty of stealing from Capt. James Clarke, General Court of Trials, 1671–1729, January 1719/1729, vol. A, p. 285, JA-SC.

120. Mercy, a free black woman, was found guilty of stealing from Jeremiah Wilcox, General Court of Trials, 1671–1729, 1722, vol. A, p. 397, JA-SC.

Notes to Chapter 2

1. Hager was to be "kept" in Green's wife's house for her use, and if she outlived Green's wife she would go to his executors. The will of Capt. Peter Green was part of the court case Peter Green, John Green, and William Green v. Elisha Green, Newport, Rhode Island, July 28, 1725, in Jane Fletcher Fiske, *Gleanings from Newport Court Files, 1659–1783* (Boxford: J. F. Fiske, 1998), #243.

2. Will of Joseph Wanton, part of the following suit: Benjamin Holland, an infant who sues by his Guardian Gilbert Devol v. Mary Richardson, Joseph G. Wanton, John G. Wanton, Gideon Wanton, Edward Wanton, Henry Bowers and Mary his wife, Abraham Borden, Thomas Howland, Charles Whitfield and Elizabeth his wife, in Newport, Rhode Island, August 14, 1749, in Fiske, *Gleanings*, #1129.

3. Deposition of Christopher Gardner at North Kingstown, May 22, 1772, part of the following suit: Susanna Womsley, an infant within the age of twenty-one years, who sues by Mary Womsley, her mother and next friend, v. Jeffrey Watson, Newport, Rhode Island, April 25, 1772, in Fiske, *Gleanings*, # 1130.

4. In reference to people of color. Joanne Pope Melish, "The Racial Vernacular: Contesting the Black/White Binary in Nineteenth-Century Rhode Island," in *Race, Nation and Empire in American History*, ed. James T. Campbell, Matthew Pratt Guterl, and Robert G. Lee (Chapel Hill: University of North Carolina Press, 2007).

5. William Dillion Piersen, *Black Yankees: The Development of an Afro-American Subculture in Eighteenth-Century New England* (Amherst: University of Massachusetts Press, 1988).

6. Catherine Adams and Elizabeth H. Pleck, *Love of Freedom: Black Women in Colonial and Revolutionary New England* (New York: Oxford University Press, 2010), 117.

7. Piersen's study put the social lives of African Americans front and center. He chose to focus on the cultural impact Africans and African Americans had on the North, rather than on the impact that the institution of slavery had on the region and blacks. Piersen, *Black Yankees*, ix, 18, 61.

8. Louis P. Masur, "Slavery in Eighteenth-Century Rhode Island: Evidence from the Census of 1774," *Slavery and Abolition: A Journal of Slave and Post-Slave Studies* 6, no. 2 (1985): 139–50.

9. Margaret Ellen Newell, "The Changing Nature of Indian Slavery in New England," in *Reinterpreting the Native American Past and the Colonial Experience*, ed. Colin Calloway and Neal Salisbury (Boston: Colonial Society of Massachusetts, 2003), 107.

10. James David Drake, *King Phillip's War: Civil War in New England, 1675–1676* (Amherst: University of Massachusetts, 1999); Newell, "Changing Nature"; John A. Sainsbury, "Indian Labor in Early Rhode Island," in *New England Encounters: Indians and Euromericans, 1600–1850*, ed. Alden T. Vaughan (Boston: Northeastern University Press, 1999), 262.

11. It is unclear whether the first generations of bondsmen of African descent were slaves for life or bound for ten years as stipulated in the 1652 law; regardless, race-based lifetime slavery was a legally acknowledged and socially acceptable practice by the eighteenth century. Robert J. Cottrol, *The Afro-Yankees: Providence's Black Community in the Antebellum Era* (Westport, CT: Greenwood Press, 1982), 14.

12. The first documented evidence of Rhode Islanders buying enslaved people directly from Africa was in 1696, when fourteen Africans of a "cargo" of forty-seven were purchased, for thirty to thirty-five pounds each, from the *Seaflower* in Newport. John Russell Bartlett, trans., *Records of the Colony of Rhode Island and Providence Plantations in New England*, vol. 5, *1741–1756* (New York: AMS Press,1968), 54; Irving H. Bartlett, *From Slave to Citizen: The Story of the Negro in Rhode Island* (Providence, RI: Urban League of Greater Providence, 1954), 11.

13. Edgar J. McManus, *Black Bondage in the North* (New York: Syracuse University Press, 1973), 202, 203.

14. A public auction of four "Mustees," one "Mulatto," and four "Negroes," 1745, in the Rhode Island Historical Society Manuscripts, MSS 9003, vol. 11, p. 98, RIHS.

15. Elaine Forman Crane, *A Dependent People: Newport, Rhode Island in the Revolutionary Era* (New York: Fordham University Press, 1985).

16. Masur, "Slavery," 143.

17. Richard C. Youngken, *African Americans in Newport: An Introduction to the Heritage of African Americans in Newport, Rhode Island, 1700–1945* (Providence: Rhode Island Historical Preservation and Heritage Commission, RIBHS, 1998), 11.

18. Most slaveholders in Newport owned just one or two slaves; however, there were notable exceptions. In 1730 Edward Smith willed his wife and children a total of eight enslaved woman and children. Fiske, *Gleanings*, #1014.

19. Adams and Pleck, *Love of Freedom*, 34–41.

20. Ibid.; Cottrol, *Afro-Yankees*, 16–17.

21. Adams and Pleck, *Love of Freedom*, 84–92; Youngken, *African Americans in Newport*, 18–19; Thomas B. Stockwell, *A History of Public Education in Rhode Island* (Providence, RI: Providence Press, 1876), 10.

22. John Russell Bartlett, trans., *Records of the Colony of Rhode Island and Providence Plantations in New England*, vol. 3, *1678–1706* (New York: AMS Press, 1968), 492; Bartlett, *Records*, 5:320.

23. *Providence Gazette*, September 1, 1770; Cottrol, *Afro-Yankees*, 20.

24. *Providence Gazette and Country Journal*, August 25, 1770.

25. Masur, "Slavery," 143.

26. Caesar Lyndon died in 1796; he was free but destitute. Akeia F. Benard, "The Free African American Cultural Landscape: Newport, RI, 1774–1826" (PhD diss., University of Connecticut, 2008), 52–56; Accounts, 1736–70, Rhode Island Manuscripts Collection, MSS 9004, vol. 10, pp. 84–85, RIHS; Lyndon, Caesar, Sundry account with Caesar Lyndon, July 28, 1762, Rhode Island Manuscripts Collection MSS 9004, vol. 10, p. 81, RIHS.

27. Unlike Boston, Newport had a black female majority. Adams and Pleck, *Love of Freedom*, 31.

28. Saint Jago was manumitted in 1772 and died a property holder. Donald R. Hopkins, "A Slave Called Saint Jago," *Rhode Island History* 69, no. 1 (Winter/ Spring 2011): 30–39.

29. John Banister's Daybook, December 1746 through February 1750, in John Banister Account Books, MSS 919, vol. 1, pp. 20, 111, 157, 331, 387, 477, 485, 479, 493, 512, 516, 527, 528, RIHS.

30. Accounts of cash disbursements (1764), including payments to various owners of slaves for labor (slaves are not named individually), in the Miscellaneous Manuscript Collection, Mss 9001-A Apollo (Brigantine), Box 11, RIHS.

31. Philip D. Morgan, "Maritime Slavery," *Slavery and Abolition* 31, no. 3 (September 2010): 311–26.

32. Benjamin Freebody to Samuel Freebody, April 8, 1784, Rhode Island Historical Society Manuscripts, MSS 9003, vol. 16, RIHS.

33. Benjamin Freebody to Samuel Freebody, June 16, 1784, Rhode Island Historical Society Manuscripts, MSS 9003, vol. 16, RIHS, and Deposition of Col. George Irish, July 1, 1786, Rhode Island Historical Society Manuscripts, MSS 9003, vol. 16, RIHS. Although the letter is dated 1774, it is most likely a misprint and should be dated 1784. There is evidence to support this claim. First, Benjamin Freebody refers to the "last fall after the British left," and the British ended their occupation of New York in November of 1783. Moreover, according to Samuel Freebody, Benjamin Freebody left New York in 1784 and arrived in Rhode Island in August 1784 after being gone about nine years.

34. First Census of the United States, 1790; First Census of the United States, 1790, US Census Bureau, www.census.gov/history/www/through_the_ decades/overview/1790.html; John W. Freebody, *Eight Centuries of Freebodys* (Fairlawn, NJ: John W. Freebody, 1974), 122–23.

35. Robert K. Fitts, *Inventing New England's Slave Paradise: Master/Slave Relations in Eighteenth-Century Narragansett, Rhode Island* (New York: Garland, 1998), 108.

36. Rhett S. Jones, "Plantation Slavery in the Narragansett Country of Rhode Island, 1690–1790: A Preliminary Study," *Plantation Society* 2, no. 2 (1986): 161–62; Piersen, *Black Yankees*.

37. Fitts, *Inventing New England's Slave Paradise*, 104–8, 142.

38. Bartlett, *From Slave to Citizen*, 9.

39. Piersen, *Black Yankees*.

40. William Davis Miller, *The Narragansett Planters* (Worcester, MA: American Antiquarian Society, 1934), 20–41.

41. Masur, "Slavery," 144.

42. See Fitts, *Inventing New England's Slave Paradise*, 106–57.

43. George, a "negro" servant belonging to Sarah Davis, was found guilty committing fornication with Maria, a "negro" servant of Mr. Francis Brimley, General Court of Trials, 1671–1729, 1673, vol. A, p. 11, JA-SC.

44. John Russell Bartlett, trans., *Records of the Colony of Rhode Island and Providence Plantations in New England*, vol. 4, *1707–1740* (New York: AMS Press, 1968), 27.

45. Thomas Peckham v. John Scott, Newport, Rhode Island, December 1714, in Fiske, *Gleanings*, # 40.

46. Samuel Swan v. Robert Wilcox, Newport, Rhode Island, March 24, 1728/9, in Fiske, *Gleanings*, #463.

47. Hezekiah Gorton's "negro man" was ordered whipped for poisoning Ann Markham and Rebecca French, July 25, 1734. Miscellaneous Manuscript Collection, MSS 9001-G, Box 5, Folder Newport Gorton, RIHS.

48. Bartlett, *Records*, 4:179.

49. The act read: Whereas, it frequently happens that the commanders of privateers and masters of other vessels, do carry off slaves that are the property of inhabitants of this colony, and the that without the privy or consent of their masters or mistresses; whereas, there is no law of this colony for remedying so great an evil, Be it therefore enacted by this General Assembly, and by the authority of the same, it is enacted, that from and after the publication of this act, if any commander of private man of war, or master of a merchant ship or other vessel, shall knowingly carry away from, or out of this colony, a slave or slaves, the property of ay inhabitant thereof, the commander of such privateer, or the master of the said merchant ship or vessel, shall pay, as a fine, the sum of £500, to be recovered by the general treasurer of this colony for the time being, by bill, plaint, or information in any court of record within this colony. John Russell Bartlett, trans., *Records of the Colony of Rhode Island and Providence Plantations in New England*, vol. 6, *1757–1769* (New York: AMS Press, 1968), 64.

50. An excerpt taken from the journal of Dr. James MacSparran, a prominent Episcopal minister in Narragansett. Bartlett, *From Slave to Citizen*, 15.

51. Ibid.

52. These numbers represent only those identified as slaves who ran away from town and cities in Rhode Island. Maureen Alice Taylor and John Wood Sweet, eds., *Runaways, Deserters, and Notorious Villains from Rhode Island Newspapers*, vol. 2, *Additional Notices from the Providence Gazette, 1762–1800, as Well as Advertisements from All Other Rhode Island Newspapers from 1732–1800* (Rockport, ME: Picton Press, 2001).

53. These calculations are based on runaway slave advertisements placed in local and regional papers in Rhode Island and New England. Ibid.

54. Ibid.

55. Newport Country Supreme Court Record Book, vol. E, pp. 183–84 (March 1762), JA-SC; "Extract of a Letter from London," *New-London Summary*, February 26, 1762.

56. *Newport Mercury*, February 15, 1773.

57. *Boston Evening Post*, April 27, 1774; *Essex Gazette*, March 12, 1772.

58. Jobba, a "negro" servant belonging to Caleb Carr, was found not guilty of fornication with James Gray, General Court of Trials, 1671–1729, 1673, vol. A, p. 10, JA-SC.

59. Hope, a "negro" servant belonging to Sillima Coddington, was found guilty of fornication with James Pass/Pazz, General Court of Trials, 1671–1729, 1673, vol. A, p. 11, JA-SC.

60. Joanne Pope Melish, *Disowning Slavery: Gradual Emancipation and "Race" in New England, 1780–1860* (Ithaca, NY: Cornell University Press, 1998), 12; Adams and Pleck, *Love of Freedom*, 111.

61. Bartlett, *Records*, 3:492; Bartlett, *Records*, 4:50, 320–21.

62. Stephanie Camp, "The Pleasures of Resistance: Enslaved Women and Body Politics in the Plantation South, 1830–1861," *Journal of Southern History* 68, no. 3 (August 2002): 533–72.

63. Bartlett, *From Slave to Citizen*, 13; Lyndon, Ceaser (Caesar), Accounts, 1736–70, Rhode Island Manuscripts Collection, MSS 9004, vol. 10, pp. 84–85, RIHS.

64. The festivals usually lasted from three days to a full week. Sterling Stuckey, *Going through the Storm: The Influence of African American Art in History* (New York: Oxford University Press, 1994), 53–73; Shane White, "'It Was a Proud Day': African Americans, Festivals, and Parades in the North, 1741–1834," *Journal of American History* 81, no. 1 (June 1994): 13–50.

65. Stuckey, *Going through the Storm*, 53.

66. White, "'It Was a Proud Day,'" 46.

67. Ibid., 14.

68. Shane White, *Somewhat More Independent: The End of Slavery in New York City, 1770–1810* (Athens: University of Georgia Press, 1991), 95–106.

69. Stuckey, *Going through the Storm*, 55.

70. Christian M. McBurney, "The Rise and Decline of the South Kingstown Planters, 1660–1783" (BA honors thesis, Brown University, 1981), i–vi, 55.

71. A reference to the title of Fitts's *Inventing New England's Slave Paradise*.

72. Meeting Minutes, 1723, in the South Kingstown Town Meeting Records, Vitals, vol. 1, p. 13, South Kingstown Town Hall, Office of the Clerk.

73. In Rhode Island, "Negro" Election Day was traditionally celebrated on the last Saturday in June, and recollections of "Negro" Election Days often mention Native Americans. White, "'It Was a Proud Day,'" 17, 19.

74. Ibid., 22.

75. Shane White, "Slavery in the North," *Organization of American History Magazine* 17, no. 3 (April 2003): 20.

76. William J. Brown, *The Life of William J. Brown of Providence, Rhode Island, with Personal Recollections of the Incidents in Rhode Island* (Durham: University of New Hampshire Press, 2006); Frances Harriet Green, *Memoirs of Elleanor Eldridge, 1784–1845* (Chapel Hill: University of North Carolina Press, 2000); Cottrol, *Afro-Yankees*, 23–24.

Notes to Chapter 3

1. Richard Gardner/Gardiner deed for the sale of an infant, October 1798, in the Miscellaneous Manuscript Collection, MSS 9001-G, Box 2, Folder Richard Gardner, RIHS.

2. John Russell Bartlett, trans., *Records of the Colony of Rhode Island and Providence Plantations in New England*, vol. 6, *1757–1769* (New York: AMS Press, 1968), 379.

3. Ibid., 6:379.

4. Ibid., 6:379–80.

5. Elaine Forman Crane, *A Dependent People: Newport, Rhode Island in the Revolutionary Era* (New York: Fordham University Press, 1985), 25–29.

6. Elizabeth Donnan, "The New England Slave Trade after the Revolution," *New England Quarterly* 3, no. 2 (April 1930): 252.

7. Trans-Atlantic Slave Trade Database, accessed December 17, 2014, www. slavevoyages.org/tast/index.faces.

8. John Russell Bartlett, trans., *Records of the State of Rhode Island and Providence Plantations in New England*, vol. 10, *1784–1792* (New York: AMS Press, 1968), 7;Trans-Atlantic Slave Trade Database.

9. Douglass Harper, "Slavery in the North," 2003, www.slavenorth.com/index.html.

10. Jacob Shoemaker died with no heirs. Irving H. Bartlett, *From Slave to Citizen: The Story of the Negro in Rhode Island* (Providence, RI: Urban League of Greater Providence, 1954), 25.

11. It is difficult to assess how many Quakers were in British North America. However, it is clear that the Quaker population was heavily concentrated in Pennsylvania and New England—especially Rhode Island. There were an estimated 145,000 Quakers in Pennsylvania in 1775; and in Philadelphia one-seventh of the population professed to be "Friends." Arthur J. Mekeel, *The Quakers and the American Revolution* (York: Sessions Book Trust, 1996), 2, 388.

12. Charles II granted Pennsylvania to William in payment for a debt; the king also hoped the colony would serve as magnet for troublesome Quakers throughout the Americas. The vast majority of colonial settlers in Pennsylvania were Quakers. Hugh Barbour and Jerry William Frost, *The Quakers* (Westport, CT: Greenwood Press, 1988), 74–75.

13. Roger Williams disliked what he perceived as dogmatic teachings in Quakerism; in fact, he considered Quakers just as bothersome as the Puritans. Ibid., 53–54.

14. *Inner light* refers to the Quaker belief that the light of Christ is in every man and woman. Thomas Drake, *Quakers and Slavery in America* (New Haven, CT: Yale University Press, 1950), 1; David S. Lovejoy, "Samuel Hopkins: Religion, Slavery and the Revolution," *New England Quarterly* 40, no. 2 (June 1976): 229.

15. Drake, *Quakers and Slavery*, 4–7.

16. There were a couple of notable exceptions. In 1688 a group of Mennonite farmers in Germantown, Pennsylvania (a Quaker colony), protested

slaveholding because they believed it was un-Christian to trade and hold slaves. In 1700 Samuel Sewall, a Puritan old-time Congregationalist, published "The Selling of Joseph," which argued that slavery and the slave trade was a form of man-stealing, which was clearly prohibited in the Bible. Lovejoy, "Samuel Hopkins," 228.

17. Gary B. Nash and Jean R. Soderlund, *Freedom by Degrees: Emancipation in Pennsylvania and Its Aftermath* (New York: Oxford University Press, 1991), 42.

18. Drake, *Quakers and Slavery*, 39–42.

19. Lovejoy, "Samuel Hopkins."

20. Drake, *Quakers and Slavery*, 78–79.

21. New England Yearly Meeting Collection, Rhode Island Monthly Meeting, Box 10, Microfilm Reel 1 of 7, RIHS.

22. Manumission record of Robert Lawton to Samuel, New England Yearly Meeting Collection, Rhode Island Monthly Meeting, Box 10, Microfilm Reel 1 of 7, RIHS.

23. "To the Printer of the United States Chronicle You Are Desired to Republish the Enclosed," *United States Chronicle*, October 27, 1784, [1].

24. Ibid.

25. John Ferguson, *Memoir of the Life and Character of Rev. Samuel Hopkins D.D. Formerly the Pastor of the First Congregational Church in Newport, Rhode Island* (Boston: L. W. Kimball, 1830), 9–14.

26. In 1769, largely because of his strict Calvinistic beliefs, Hopkins lost the support of his congregants in Massachusetts. They were so disillusioned with him that they refused to contribute to his salary. Hopkins planned to farm to support his family. However, before he could plant his first field, he received an invitation to preach in Newport. Sheryl A. Kujawa, "'The Path of Duty Plain': Samuel Hopkins, Sarah Osborn and Revolutionary Newport," *Rhode Island History* 58, no. 3 (2000): 75–89; Joseph Conforti, "Samuel Hopkins and the Revolutionary Antislavery Movement," *Rhode Island History* 38, no. 2 (1979): 39–49.

27. See Conforti, "Samuel Hopkins," 40.

28. Bryan Rommel-Ruiz, "Colonizing the Black Atlantic," *Slavery and Abolition* 27, no. 3 (December 2006): 349–65; Ferguson, *Memoir*, 87.

29. Ferguson, *Memoir*, 85–86.

30. John Russell Bartlett, trans., *Records of the Colony of Rhode Island and Providence Plantations in New England*, vol. 7, *1770–1776* (New York: AMS Press, 1968), 251–52.

31. Ibid., 251–53.

32. The vast majority of African Americans threw their support behind the British when in 1775 Lord Dunmore issued a proclamation offering freedom in exchange for service; thousands of African Americans joined his ranks. Douglass Egerton, *Death or Liberty: African Americans and Revolutionary America* (Oxford: Oxford University Press, 2009), 6.

33. Pete Maslowski, "National Policy toward the Use of Black Troops in the Revolution," *South Carolina Historical Magazine*, 73, no. 1 (1972): 1–17.

34. Benjamin Quarles, *The Negro in the American Revolution* (Chapel Hill: University of North Carolina Press, 1961), ix.

35. Philip S. Foner, *Blacks in the American Revolution* (Westport, CT: Greenwood Press, 1976), 59.

36. Quarles, *Negro*, viii–xi.

37. Lorenzo Greene, "Some Observations on the Black Regiment of Rhode Island in the American Revolution," *Journal of Negro History* 37, no. 2 (April 1952): 142–72.

38. Foner, *Blacks*, 57–59.

39. Berlin, *Many Thousands Gone: The First Two Centuries of Slavery in North America* (Cambridge, MA: Harvard University Press, 1998), 230.

40. Foner, *Blacks*, 58.

41. Quarles, *Negro*, 73.

42. While these previously oppressed men were commissioned to fight for freedom, their monetary value was also assessed. A committee of five consisting of one representative from each county was to set a price for each man after he passed muster. Slaves were valued between £30 and £120, depending on their skill, age, and ability. John Russell Bartlett, trans., *Records of the State of Rhode Island and Providence Plantations in New England*, vol. 8, *1776–1779* (New York: AMS Press, 1968), 360. Greene, "Some Observations," 166.

43. Bartlett, *Records*, 8:359.

44. Ibid., 8:359–60.

45. Greene, "Some Observations," 161.

46. The specific date is not noted in the records. Bartlett, *Records*, 8:361.

47. Ibid.

48. Ibid.

49. Greene, "Some Observations," 163.

50. The General Assembly appointed Thomas Wells, John Smith, Benjamin Howland, Stephen Steere, Joseph Noyes, Nathan Miller, and Abraham Lippitt to report on the matter of emancipation. I have been unable to find any such report in the colonial records. John Russell Bartlett, trans., *Records of the State of Rhode Island and Providence Plantations in New England*, vol. 9, *1780–1783* (New York: AMS Press, 1968), 735; Bartlett, *Records*, 10:7–8; *United States Chronicle*, January 1, 1784, 3.

51. Egerton, *Death or Liberty*, 109–10; Arthur Zilversmit, *The First Emancipation: The Abolition of Slavery in the North* (Chicago: University of Chicago Press, 1967), 120–21; Charles Rappleye, *Sons of Providence: The Brown Brothers, the Slave Trade, and the American Revolution* (New York: Simon and Schuster, 2006), 226–29.

52. Bartlett, *Records*, 10:7.

53. Individual towns were responsible for supporting and educating freed children until age eighteen for females and twenty-one for males. Ibid.

54. Ibid., 10:132.

55. The state did not appoint an individual, committee, or commission to ensure that slaveholders adhered to the law. The Providence Society for

Promoting the Abolition of Slavery was a self-appointed gatekeeper of the gradual emancipation law. This private organization did the job the state should have been doing. They brought suit against questionable claims of ownership, and they policed their neighbors' attempts to sell indentured and apprenticed African Americans out of the state. Providence Abolition Society Minute Meetings, Moses Brown Papers, RIHS.

56. A manumission of Nab by Henry Reynolds, March 1, 1784, Reynolds Family Papers, MSS 663, Folder dated 1774–1787, RIHS. See also Joanne Pope Melish, "The Manumission of Nab," *Rhode Island History* 68, no. 1 (Winter/ Spring 2010): 36–41.

57. Edgar J. McManus, *Black Bondage in the North* (Syracuse, NY: Syracuse University Press, 1973), 203–5.

58. Berlin, *Many Thousands Gone*, 372.

59. Herbert Aptheker, *The Negro in the American Revolution* (New York: International Publishers, 1940), 5–8.

60. Most of the runaway ads include date of escape, owner, and place of escape, as well as the name, age, sex, and physical description of the slave. They differentiate between slaves, indentured servants, and apprentices. Maureen Alice Taylor and John Wood Sweet, eds., *Runaways, Deserters, and Notorious Villains from Rhode Island Newspapers*, vol. 2, *Additional Notices from the Providence Gazette, 1762–1800, as Well as Advertisements from All Other Rhode Island Newspapers from 1732–1800* (Rockport, ME: Picton Press, 2001). A curiously high number of enslaved people fled in the five years prior to the outbreak of the war. Some historians have attributed runaways after 1772 to a response to the *Somerset* case, in which slavery was deemed to be inconsistent with English common law. William R. Cotter, "The Somerset Case and the Abolition of Slavery in England," *History: The Journal of the Historical Association* 79, no. 225 (February 1994): 31–54.

61. Irene Burnham et al., *Creative Survival: The Providence Black Community in the Nineteenth Century* (Providence: RIBHS, 1985), 32.

62. Rhode Island Quakers kept a record of their members' manumissions; the emancipations were indexed according to the slaveholder's last name. Slave Manumissions, 1708–1827, New England Yearly Meeting Collection, Rhode Island Monthly Meeting, Box 10, Microfilm Reel 1 of 7, RIHS.

63. Two slaves were freed in exchange for cash; two were freed in return for loyal service; one was freed as a death request; 18 were freed for religious reasons.

64. Manumission Record of Hannah Rivera to Phyllis, New England Yearly Meeting Collection, Rhode Island Monthly Meeting, Box 10, Microfilm Reel 1 of 7, RIHS.

65. Manumission Record of Daniel Weeden to Caesar, New England Yearly Meeting Collection, Rhode Island Monthly Meeting, Box 10, Microfilm Reel 1 of 7, RIHS.

66. Manumission Records of John Bowen to Experience, Benjamin, Daniel and Freelove, New England Yearly Meeting Collection, Rhode Island Monthly Meeting, Box 10, Microfilm Reel 1 of 7, RIHS.

67. Bartlett, *Records,* 8:358–60.

68. Greene, "Some Observations," 157.

69. The number of soldiers that served in the Rhode Island First is difficult to nail down. Charles Battle, a local Rhode Island historian, claims that 210 men were enlisted; historian Bernard Nalty asserts that 150 men served, and according to Debra Newman Ham's list of black servicemen, complied from the War Department Collection of Revolutionary Records, 115 blacks were enlisted in the Rhode Island First. On the other hand, Philip Foner and Lorenzo Greene, relying on incomplete muster rolls, treasurer lists, payrolls, and casualty lists, claim that between 225 and 250 black men enlisted. I am inclined toward the number given by Greene and Foner because they relied on not only War Department records but also muster rolls, treasurer lists, payrolls, and casualty lists. Charles A. Battle, *Negroes on the Island of Rhode Island* (N.p.: n.p., 1932), 10; Debra Newman Ham, *List of Black Servicemen Compiled for the War Department Collection of Revolutionary War Department Records* [microfilm] (Washington, DC: National Archives and Records Service Administration, 1974); Bernard Nalty, "Record of Valor: Black Soldiers before Independence," *American Visions* 3, no. 4 (1988): 18–27; Greene, "Some Observations," 164–65.

70. African Americans, free and enslaved, were motivated to fight by the promise of both literal and political freedom; they served officially and unofficially. For example, in Massachusetts, black soldiers were enlisted in 1775 and 1776, although the state did not legally allow for their enlistment until 1778. It is nearly impossible to determine exactly how many slaves or free blacks served in the various state militias because each state had different policies and time lines for accepting or rejecting black soldiers; and perhaps more importantly, each state had different policies for keeping track of how many black men served. Foner, *Blacks,* 58.

71. Battle, *Negroes,* 14.

72. Greene, "Some Observations," 172.

73. The state of Vermont ended lifelong slavery in 1777, six years later, in 1783, the Massachusetts Supreme Court declared slavery unconstitutional; however, the burden of action was on the enslaved. In 1780, the Pennsylvania state legislature passed the nation's first gradual emancipation law, and legislators in Rhode Island and Connecticut followed in 1784. New York and New Jersey were among the last northern states to pass gradual emancipation laws, in 1799 and 1804, respectively. New York (1827), Rhode Island (1842), and Connecticut (1848) all abolished slavery in the first half of the nineteenth century; the institution of slavery was never abolished in New Jersey or New Hampshire. Berlin, *Many Thousands Gone,* 232–33; Margot Minardi, *Making Slavery History: Abolitionism and the Politics of Memory in Massachusetts* (Oxford: Oxford University Press, 2010), 18–19, 125–31.

74. John Wood Sweet, "'More Than Tears:' The Ordeal of Abolition in Revolutionary New England," *Explorations in Early American Culture* 5 (2001): 151–52.

75. Melish, "Manumission of Nab."

76. Connecticut was the only other northern state to prohibit its citizens from participating in the slave trade. Bartlett, *Records*, 10:262–63.

77. Jay Coughtry, *The Notorious Triangle: Rhode Island and the African Slave Trade, 1700–1807* (Philadelphia: Temple University Press, 1981), 18.

78. Bartlett, *Records*, 10:262–63.

79. Coughtry, *Notorious Triangle*, 31.

80. Ibid., 28.

81. James Tallmadge, "An Oration upon the Infringement of Rights of Man, to Be Delivered at the Commencement of Rhode Island College," September 1798, John Carter Brown Library, 5.

82. Ibid., 13.

83. Ibid., 6, 7.

84. Brown University Steering Committee on Slavery and Justice, "Slavery and Justice Report," 2006, accessed December 17, 2014, www.brown.edu/Research/Slavery_Justice/; Walter C. Brunson, *The History of Brown University, 1764–1914* (Providence, RI: The University, 1914), 500.

85. From the colonial period college graduates exploited the links between higher education and the Atlantic economy, apprenticing under slave traders, ministers, lawyers, doctors, politicians, and merchants. In the antebellum era the wealth of the cotton planters funded the expansion of the education infrastructure in the North and the South. Craig Steven Wilder, *Ebony and Ivy: Race, Slavery, and the Troubled History of America's Universities* (New York: Bloomsbury Press, 2013).

86. Coughtry, *Notorious Triangle*, 28.

87. Several members of the DeWolf (sometimes spelled D'Wolf) family were prominent merchants in Bristol; their economic enterprises included slave trading, privateering, merchant marine, insurance, banking, and Cuban sugar and coffee plantations. Phoebe Simpson, "DeWolf Papers," RIHS.

88. Representative John Brown, a slaver who flouted the law, was instrumental in the approval and building of the Bristol Custom House. Cynthia Mestad Johnson, "James DeWolf: Slaving Practices, Business Enterprise and Politics" (MA thesis, California State University, 2010), 78–80; Coughtry, *Notorious Triangle*, 39.

89. Coughtry, *Notorious Triangle*, 58; Johnson, "James DeWolf," 40–50.

90. Johnson, "James DeWolf," 30, 37, 72–75, 85–94.

91. Providence Abolition Society Minute Meetings, February 20, 1789, Moses Brown Papers, RIHS.

92. Most of the members of the Society were Quakers, and Quakers from Massachusetts and Connecticut were often physically closer to meetings (both religious and abolitionist) in nearby Rhode Island. Bartlett, *Records*, 10:382.

93. Ibid.

94. See Rappleye, *Sons of Providence*.

95. Brown University Steering Committee, "Slavery and Justice Report."

96. Coughtry, *Notorious Triangle*, 28–32.

97. Trans-Atlantic Slave Trade Database, accessed December 16, 2014, www.slavevoyages.org/tast/index.faces.

98. Johnson, "James DeWolf," 92–111; Hugh Thomas, *The Slave Trade: The Story of the Atlantic Slave Trade, 1440–1870* (New York: Simon and Schuster, 1997); Jenny S. Martinez, *The Slave Trade and the Origins of International Human Rights Law* (Oxford: Oxford University Press, 2012).

Notes to Chapter 4

1. As the title of his memoir suggests, Cato Pearce was did not write his own story but dictated it; the writer/publisher of his memoir chose to remain anonymous. Cato Pearce, *A Brief Memoir of the Life and Religious Experience of Cato Pearce, A Man of Color. Taken Verbatim From His Lips and Published for His Benefit* (Pawtucket, RI, 1842), 5.

2. See Joanne Pope Melish, *Disowning Slavery: Gradual Emancipation and "Race" in New England, 1780–1860* (Ithaca, NY: Cornell University Press, 1998); William Wieck, "The Statutory Law of Slavery and Race in the Thirteen Mainland Colonies of British America," *William and Mary Quarterly*, 3rd ser., 34, no. 2 (1977): 258–80.

3. Pearce, *Brief Memoir*, 5; "Ten Dollars Reward," *United States Chronicle*, March 10, 1796.

4. Christian McBurney, *Jailed for Preaching: The Autobiography of Cato Pearce, a Freed Slave from Washington County, Rhode Island with an Historical Introduction by Christian M. McBurney* (Kingstown, RI: Pettaquamscutt Historical Society, 2006), 4–10.

5. Pearce, *Brief Memoir*, 5–6, 15–31; see also McBurney, *Jailed for Preaching*, 1–25.

6. Christian M. McBurney, "Cato Pearce's Memoir: A Rhode Island Slave Narrative," *Rhode Island History* 67, no. 1 (Spring 2009): 12–16.

7. First Census of the United States, Rhode Island, 1790, US Census Bureau, www.census.gov/history/www/through_the_decades/overview/1790. html; Fourth Census of the United States, Rhode Island, 1820, https://archive.org/details/1820_census; Fifth Census of the United States, Rhode Island, 1830, https://archive.org/details/populationsc18300168unit; Sixth Census of the United States, Rhode Island, 1840, https://archive.org/details/populationsch1840504unit.

8. Leonard P. Curry, *The Free Black in Urban America, 1800–1850: The Shadow of the Dream* (Chicago: University of Chicago Press, 1981), 246–57.

9. Following the American Revolution, members of the DeWolf family were responsible for a third of the slave trade commerce in Rhode Island. Johnson, "James DeWolf," 12–15, 32, 47–54.

10. Sowande' Mustakeem, "'She Must Go Overboard and Shall Go Overboard': Diseased Bodies and the Spectacle of Murder at Sea," *Atlantic Studies* 8, no. 3 (September 2011): 301–2.

11. Marcus Redicker has suggested that the entire trial in St. Eustatius was orchestrated by DeWolf in an attempt to avoid a real trial in Rhode Island. Isaac Manchester went on to captain several DeWolf ships after the trial. Marcus Redicker, *The Slave Ship: A Human History* (New York: Viking, 2007), 343–45; Johnson, "James DeWolf," 41–75.

12. McBurney, "Cato Pearce's Memoir," 4.

13. Frederick Douglass was one of the first enslaved people to provide a detailed description of "negro cloth" and how it was allotted. Frederick Douglass, *Narrative of the Life of Frederick Douglass: An American Slave Written by Himself* (New York: Signet, 1997), 26; Myron O. Stachiw, "'For the Sake of Commerce': Slavery, Antislavery, and Northern Industry," in *The Meaning of Slavery in the North*, ed. David R. Roediger and Martin Henry Blatt (New York: Garland, 1998), 33–36; Myron Stachiw, *"For the Sake of Commerce": Rhode Island, Slavery and the Textile Industry: An Essay to Accompany the Exhibit "The Loom and the Lash: Northern Industry and Southern Slavery,"* pamphlet (Providence: RIHS, 1982), 10.

14. Rowland Hazard Sr. was the first American to employ water power for carding wool and using power looms. Tony Horowitz, "La Chanson de Roland: A Short History of Peace Dale Rhode Island," student paper, January 23, 1977, RIHS; Stachiw, "'For the Sake of Commerce,'" 33–36.

15. Enslaved African Americans in the southern United States produced the bulk of the world's cotton and almost all of the cotton consumed by the US textile industry during the antebellum era (1820–65). Of the 2.3 million slaves in the American South in 1850, nearly 2 million were involved in cotton cultivation. Northerners, especially New Yorkers, were buying, selling, and shipping it. By 1860, cotton represented more than half of all US exports, and Lower Manhattan was populated with cotton brokers, bankers, merchants, shippers, auctioneers, and insurers who profited from that export. Only New York banks were big enough to extend massive lines of credit to plantation owners so they could buy seed, farming equipment, and slaves. New York was also home to water and rail transportation companies that shipped cotton from the South to the North and abroad. Over the nineteenth century, the textile industry transformed northern towns. In 1816, large-scale textile factories employed 1 percent of the New England workforce; thirty-six years later, in 1852, the industry employed 14 percent of the labor force, and by 1860 New England was home to 472 cotton mills. These textile factories were often the sole employers in towns throughout the region and were a direct link between New England wealth and southern slaveholding. Ronald Bailey, "Those Valuable People, the Africans," in Roediger and Blatt, *Meaning of Slavery*, 13; Jacqueline Jones, *American Work: Black and White Labor* (New York: Norton, 1998), 160; Anne Farrow, Joel Lang, and Jenifer Frank, *Complicity: How the North Promoted, Prolonged, and Profited from Slavery* (New York: Ballantine Books, 2005), 4–23; Mary Blewett, *Constant Turmoil: The Politics of Industrial Life in Nineteenth-Century New England* (Amherst: University of Massachusetts Press, 2000); Jonathan Prude, *The Coming of Industrial Order, Town and Factory Life in Rural Massachusetts, 1810–1860* (Cambridge: Cambridge University Press, 1983); and Steve Dunwell, *The Run of the Mill: A Pictorial Narrative of the Expansion, Dominion, Decline and Enduring Impact of the New England Textile Industry* (Boston: David R. Godine, 1978).

16. Gavin Wright, *Slavery and American Economic Development* (Baton Rouge: Louisiana State University Press, 2006).

17. Christy Clark-Pujara, "The Business of Slavery and Antislavery Sentiment: The Case of Rowland Gibson Hazard—An Antislavery 'Negro Cloth' Dealer," *Rhode Island History* 71, no. 2 (Summer/Fall 2013): 35–56.

18. Mary Peace Hazard was born and raised in South Carolina. Her parents, Isaac Peace and Elizabeth Gibson, were originally from Barbados, an old and established slave society. Rick Stattler, "Guide to Rowland and Mary (Peace) Hazard Papers," 1997, RIHS. See also Caroline E. Robinson, *The Hazard Family of Rhode Island; Being a Genealogy and History of the Descendants of Thomas Hazard, with Sketches of the Worthies of the Family, and Anecdotes Illustrative of Their Traits and Also of the Times in Which They Lived* (Boston: Printed for the Author, 1896), 77–78. The Hazard brothers' success in the textile industry provided funding for their other business interests, including a general store in Providence, part ownership in Pier Railroads (Providence, Stonington, and Narragansett), and the Wisconsin Central Railroad. Horowitz, "Chanson de Roland," 4–6. Also see "Historic and Architectural Resources of South Kingstown, Rhode Island: A Preliminary Report" (Providence: Rhode Island Historical Preservation Commission, 1984), and the Peace Dale Manufacturing Company Records, Baker Library Historical Collections, Harvard Business School.

19. Rowland Gibson Hazard to Isaac Peace Hazard, February 15, 1835, Isaac P. Hazard Papers, MSS 483, sg 12, Box 2, Folder 7, RIHS; Rowland Gibson Hazard to Agents in New Orleans, January 1836, Rowland G. and Caroline (Newbold) Hazard Papers, MSS 483, sg 5, Box 2, Folder 21, RIHS; Isaac Peace Hazard to Rowland Gibson Hazard, January 13, 1836, Isaac P. Hazard Papers, MSS 483, sg 12, Box 2, Folder 25, RIHS; Rowland Gibson Hazard to Jonathan Bouses, "By Direction of James Hamilton," August 11 1828, Isaac P. Hazard Papers, MSS 483, sg 12, Box 1, RIHS.

20. Caroline Hazard, ed., *Economics and Politics: A Series of Papers upon Public Questions Written on Various Occasions from 1840 to 1885 by Rowland Gibson Hazard, LL.D.* (Boston: Houghton Mifflin, 1889), 26–30.

21. See Wright, *Slavery*.

22. Clark-Pujara, "Business of Slavery."

23. I exclusively use *people of color* when I am referring to specific segments of the population like transients, those warned out of towns, and seamen, because they were identified by both state officials and individuals themselves as black, Indian, "mustee" and "mulatto," or various mixtures. I use *black*, *African American*, or *people of color* when referring to the black population in general.

24. Despite the ban on interracial marriages, the 1860 census record acknowledges seven interracial couples residing in the city. Robert J. Cottrol, *The Afro-Yankees: Providence's Black Community in the Antebellum Era* (Westport, CT: Greenwood Press, 1982), 131.

25. Jones, *American Work*, 163.

26. Ibid., 238.

27. Many historians and scholars have contended this for decades. Shane White, *Somewhat More Independent: The End of Slavery in New York City,*

1770–1810 (Athens: University of Georgia Press, 1991); Gary B. Nash and Jean R. Soderlund, *Freedom by Degrees: Emancipation in Pennsylvania and Its Aftermath* (New York: Oxford University Press, 1991); James Horton and Lois Horton, *In Hope of Liberty: Culture, Community, and Protest among Northern Free Blacks, 1700–1860* (New York: Oxford University Press, 1997).

28. Catherine Adams and Elizabeth H. Pleck, *Love of Freedom: Black Women in Colonial and Revolutionary New England* (New York: Oxford University Press, 2010), 11–12.

29. Irene Burnham et al., *Creative Survival: The Providence Black Community in the Nineteenth Century* (Providence: RIBHS, 1985), 46–47.

30. Frances Harriet Green, *Memoirs of Elleanor Eldridge, 1784–1845* (Chapel Hill: University of North Carolina Press, 2000); Jennifer D. Brody and Sharon P. Holland, "An/Other Case of New England Underwriting: Negotiating Race and Property in Memoirs of Elleanor Eldridge," in *Crossing Waters, Crossing Worlds: The African Diaspora in Indian Country*, ed. Tiya Miles and Sharon P. Holland (Durham, NC: Duke University Press, 2006); Jane Lancaster, "A Web of Iniquity? Race, Gender, Foreclosure and Respectability in Antebellum Rhode Island," *Rhode Island History* 69, no. 2 (Summer/Fall 2011): 72–92.

31. Curry, *Free Black*.

32. Lydia Pecker, "'A View of Power': People of Color in Antebellum Providence, Rhode Island" (BA honors thesis, Brown University, 2003), 35–40.

33. Cottrol, *Afro-Yankees*, 121–30.

34. Burnham et al., *Creative Survival*, 40–51; Richard C. Youngken, *African Americans in Newport: An Introduction to the Heritage of African Americans in Newport, Rhode Island, 1700–1945* (Providence: Rhode Island Historical Preservation and Heritage Commission, RIBHS, 1998); Cottrol, *Afro-Yankees*, 119–21.

35. W. Jeffrey Bolster, "To Feel Like a Man: Black Seamen in the Northern States, 1800–1860," *Journal of American History* 76, no. 4 (March 1990): 1174.

36. Jeffrey Howe, "Black and Indian Sailors Born in Rhode Island: Bristol Custom House Protection Papers," *Rhode Island Roots* 31 (June 2005): 91–98; Jeffrey Howe, "Black and Indian Sailors from Rhode Island: Bristol Crew Lists," *Rhode Island Roots* 31 (September 2005): 143–55; Jeffrey Howe, "Black and Indian Sailors Born in Rhode Island: New London, Connecticut Protection Records," *Rhode Island Roots* 31 (December 2005) 196–200; Jeffrey Howe, "Black and Indian Sailors Born in Rhode Island: From New Bedford Custom House Protection Oaths, 1837–1857," *Rhode Island Roots* 32 (March 2006): 43–44; Jeffrey Howe, "Black and Indian Sailors from Rhode Island: New Bedford Crew Lists," *Rhode Island Roots* 32 (June 2006): 91–93; Jeffrey Howe, "Black and Indian Sailors from Rhode Island: From Providence Customs House Records (Part 1, A-C)," *Rhode Island Roots* 32 (September 2006): 156–63; Jeffrey Howe, "Black and Indian Sailors from Rhode Island: From Providence Customs House Records (Part 2, D-J)," *Rhode Island Roots* 32 (December 2006): 197–207; Jeffrey Howe, "Black and Indian Sailors from Rhode Island: From Providence Customs House Records (Part 3, K-Y)," *Rhode Island Roots* 33 (March 2007): 34–49.

37. Martha S. Putney, "Black Merchant Seamen of Newport, 1803–1865: A Case Study in Foreign Commerce," *Journal of Negro History* 57, no. 2 (April 1972): 157, 166.

38. W. Jeffrey Bolster, *Black Jacks: African American Seamen in the Age of Sail* (Cambridge, MA: Harvard University Press, 1997), 73.

39. Bolster, "To Feel Like a Man," 1178–91, 1197.

40. Nash and Soderlund, *Freedom by Degrees*; White, *Somewhat More Independent*; Elise Virginia Lemire, *Black Walden: Slavery and Its Aftermath in Concord, Massachusetts* (Philadelphia: University of Pennsylvania Press, 2009).

41. Billy G. Smith, ed., *Down and Out in Early America* (University Park: Pennsylvania State University Press, 2004), 7–9, xviii.

42. Rhode Island officials were more concerned about the indigent population than their neighbors because so many Rhode Island men made their living as seamen and were more likely to die and leave their families destitute. Ruth Wallis Herndon, "Women of 'No Particular Home': Town Leaders and Female Transients in Rhode Island, 1750–1800," in *Women and Freedom in Early America*, ed. Larry D. Eldridge (New York: New York University Press, 1997), 269–87; Ruth Wallis Herndon, "'Who Died an Expence to This Town': Poor Relief in 18th-Century Rhode Island," in Smith, *Down and Out*, 132–39; Adams and Pleck, *Love of Freedom*, 150–61.

43. Herndon, "'Who Died an Expence,'" 147.

44. I use Providence Town Council Records from two separate depositories: the RIHS and the RIBHS. The papers from the RIHS are from the original town council books, while the papers from the RIBHS are copies from an unknown source. The minutes from the RIHS include removal orders, complaints, indentures, fines, receipts, and warrants dating from 1751 to 1830. The minutes from the RIBHS contain residency exams dating from 1755 to 1800. Bonds for Hope, who was identified as a mulatto, and Thomas Angol, March 27, 1708, in the Providence Town Papers, MSS 214, ser. 2, vol. 3, #0931, RIHS.

45. Crane asserts that the Revolutionary War destroyed the Newport economy–its population was reduced by half and the physical destruction of the city was devastating. There was also a housing shortage despite the decline in population. Elaine Forman Crane, *A Dependent People: Newport, Rhode Island in the Revolutionary Era* (New York: Fordham University Press, 1985), 126–40.

46. Youngken, *African Americans in Newport*, 23.

47. Overseer of the Poor Report, December 1819 and June 1820, Providence Town Papers, MSS 214, vol. 105, #0034531, RIHS.

48. Melish has argued that this type of racial ambiguity in warned-out records is evidence of passive resistance on the part of some free people of color. They refused to "engage in the racial naming game" by clarifying their racial identities for town clerks. Melish, *Disowning Slavery*, 239.

49. Order of removal for Jane Whipple, October 1, 1787, Providence Town Minutes, Folder: Residency Exams, Providence Blacks, 1787–1799, RIBHS.

50. Hilda Abbey residency exam, November 7, 1787, Providence Town Minutes, Folder: Residency Exams, Providence Blacks, 1787–1799, RIBHS.

51. Bristol Rhodes residency exam, September 9, 1794, Providence Town Minutes, Folder: Residency Exams, Providence Blacks, 1787–1799, RIBHS.

52. In the eighteenth century, *transient* referred not to a traveler or homeless person but to an individual who was living in a town without legal residency. Ruth Wallis Herndon, "Women," 270.

53. Order of removal for Prince Thurston, June 5, 1793, Providence Town Papers, MSS 214, vol. 18, #7980, RIHS.

54. Order of removal for Cato Gardner, October 6, 1796, Providence Town Papers, MSS 214, vol. 26, #11261, RIHS; order of removal for Mary Ceasar, September 5, 1796, Providence Town Papers, MSS 214, vol. 26, #11401 and 2, RIHS; order of removal for Watty Greene, December 17, 1794, Providence Town Papers, MSS 214, vol. 23, #10142, RIHS; orders of expulsion for Cuff Roberts and family, John Thomas, Lucy Gardner, Newport Kelly and wife, October 9, 1806, Providence Town Papers, MSS 214, vol. 60, #008728, RIHS; orders of expulsion for Mary/Martha Ceasar and her daughters Martha (12), Clarissa (8) and Fanny (2), Providence Town Papers, MSS 214, vol. 60, #008746, RIHS.

55. Complaint about Moses Staunton, April 27, 1826, "Providence Town Papers," MSS 214, vol. 88, #0024971, RIHS; indenture lease for Cuff Robard, September 21, 1795, Providence Town Papers, MSS 214, vol. 23, #10059, RIHS.

56. Warrant for Patience Ingraham via Nancy Brown, alias Nancy Clarkson, July 23, 1780, Providence Town Papers, MSS 214, vol. 6, #2745, RIHS.

57. Notice for Ishmael Brown, John Hex, Jack Greene, and Samuel Strange, September 7, 1789, Providence Town Papers, MSS 214, vol. 12, #5260, RIHS.

58. Cottrol, *Afro-Yankees*, 48.

59. Gilje excludes criminal activity, uprisings, and rebellions in his definition of riots, which I adopt. Paul Gilje, *Rioting in America* (Bloomington: University of Indiana Press, 1996), 5, 87.

60. Ibid., 88–90.

61. David Grimstead, *American Mobbing, 1828–1860: Toward the Civil War* (New York: Oxford University Press, 1998), 4, 16.

62. Ibid., 173–75.

63. William J. Brown, *The Life of William J. Brown of Providence, Rhode Island, with Personal Recollections of the Incidents in Rhode Island* (Durham: University of New Hampshire Press, 2006), 18.

64. Gilje, *Rioting in America*, 5; Howard P. Chudacoff, "Social Turmoil and Governmental Reform in Providence, 1830–1832," *Rhode Island History* 31, no. 1 (1972): 21–32.

65. The Report of the 1824 Hardscrabble Riot is not a transcript of the court trial but a summation of the major arguments and comments made by lawyers, the judge, and witnesses. *Hard-Scrabble Calendar Report of the Trials of Oliver Cummins, Nathaniel G. Metcalf, Gilbert Humes, and Arthur Farrier; Who Were Indicted with Six Other for a Riot, And for Aiding in Pulling Down a Dwelling House, on the 18th of October at Hard-Scrabble* (Providence, RI: Printed for the Purchaser, 1824), Rider Collection, Box 217 no. 11, Brown University Hay Library.

66. Burnham et al., *Creative Survival*, 40.

67. *Hardscrabble Calendar*.

68. Ibid., 5.

69. Ibid., 7–9.

70. Ibid., Introduction.

71. Ibid.

72. Burnham et al., *Creative Survival*, 59.

73. Charles Hoffman and Tess Hoffman, *North by South: The Two Lives of Richard James Arnold* (Athens: University of Georgia Press, 1988), 84–85.

74. The Committee's Report was published in the *Providence Daily Journal*. It was the official accounting of the Snowtown Riot. The report details the events as well as the damage caused by the riots. It is based on the testimonies of the sheriff, governor, militiamen, and witnesses (white). "Committee's Report," *Providence Daily Journal*, September 29, 1831.

75. Ibid.

76. Ibid.

77. Ibid.

78. Ibid.

79. Ibid.

80. Ibid.

81. "Town-Meeting Resolutions from September 25, 1831," *Providence Daily Journal*, September 29, 1831.

82. Hoffman and Hoffman, *North by South*, 88–89.

83. "Committee's Report."

84. *American Providence*, evening ed., September 24, 1831.

85. Ibid.

Notes to Chapter 5

1. William Robinson published and translated correspondence and meeting minutes of the Free African Union Society and the African Benevolent Society. Both record groups were presented to Colored Union Congregation Church in 1844 for safekeeping. The church handed them over to the Newport Historical Society in 1963. Anthony Taylor and Saimar Nubia to Cato Gardner and London Spear for all the Africans in Providence, December 24, 1787, in *The Proceedings of the Free African Union Society and the African Benevolent Society Newport Rhode Island 1780–1824*, ed. and trans. William Robinson (Providence: Urban League of Rhode Island, 1976), 19.

2. Hosea Easton claimed African, Wampanoag, and Narragansett heritage. Easton was a minister, lecturer, abolitionist, and writer; he was one of the most important intellectuals of his day. He was born free, of free parents in Middleborough, Massachusetts, in 1798; however, his ancestors had been enslaved by one of the founders of Newport, Rhode Island—Nicholas Easton. George R. Price and James Brewer Stewart, eds., *To Heal the Scourge of Prejudice: The Life and Writing of Hosea Easton* (Amherst: University of Massachusetts Press, 1999), 54.

3. Robert L. Harris Jr., "Early Black Benevolent Societies, 1780–1830," *Massachusetts Review* 20, no. 3 (1979): 603–25; Leslie M. Alexander, *African or American? Black Identity and Political Activism in New York City, 1784–1861* (Chicago: University of Illinois Press, 2008), preface; James Horton and Lois Horton, *In Hope of Liberty: Culture, Community, and Protest among Northern Free Blacks, 1700–1860* (New York: Oxford University Press, 1997).

4. Historian Leone Bennet Jr. described the period from 1787 to 1837 "as arguably the most important era in African American history." Historian Robert Harris also asserts that voluntary associations were the basis of black institutional life. Harris, "Early Black Benevolent Societies," 603–25.

5. Being a head of a household in the nineteenth century indicated that an individual was fairly economically stable. *1800 United States Census*, Newport, RI, Roll 46, p. 249, Image 102, Wisconsin Historical Society, Madison, WI.

6. Levine Street, in Newport, Rhode Island, was home to several middle-class free black Rhode Island families in the postcolonial period. Richard C. Youngken, *African Americans in Newport: An Introduction to the Heritage of African Americans in Newport, Rhode Island, 1700–1945* (Providence: Rhode Island Historical Preservation and Heritage Commission, RIBHS, 1998), 24–26.

7. Union members attended meetings quarterly, while committee members met monthly and the annual meeting took place every August. The committee consisted of a president, a vice president, a judge, a secretary, a treasurer, and twelve representatives. At the invitation of the Newport organization, a second chapter of FAUS was established in Providence (FAUS–PVD) in 1789. Caesar Lyndon (by order of the president Anthony Taylor) to Cato Gardner and London Spear, August 24, 1789, in Robinson, *Proceedings*, 23.

8. Harris, "Early Black Benevolent Societies," 611–13.

9. The separation of black male and female groups simply reflects gender conventions of the time. James Oliver Horton, "Freedom's Yoke: Gender Conventions among Antebellum Free Blacks," *Feminist Studies* 12, no. 1 (1986): 66; Irene Burnham et al., *Creative Survival: The Providence Black Community in the Nineteenth Century* (Providence: RIBHS, 1985), 52.

10. Youngken, *African Americans in Newport*, 23.

11. Newport Gardner to Arthur Tikey [*sic* Taylor], July 26, 1794, and Newport Gardner to Unknown, December 9, 1793, both in Robinson, *Proceedings*, 42–43, 47.

12. Lymas Keith on behalf of FAUS to Kingston Pease, March 4, 1791; Caesar Lyndon to Kingston Pease, July 28, 1792; and Kingston Pease to Caesar Lyndon, August 7, 1792, all in Robinson, *Proceedings*, 37–40.

13. See Horton, "Freedom's Yoke," 51–76.

14. The men of FAUS were demonstrating the same kind of "politics of respectability" as discussed in Evelyn Higginbotham's study of female participation in the black church. See Evelyn Brooks Higginbotham, *Righteous Discontent: The Women's Movement in the Black Baptist Church, 1880–1920* (Cambridge, MA: Harvard University Press, 1993); Horton, "Freedom's Yoke," 65.

15. FAUS to Prince Hall, n.d., but a reply to Hall's letter of September 16, 1789, in Robinson, *Proceedings*, 29.

16. Alexander, *African or American?*, xiv; Patrick Rael, *Black Identity and Black Protest in the Antebellum North* (Chapel Hill: University of North Carolina Press, 2002).

17. Gardner was the first black musician acknowledged within the mainstream community as a professional musician and singing school master. He was instrumental in establishing FAUS, served as a sexton in Samuel Hopkins's church, and was a teacher in the African Benevolent Society School. He retained his mother's tongue and spoke it fluently his entire life. "Newport Gardner, 1746–1826," *Black Perspective in Music* 4, no. 2 (July 1976): 202–7; John Ferguson, *Memoir of the Life and Character of Rev. Samuel Hopkins, D.D.: Formerly Pastor of the First Congregational Church in Newport, Rhode Island* (Boston: L. W. Kimball, 1830).

18. Youngken, *African Americans in Newport*, 24–28.

19. Ibid.

20. James Campbell, *Middle Passages: African American Journeys to Africa, 1787–2005* (New York: Penguin Press, 2006), 20.

21. George E. Brooks, "The Providence African Society's Sierra Leone Emigration Scheme, 1794–1795: Prologue to The African Colonization Movement," *International Journal of African Historical Studies* 7, no. 2 (1974): 185–87.

22. Anthony Taylor and Saimar Nubia to Cato Gardner and London Spear for all the Africans in Providence, December 24, 1787, in Robinson, *Proceedings*, 19.

23. Alexander, *African or American?*, 26–30.

24. *Boston Evening Post*, September 22, 1735.

25. Campbell, *Middle Passages*, 23.

26. Brooks, "Providence," 187–90.

27. Cecil Magbaily Fyle, *The History of Sierra Leone* (London: Evans Brothers, 1981), 34; Alexander Peter Kup, *Sierra Leone: A Concise History* (New York: St. Martin's Press, 1975).

28. Fyle, *History of Sierra Leone*, 36.

29. Bryan Rommel-Ruiz, "Colonizing the Black Atlantic," *Slavery and Abolition* 27, no. 3 (December 2006): 349–65.

30. Henry Noble Sherwood, "The Formation of the American Colonization Society," *Journal of Negro History* 2, no. 3 (1917): 209–28.

31. Trans-Atlantic Slave Trade Database, accessed December 18, 2014, www.slavevoyages.org/tast/index.faces; Brooks, "Providence," 184.

32. Louis R. Mehlinger, "The Attitude of the Free Negro toward African Colonization," *Journal of Negro History* 1, no. 3 (1916): 276–301.

33. Rommel-Ruiz, "Colonizing the Black Atlantic," 349–65.

34. Quamine died in 1779 serving on a ship; he was fighting for prize money to buy his wife's freedom. Brooks, "Providence," 186.

35. Thornton was born into a West Indian slaveholding family but denounced his wealth and human property and came to the United States and joined the abolition movement. Brooks, "Providence," 187.

36. C. Ford Peatross, ed., *Capital Drawings: Architectural Designs for Washington, D.C., from the Library of Congress* (Baltimore: Johns Hopkins University Press, 2005).

37. Joanne Pope Melish, *Disowning Slavery: Gradual Emancipation and "Race" in New England, 1780–1860* (Ithaca, NY: Cornell University Press, 1998), 192–98.

38. Brooks, "Providence," 183.

39. Anthony Taylor and Saimar Nubia to Cato Gardner and London Spear for all the Africans in Providence, December 24, 1787, in Robinson, *Proceedings*, 19.

40. Anthony Taylor to Unknown, December 24, 1787, in Robinson, *Proceedings*, 16. William Thornton was the son of a slaveholder who in his twenties decided to dedicate his life to abolition and the African colonization movement. "William Thornton and Negro Colonization," *Proceedings of the American Antiquarian Society* 30, no. 1 (April 14, 1921): 32–61.

41. FAUS (Providence) to FAUS (Newport), February 25, 1794, in Robinson, *Proceedings*, 45–46.

42. William Thornton to the Elders and Members of the Union Society, March 6, 1787, in Robinson, *Proceedings*, 17.

43. Samuel Stevens to Anthony Tiler [*sic* Taylor], June 1, 1787, in Robinson, *Proceedings*, 17–18.

44. Samuel Stevens to African Company at Boston, October 4, 1787, in Robinson, *Proceedings*, 18–19.

45. African Americans in Massachusetts and Rhode Island sought help from their local governments to settle in Africa. In 1774, blacks in Massachusetts requested that the colonial legislature emancipate them, with the hope that they would be able to leave the colony for someplace in Africa. Thirteen years later, in 1787, they petitioned the Massachusetts General Court for funds because they did not have the means to send a scout. Rommel-Ruiz, "Colonizing the Black Atlantic," 349. Samuel Stevens to Anthony Tiler [*sic* Taylor], Boston, June 1, 1787, and Anthony Taylor to Samuel Stevens and the African Company at Boston, November 4, 1787, both in Robinson, *Proceedings*, 17–19.

46. FAUS (Providence) to FAUS (Newport), January 15, 1794, in Robinson, *Proceedings*, 43.

47. FAUS (Newport) to FAUS (Providence), February 26, 1794, in Robinson, *Proceedings*, 46–47.

48. Owned by Nicholas Brown Jr., George Benson, and Thomas P. Ives, the *Charlotte* carried American rum, tobacco, lumber, and foodstuffs to Sierra Leone. Ship captain Martin Benson held Mackenzie in contempt, viewing him as a liability to the crew. Mackenzie had the support of Moses Brown and George Benson, so he was allowed passage and appointed second mate. See Brooks, "Providence," 192–94. FAUS (Newport) to FAUS (Providence) [A direct response to a letter sent on January 15, 1794], n.d., in Robinson, *Proceedings*, 44.

49. Brooks, "Providence," 196–97.

50. Burnham et al., *Creative Survival*, 54.

51. Brooks, "Providence," 183.

52. Youngken, *African Americans in Newport*, 23.

53. Frederick Cooper, "Elevating the Race: The Social Thought of Black Leaders, 1827–50," in *African American Activism before the Civil War*, ed. Patrick Rael (New York: Routledge, 2008), 58–60; Patrick Rael, *Black Identity and Black Protest in the Antebellum North* (Chapel Hill: University of North Carolina Press, 2002), 119–20; Alexander, *African or American?*, 1–8.

54. Minutes of a General Meeting of Africans 1807, in Robinson, *Proceedings*, 153.

55. Caleb J. Tenney (Clerk of Directors), Annual Directors' Report to the Society, December 31, 1809, in Robinson, *Proceedings*, 172.

56. Meeting Minutes of the ABS, 1808, in Robinson, *Proceedings*, 153.

57. Meeting Minutes of the ABS, January 17, 1810, Robinson, *Proceedings*, 169–71.

58. Rhode Island schools were legally desegregated in 1866. Lawrence Grossman, "George T. Downing and Desegregation of Rhode Island Public Schools," *Rhode Island History* 36, no. 4 (November 1977): 100–107.

59. In many rural towns African American students accounted for less than 1 or 2 percent of the total school-aged population. In the 1850s George T. Downing along with established local leaders led an unsuccessful campaign to integrate Rhode Island schools. Downing was the son of a successful New York restaurateur; he owned a luxury hotel in Newport and ran a catering business in Providence. Although the campaign was not successful, it laid the groundwork for future desegregation legislation in the 1860s. Robert J. Cottrol, *The Afro-Yankees: Providence's Black Community in the Antebellum Era* (Westport, CT: Greenwood Press, 1982), 90–101.

60. Meeting Minutes of the ABS, 1809, in Robinson, *Proceedings*, 159–62.

61. Meeting Minutes of the ABS, March 16, 1810, in Robinson, *Proceedings*, 157.

62. Youngken, *African Americans in Newport*, 49.

63. Patten delivered anti–slave trade sermons at the Second Congregation Church in Newport, Rhode Island. William Patten, *On the Inhumanity of the Slave Trade and the Importance of Correcting It: A Sermon Delivered in the Second Congregational Church, Newport, Rhode-Island, 12 August 1792* (Providence, RI: J. Carter, 1793).

64. Meeting Minutes of the ABS, January 13, 1809, in Robinson, *The Proceedings*, 154–162.

65. Obour Tanner was enslaved by a Newport silversmith, John Tanner. She was baptized in 1768 at First Congregational Church. She died on June 21, 1835. Catherine Adams and Elizabeth H. Pleck, *Love of Freedom: Black Women in Colonial and Revolutionary New England* (New York: Oxford University Press, 2010), 21, 91, 100. "Obour Tanner," *Blood at the Root*, n.d., accessed June 18, 2014, http://blogs.umb.edu/bloodrootdemo/people/enslaved/obour-tanner/.

66. Thomas B. Stockwell, *A History of Public Education in Rhode Island, 1636 to 1876* (Providence, RI: Providence Press, 1876), 30.

67. Ibid.

68. Meeting Minutes of the ABS, October 25, 1809, in Robinson, *Proceedings*, 165–66.

69. Meeting Minutes of the AFBS, January 20, 1810, in Robinson, *Proceedings*, 172–73.

70. Meeting Minutes of the ABS, February 21, 1814, Newport, and March 2, 1814, in Robinson, *Proceedings*, 182.

71. Meeting Minutes of the ABS, January 7, 1819, in Robinson, *Proceedings*, 186.

72. Meeting Minutes of the ABS, January 2, 1811, in Robinson, *Proceedings*, 174–75.

73. Meeting Minutes of the ABS, 1809, in Robinson, *Proceedings*, 159–62; Meeting Minutes of the ABS, January 29, 1812, in Robinson, *Proceedings*, 178.

74. Meeting Minutes of the ABS, January 3, 1816, in Robinson, *Proceedings*, 183–84.

75. Meeting Minutes of the ABS, March 6, 1816, in Robinson, *Proceedings*, *Proceedings*, 188.

76. Meeting Minutes of the ABS, March 6, 1816, in Robinson, *Proceedings*, 188.

77. Meeting Minutes of the ABS, January 3, 1822, in Robinson, *Proceedings*, 191.

78. Cottrol, *Afro-Yankees*, 60.

79. Moses Brown, *A Short History of the African Union Meeting and School House, Erected in Providence (R.I.) In the Years 1819, '20, '21: With Rule for Its Future Government* (Providence, RI: Brown and Danforth, 1821), 3.

80. Ibid., 4.

81. Ibid., 13.

82. Lydia Pecker, "'A View of Power': People of Color in Antebellum Providence, Rhode Island" (BA honors thesis, Brown University, 2003), 30.

83. The Prince Hall Freemasons probably participated in the dedication by performing a cornerstone ceremony. A branch of Prince Hall Masons was established in Rhode Island in 1790s, and one of the fraternity's primary functions in the black community was cornerstone laying at newly built churches, colleges, and schools. William A. Muraskin, *Middle-Class Blacks in a White Society: Prince Hall Freemasonry in America* (Berkeley: University of California Press, 1975), 34, 174; Burnham et al., *Creative Survival*, 56.

84. William J. Brown, *The Life of William J. Brown of Providence, Rhode Island, with Personal Recollections of the Incidents in Rhode Island* (Durham: University of New Hampshire Press, 2006), 47.

85. An official state-sanctioned black company was not raised until the Dorr Rebellion. Cottrol, *Afro-Yankees*, 76.

86. Free black New Yorkers were also creating African American culture. They created a distinctive style of language, dress, hairstyle, and even body movement (walks). Throughout the North, free blacks were pursuing their cultural independence. Shane White, *Somewhat More Independent: The End of*

Slavery in New York City, 1770–1810 (Athens: University of Georgia Press, 1991), 185–200.

87. Cultural historian Shane White asserts that parades, "with their overtly public and political cast, prominently, even intrusively, displayed the newly freed northern blacks to whites and to themselves as both African Americans and citizens of the new nation." Shane White, "'It Was a Proud Day': African Americans, Festivals, and Parades in the North, 1741–1834," *Journal of American History* 81, no. 1 (June 1994): 15–16.

88. W. Brown, *Life of William J. Brown*, 26.

89. Ibid., 27.

90. Burnham et al., *Creative Survival*, 57.

91. Historians Sterling Stuckey and Patrick Rael have identified major characteristics of black nationalist sentiment and ideology. Stuckey saw black nationalism as an acknowledgment of group oppression, a preference for African traits, a consciousness of the bonds of Africans everywhere, and an assertion that Africans must free themselves. Rael recognized three basic elements of black nationalism: group consciousness built on racial identity and pride, a desire to develop social and political institutions autonomous from those of whites, and the expression of a distinct black cultural heritage. Rael, *Black Identity*, 210; Sterling Stuckey, *The Ideological Origins of Black Nationalism* (Boston: Beacon Press, 1972), 5–7.

92. Alexander offers a fuller discussion of how black northerners, particularly in New York, which boasted the largest urban black population, used the term *African* politically. Alexander, *African or American?*, 83–84.

93. Anthony Taylor and Saimar Nubia to Cato Gardner and London Spear for all the Africans in Providence, December 24, 1787, in Robinson, *Proceedings*, 19.

94. Tommie Shelby, "Two Conceptions of Black Nationalism: Martin Delany on the Meaning of Black Political Solidarity," *Political Theory* 3, no. 5 (October 2003): 665.

95. Stuckey, *Ideological Origins*, 3.

96. The group had been in Liberia for only a few months before a yellow fever outbreak wiped out their small community. Brooks, "Providence," 202; Charles Hoffman and Tess Hoffman, *North by South: The Two Lives of Richard James Arnold* (Athens: University of Georgia Press, 1988), 87.

97. J. Stanley Lemons and Michael A. McKenna, "Re-enfranchisement of Rhode Island Negroes," *Rhode Island History* 30 (February 1971): 4; Robert Glenn Sherer Jr., "Negro Churches in Rhode Island before 1860," *Rhode Island History* 25, no. 9 (January 1966): 9–25; Burnham et al., *Creative Survival*, 57.

98. Cottrol, *Afro-Yankees*, 49.

Notes to Chapter 6

1. The members of the Third Battalion pooled their money "to buy a printing press, type, and all the materials to print a small newspaper." A semimonthly paper, the *Black Warrior*, was printed at Fort Parapet starting sometime in

1864. The paper ran, according to one proud soldier, "for a long time." Above the title ran a succinct banner: "Freedom to All. Death to Copperheads and Traitors." Nelson Viall, "Fourteenth Rhode Island Heavy Artillery (Colored)," October 20, 1891, Soldiers and Sailors Historical Society, MSS 723, folder 18, pp. 20 and 22, RIHS. A page of the *Black Warrior* was reprinted in the history of the Rhode Island Fourteenth. William H. Chenery, *The Fourteenth Regiment Rhode Island Heavy Artillery (Colored), 1861–1865* (Providence, RI: Snow and Farnham, 1898), 49.

2. Robert J. Cottrol, *The Afro-Yankees: Providence's Black Community in the Antebellum Era* (Westport, CT: Greenwood Press, 1982), 70–74.

3. J. Stanley Lemons and Michael A. McKenna, "Re-enfranchisement of Rhode Island Negroes," *Rhode Island History* 30 (February 1971): 7; Patrick T. Conley, *The Dorr Rebellion: Rhode Island's Crisis in Constitutional Government* (Providence: Rhode Island Bicentennial Foundation,1976), 1–3.

4. William J. Brown, *The Life of William J. Brown of Providence, Rhode Island, with Personal Recollections of the Incidents in Rhode Island* (Durham: University of New Hampshire Press, 2006), 48–49.

5. Rhode Island's property qualification for voting was unique. The vast majority of the states had dropped property requirements in the first three decades of the nineteenth century. On the other hand, like many northern states Rhode Island banned or restricted blacks from voting. For example, the state of New York had a property qualification only for black men, and in 1817 Connecticut eliminated black voting entirely. Lemons and McKenna, "Re-enfranchisement," 2–3; Cottrol, *Afro-Yankees*, 79.

6. "Do nothing" constitutional conventions in 1824 and 1834 failed to reform or replace the outdated 1663 Charter that restricted the vote and reaffirmed the power of state legislatures. Cottrol, *Afro-Yankees*, 70–74.

7. The petition was signed by James Hazard, Ransom Parker, Ichabod Northup, Samuel Rodman, and George Smith. Lemons and McKenna, "Re-enfranchisement," 8.

8. Ibid., 9.

9. Cottrol, *Afro-Yankees*, 74–77; Conley, *Dorr Rebellion*, 3–7.

10. Conley, *Dorr Rebellion*, 3–7.

11. In 1851 a Democratic General Assembly overturned Dorr's conviction. Conley, *Dorr Rebellion*, 6–12.

12. Cottrol, *Afro-Yankees*, 76; Lemons and McKenna, "Re-enfranchisement," 12.

13. Lemons and McKenna, "Re-enfranchisement," 2–13; Cottrol, *Afro-Yankees*, 77.

14. Sixth Census of the United States, Rhode Island, 1840, https://archive.org/details/populationsch1840504unit.

15. Irene Burnham et al., *Creative Survival: The Providence Black Community in the Nineteenth Century* (Providence: RIBHS, 1985), 65.

16. Irving H. Bartlett, *From Slave to Citizen: The Story of the Negro In Rhode Island* (Providence, RI: Urban League of Greater Providence, 1954), 45–46.

17. The Bethel A.M.E. Church and Isaac Rice's home were among the "known" black stops on the Underground Railroad in Rhode Island. Matthew M. Rillovick, Richard R. Kuns, and John Sabino, *The Underground Railroad in New England* (n.p.: American Revolution Bicentennial Administration, Region 1, [1976?]).

18. See Stephen David Kantrowitz, *More Than Freedom: Fighting for Black Citizenship in a White Republic, 1829–1889* (New York: Penguin Press, 2012).

19. George T. Downing was a direct descendant of a slave; however, he grew up with extraordinary privilege. Downing's father, Thomas, was educated and freed by his master, who was also most likely his father. Thomas Downing came to New York to fight in the War of 1812. After he was released from service, he opened a very successful oyster restaurant and catering company in the city. George Downing grew up in a polarized environment. Prominent politicians, artists, and businessmen like Charles Dickens and Samuel J. Tilden frequented his father's restaurant. However, when he walked down the streets of New York he endured daily humiliations of racism, such as the stoning of black children by white gangs. In many ways racism trumped his class privilege. At twenty-seven, in 1846, Downing opened a summer branch of his father's business in Newport—the fashionable playground of the rich. Five years later, in 1851, he opened a catering business in Providence, and in 1855 he built a luxury hotel in Newport—Sea Grit House. Despite his economic success and connections, Downing was unable to enroll his black children in the Newport common schools. Cottrol, *Afro-Yankees,* 95; Lawrence Grossman, "George T. Downing and Desegregation of Rhode Island Public Schools," *Rhode Island History* 36, no. 4 (November 1977): 99–101.

20. Grossman, "George T. Downing," 101.

21. Ichabod Northup, a porter who owned over $3,000 worth of real estate, James M. Cheeves, a gunsmith who owned nearly $4,000 worth of property, and Walter Booth, a laborer who owned nearly $2,000 worth of real estate, signed the school integration petition. Cottrol, *Afro-Yankees,* 99; *Will the General Assembly Put Down Caste Schools?* [Providence, RI: n.p., 1857].

22. Cottrol, *Afro-Yankees,* 95; Bartlett, *From Slave to Citizen,* 52–53.

23. Cottrol, *Afro-Yankees,* 98.

24. In 1838, thirty-eight years after the state General Assembly passed a law stipulating that each town have at least one school for white citizens between the ages of six and twenty, the Providence Town Council had established both schools. Bartlett, *From Slave to Citizen,* 50–51.

25. *Will the General Assembly,* 6.

26. Ichabod Northup, James M. Cheeves, Rev. Peter Ross, John Banks, Walther Booth, William H. C. Stephenson, James Jefferson, and Henry Bowen all signed the school integration petition to the Rhode Island General Assembly. *Will the General Assembly,* 14; Grossman, "George T. Downing," 101–2.

27. *Will the General Assembly,* 1.

28. Ibid., 12.

29. Ibid., 3.

30. Ibid.

31. William Cooper Nell, Robert Morris, and John T. Hilton—known as the School Abolishing Party—brought "colored citizens," white abolitionists, and white antislavery politicians together in a coalition to challenge segregation in Boston's public schools. Much of the fight centered on the Smith school, where black children had been mistreated by their white teacher. The abolitionists claimed that the degraded state of many free blacks could be traced back to inferior and segregated schooling. In 1855, after decades of protracted battles over school integration, the Know-Nothing Party pushed through legislation abolishing segregated schools in Boston in order to keep the black vote. Kantrowitz, *More Than Freedom*, 124–33, 162–69.

32. *Will the General Assembly*, 10.

33. Ibid., 3, 9–11.

34. Ibid., 6.

35. Grossman, "George T. Downing," 102–4; Cottrol, *Afro-Yankees*, 96–100.

36. Grossman, "George T. Downing," 104–5.

37. Ibid.; Cottrol, *Afro-Yankees*, 96–100.

38. Grossman, "George T. Downing," 104.

39. Nelson Viall, the commander of the Fourteenth Rhode Island Heavy Artillery (Colored), left a personal narrative of the regiment. The document is handwritten and thirty-five pages long. It is part of the papers of the Soldiers and Sailors Historical Society of Rhode Island, an organization founded to preserve and disseminate the history of the Civil War. Viall, "Fourteenth Rhode Island Heavy Artillery," 11–12 .

40. Eric Foner, *Forever Free: The Story of Emancipation and Reconstruction* (New York: Vintage Books, 2005), 42–43.

41. Benjamin Quarles, *The Negro in the Civil War* (Boston: Little, Brown, 1953), 22–41.

42. Foner, *Forever Free*, 43–50.

43. At the start of the war the Union had a noninterference policy, and officers were to return runaway slaves to their masters. This policy was put into place to keep the loyalty of those in border states and other loyal southerners. Enslaved people then became contraband of war. Returning slaves to disloyal masters did not make sense—militarily. In 1861 the first confiscation act authorized the seizure of all Confederate property, including slaves. In 1862 the second confiscation act freed all seized slaves of disloyal southerners. On January 1, 1863, Lincoln signed the Emancipation Proclamation freeing slaves in rebelling states. Ira Berlin, Joseph P. Reidy, and Leslie S. Rowland, eds., *Freedom's Soldiers: The Black Military Experience in the Civil War* (New York: Cambridge University Press, 1998), vii–viii; Joseph T. Glatthaar, *Forged in Battle: The Civil War Alliance of Black Soldiers and White Officers* (New York: Free Press, 1990), x.

44. Berlin, Reidy, and Rowland, *Freedom's Soldiers*, 21.

45. Quarles, *Negro*, xi.

46. Berlin, Reidy, and Rowland, *Freedom's Soldiers*, 1–2.

47. Pay discrimination was particularly insulting: "Free blacks, who were generally better educated and more cosmopolitan than slaves, marched into military service with different hopes and aspirations. The inequities of black military life thus seemed particularly galling to those black soldiers were had been free." Consequently, it was free blacks and not former slaves who were most likely to demand commissioned offices and who dominated those ranks after the army altered its policy toward the end of the war. Berlin, Reidy, and Rowland, *Freedom's Soldiers*, 26–31, 35.

48. The Rhode Island Fourteenth was designated the Eighth United States Heavy Artillery (Colored) on April 4, 1865, and then the Eleventh United States Heavy Artillery (Colored) in May of 1864. I have chosen to use the original name because black Rhode Islanders first volunteered to fight early in the war under the banner of the Rhode Island Fourteenth. Harold Barker, *History of the Rhode Island Combat Units in the Civil War, 1861–1865* (n.p.: n.p., 1964), 325; "Guide to Rhode Island Eleventh United States Heavy Artillery (Colored) [Collection], 1853–1913," Rhode Island Eleventh United States Heavy Artillery (Colored), Providence College, Phillips Memorial Library, Special and Archival Collections, 1–2.

49. Chenery, *Fourteenth Regiment*, 10–11.

50. In 1898, the Rhode Island General Assembly appointed William H. Chenery to "compile the history" of the Fourteenth Regiment. Chenery served as a first lieutenant in the Civil War. Chenery's history included numerous copies of official orders as well as several newspaper articles and editorials. Ibid., 10.

51. Viall, "Fourteenth Rhode Island Heavy Artillery," 12, 20.

52. There is also reference to "three hundred muskets" in the first battalion's parade through the city of Providence. Chas. P. Stone (brigadier-general and chief of staff) estimates that there were five hundred to six hundred men in the second battalion. Viall, "Fourteenth Rhode Island Heavy Artillery," 1, 10; *Providence Journal*, August 28, 1863; Chenery, *Fourteenth Regiment*, 31.

53. Viall, "Fourteenth Rhode Island Heavy Artillery," 2–4; John David Smith, "Let Us All Be Grateful That We Have Colored Troops Will Fight," in *Black Soldiers in Blue: African American Troops in the Civil War Era*, ed. John David Smith (Chapel Hill: University of North Carolina Press, 2002), 24; Quarles, *Negro*, 185–86; Chenery, *Fourteenth Regiment*, 5–7.

54. Chenery, *Fourteenth Regiment*, preface.

55. John T. Waugh held $1,500 in real estate in Providence in 1859; he was also involved with the school desegregation campaign in Boston. Ibid., 55.

56. Ibid., preface, 5–26.

57. Ibid., 27–28.

58. Ibid., 23–34.

59. Viall, "Fourteenth Rhode Island Heavy Artillery," 13.

60. Samuel Jefferson, Anthony King, and Samuel Mason were among the men murdered by the rebels. Chenery, *Fourteenth Regiment*, 59–62.

61. Ibid., 38.

62. Ibid., 46.

63. Viall, "Fourteenth Rhode Island Heavy Artillery," 20, 22.

64. Chenery, *Fourteenth Regiment*, 61–62, 144–50.

65. Viall, "Fourteenth Rhode Island Heavy Artillery," 29–34.

66. Captain Phanuel E. Bishop, letter to the *Providence Evening Press*, February 4, 1864, in Chenery, *Fourteenth Regiment*, 21.

67. Viall, "Fourteenth Rhode Island Heavy Artillery," 18.

Notes to Conclusion

1. Brown University Center for the Study of Slavery and Justice, "Slavery and Justice Report," 2006, www.brown.edu/initiatives/slavery-and-justice/; Brown University, "Martin Puryear Slavery Memorial," n.d., accessed July 13, 2015, www.brown.edu/about/public-art/martin-puryear-slavery-memorial.

2. Lorenzo J. Greene, *The Negro in Colonial New England* (New York: Columbia University Press, 1942; Edgar J. McManus, *Black Bondage in the North* (Syracuse, NY: Syracuse University Press, 1973); Jay Coughtry, *The Notorious Triangle: Rhode Island and the African Slave Trade, 1700–1807* (Philadelphia: Temple University Press, 1981), Gary B. Nash and Jean R. Soderlund, *Freedom by Degrees: Emancipation in Pennsylvania and its Aftermath* (New York: Oxford University Press, 1991); Graham Russell Hodges, *Slavery and Freedom in the Rural North: African Americans in Monmouth County, New Jersey, 1665–1865* (Madison, WI: Madison House, 1997); George Fishman, *The African American Struggle for Freedom and Equality: The Development of a People's Identity, New Jersey, 1624–1850* (New York: Garland, 1997); Joanne Pope Melish, *Disowning Slavery: Gradual Emancipation and "Race" in New England, 1780–1860* (Ithaca, NY: Cornell University Press, 1998); Graham Russell Hodges, *Root and Branch: African Americans in New York and East Jersey, 1613–1863* (Chapel Hill: University of North Carolina Press, 1999); Thelma Wills Foote, *Black and White Manhattan: The History of Racial Formation in Colonial New York City* (New York: Oxford University Press, 2003); Leslie Harris, *In the Shadow of Slavery: African Americans in New York City, 1626–1863* (Chicago: University of Chicago Press, 2003); Catherine Adams and Elizabeth H. Pleck, *Love of Freedom: Black Women in Colonial and Revolutionary New England* (New York: Oxford University Press, 2010); Margot Minardi, *Making Slavery History: Abolitionism and the Politics of Memory in Massachusetts* (Oxford: Oxford University Press, 2010); Craig Steven Wilder, *Ebony and Ivy: Race, Slavery, and the Troubled History of America's Universities* (New York: Bloomsbury Press, 2013).

3. The dedication ceremony for the Memorial Monument to the Negro Slaves of Barrington, RI, Princes Hill Cemetery, Barrington, RI, was held on June 12, 1903. Robert K. Fitts, *Inventing New England's Slave Paradise: Master/Slave Relations in 18th-Century Narragansett, Rhode Island* (New York: Garland, 1998), 45–47.

4. Wilder, *Ebony and Ivy*, 11.

5. RIHS, "Summer Walks 2015," accessed July 13, 2015, www.rihs.org/walking-tours/; Newport History Tours, "Historic Tours of Newport," accessed July 13, 2015, http://newporthistorytours.org/tour-descriptions/; Historic Tours of Newport, "Scheduled Tours," accessed July 13, 2015, http://historictoursofnewport.com/tour-details/scheduled-tours/.

Index

Figures, notes, and tables are indicated by f, n, and t following the page number.

Business of slavery (continued)
industry, 109; and war, 62–64;
West Indian slave trade, 13–23, 74,
164–65n14

Capitalism, 2, 152, 156
Casey, Abraham, 112, 115
Charterites, 135–36
Christians, 30, 66, 115, 162n17
Churches: and abolitionist movement,
69; African Union Meeting House,
111, 126–30; in black communities, 8;
and free blacks, 112; fugitive slaves
hidden in, 137; rioters targeting, 102;
segregation of, 53
Citizenship: for Civil War veterans, 131;
for free blacks, 8; for Revolutionary
War veterans, 79; and school
integration, 141–42, 150; and voting
rights, 137
Civil War, 138, 142–43, 198n43,
199nn47–48
Cloth industry. See Textile industry
Coggeshall, Jane, 10–11
Colonial African Burial Ground
(Newport), 155, 155–56f
Colored Union Congregation Church,
189n1
Connecticut, 181n73, 182n76
Continental Army, 70–71, 100
Cotton, 2, 16, 22, 89–90, 132, 184n15. See
also Textile industry
Cranston, Samuel, 13, 16

Dance halls, 102–3, 108
DeWolf, James, 83, 89, 183n11
DeWolf family, 2, 82–84, 89–90, 160n3,
182n87
Dorr, Thomas, 134–36
Dorrites, 134–37
Dorr Rebellion, 132, 138, 140, 150
Douglass, Frederick, 135, 184n13
Downing, George Thomas, 138, 139, 141–
43, 193n59, 197n19

Easton, Hosea, 189n2
Education. See Schools
Emancipation Proclamation (1863),
198n43

First Congregational Church (Newport), 69

Free African Union Society (FAUS), 110,
112, 138, 189n1, 190n7, 191n17
Free blacks: and business of slavery,
8–10, 89–98, 111; education of, 124,
127; employment of, 4; enslaved
people socializing with, 40, 47;
extralegal businesses operated
by, 108; institutions for, 129; in
Massachusetts, 117; and mutual aid
societies, 112–13; in Newport, 96, 112,
114, 118–19; in New York, 88, 96, 117; in
Pennsylvania, 117; population growth
of, 88; in Providence, 39, 88, 96–98,
112, 119; return to Africa by, 115–18,
121; in Revolutionary War, 71; rights
of, 38, 40; and riots, 101–2; as sailors,
4, 60, 97
Freebody, Benjamin, 50–51, 174n33
Freebody, Samuel, 50–51, 174n33
Freeman's Constitution, 135–36
Freemasons, 194n83
Fugitive Slave Law of 1850, 93, 137
Fugitive slaves: advertisements
for, 180n60; business of slavery
interrupted by, 54–55; and Civil War,
145; and emancipation, 75, 98; and
freedom of movement, 48; legislation
on, 93, 137; and Native Americans, 34

Gardner, Moll, 41–42, 52
Gardner, Newport, 115, 119–20, 123, 130,
191n17
General Assembly (Rhode Island):
abolition legislation passed by,
62; emancipation votes by, 10; and
governor's role, 13; Quakers in, 66;
and Revolutionary War, 72–74, 81; on
school integration, 139, 142; slavery
legislation passed by, 29, 33, 36–38, 54,
171n110; on voting rights, 133–35, 137
Gorton, Hezekiah, 53, 175n47
Gradual emancipation laws: and
abolitionist movement, 83–84, 180n55;
hereditary slavery ended by, 4, 7–8,
65, 86; in New England states, 79–80,
118; and poverty, 98; and Quakers,
74–76

Hager (slave), 41, 172n1
Hardscrabble, Rhode Island, 102–5,
188n65

Hazard, Rowland G., 92–93
Hereditary slavery, 4, 62, 64–65, 88
Hopkins, Samuel, 68, 69, 117, 120, 122, 178n26
Hopkins, Stephen, 49, 67
Hutchison, Anne, 164n8

Indentured servants, 6, 45, 87, 99–100
Indians. *See* Native Americans
Institution building, 121, 123, 128–30, 132
Integration, 139, 141, 143
Interracial marriages, 94

Jago, Saint, 49, 174n28
Jamaica, 16, 18–19, 28, 55
Jethro (slave), 34, 53

Know-Nothing Party, 198n31

Law and Order Party, 135
Lopez, Aaron, 23–24
Lopez family, 16, 82
Louisiana, 131, 148
Lyndon, Caesar, 49, 57, 114, 174n26
Lyndon, Josiah, 49, 57, 114

Mackenzie, James, 119, 120, 192n48
MacSparran, James, 52, 54, 175n50
Manchester, Isaac, 89, 183n11
Maryland, 71, 117
Massachusetts: abolitionist movement in, 83; emancipation cases in, 79, 87, 181n73; enslaved population in, 4, 25, 25t; free blacks in, 117; Revolutionary War enlistment of blacks in, 71, 181n70; slavery legislation in, 6–7, 11–12, 30, 35; textile industry in, 91
Merchants and tradesmen: and business of slavery, 24, 28, 40, 43–46; and emancipation, 65; and slave trade, 3, 16, 19
Metacom's War (1675–76), 32, 66, 170n86, 170n89
Middle class, 112, 124
Militias, 70–71, 103, 132
Molasses, 4, 13, 16, 20–21, 23–24, 63
Mulattoes: and business of slavery, 46; emancipation of, 70; legal status of, 37–38, 160–61n8; resistance acts by, 53, 55–56; Revolutionary War enlistment of, 78; as sailors, 97

Mutual aid societies, 111, 113

Narragansett, 26–27, 34, 45, 58, 147
Narragansett Proprietors (land company), 168n60
Native Americans, 11, 26, 29–40, 42, 45–47, 78, 169n83
New Hampshire, 4, 25, 32, 34, 59, 71
New Jersey: abolitionist movement in, 68; black culture in, 44, 57; dairy farms in, 27; enslaved population in, 3, 25, 25t, 31; gradual emancipation laws in, 7, 79–80; Quakers in, 66; Revolutionary War enlistment of blacks in, 71
New Orleans, 148–49
Newport, Rhode Island: abolitionist movement in, 69; business of slavery in, 23–24, 26, 28; Colonial African Burial Ground, 155, 155–56f; emancipation in, 81–82; enslaved population in, 12–13, 43, 45–47, 49–50, 75; founding of, 164n8; free blacks in, 96, 112, 114, 118–19; map of, 15; merchants in, 4–5, 16, 19; poverty in, 100; resistance activities in, 54–55; schools in, 122–24, 126–27, 137–40, 143; slave trade in, 35
Newport Historical Society, 28, 189n1
New York: black culture in, 44, 57; business of slavery in, 11, 18, 21, 23; Civil War enlistment of blacks in, 144, 148; dairy farms in, 27; enslaved population in, 3, 6, 25, 25t, 30–31; free blacks in, 88, 96, 117; gradual emancipation laws in, 7, 79–80, 181n73; Revolutionary War enlistment of blacks in, 71; voting rights in, 196n5
North Kingstown, Rhode Island, 12, 52, 86, 168n59
Nova Scotia, 116

Osborn, Sarah, 47, 122

Pass, James, 56, 176n59
Patronage, 120, 123
Patten, William, 123, 193n63
Peace Dale, Rhode Island, 12, 91, 92f, 168n59
Pearce, Cato, 86–89, 183n1

About the Author

Christy Clark-Pujara is Assistant Professor of History in the Department of Afro-American Studies at the University of Wisconsin–Madison.

Early American Places

Colonization and Its Discontents: Emancipation,
Emigration, and Antislavery in Antebellum Pennsylvania
Beverly C. Tomek

Empire at the Periphery: British Colonists, Anglo-Dutch Trade,
and the Development of the British Atlantic, 1621—1713
Christian J. Koot

Slavery before Race: Europeans, Africans, and Indians
at Long Island's Sylvester Manor Plantation, 1651–1884
Katherine Howlett Hayes

Faithful Bodies: Performing Religion and Race
in the Puritan Atlantic
Heather Miyano Kopelson

Against Wind and Tide: The African American Struggle
against the Colonization Movement
Ousmane K. Power-Greene

Four Steeples over the City Streets: The Social Worlds of
New York's Early Republic Congregations
Kyle T. Bulthuis

Caribbean Crossing: African Americans and the Haitian
Emigration Movement
Sara Fanning

Insatiable Appetites: Imperial Encounters with Cannibals in the
North Atlantic World
Kelly L. Watson

Unfreedom: Slavery and Dependence in
Eighteenth-Century Boston
Jared Ross Hardesty

Dark Work: The Business of Slavery in Rhode Island
Christy Clark-Pujara

CPSIA information can be obtained
at www.ICGtesting.com
Printed in the USA
BVHW031152110222
628779BV00010B/84

9 781479 855636